Educating Students with Refugee and Asylum Seeker Experiences

Maura Sellars

Maura Sellars

Educating Students with Refugee and Asylum Seeker Experiences

A Commitment to Humanity

Verlag Barbara Budrich
Opladen • Berlin • Toronto 2020

All rights reserved. No part of this publication may be reproduced, stored in or introduced into a retrieval system, or transmitted, in any form, or by any means (electronic, mechanical, photocopying, recording or otherwise) without the prior written permission of Barbara Budrich Publishers. Any person who does any unauthorized act in relation to this publication may be liable to criminal prosecution and civil claims for damages.

You must not circulate this book in any other binding or cover and you must impose this same condition on any acquirer.

A CIP catalogue record for this book is available from
Die Deutsche Bibliothek (The German Library)

© 2020 by Verlag Barbara Budrich GmbH, Opladen, Berlin & Toronto
www.barbara-budrich.net

    ISBN   978-3-8474-2289-1
    eISBN 978-3-8474-1345-5

Das Werk einschließlich aller seiner Teile ist urheberrechtlich geschützt. Jede Verwertung außerhalb der engen Grenzen des Urheberrechtsgesetzes ist ohne Zustimmung des Verlages unzulässig und strafbar. Das gilt insbesondere für Vervielfältigungen, Übersetzungen, Mikroverfilmungen und die Einspeicherung und Verarbeitung in elektronischen Systemen.

Die Deutsche Bibliothek – CIP-Einheitsaufnahme
Ein Titeldatensatz für die Publikation ist bei der Deutschen Bibliothek erhältlich.

Verlag Barbara Budrich
Stauffenbergstr. 7. D-51379 Leverkusen Opladen, Germany

86 Delma Drive. Toronto, ON M8W 4P6 Canada
www.barbara-budrich.net

Jacket illustration by Bettina Lehfeldt, Kleinmachnow –
   www.lehfeldtgraphic.de
Typographical editing: Anja Borkam, Jena – kontakt@lektorat-borkam.de
Picture credits: photo: www.istock.com
Printed in Europe on acid-free paper by docupoint GmbH, Barleben

For Matthew P Bradley
Who leads with empathy, compassion and pedagogical love.

Acknowledgements

Thanks and gratitude to Lisa Turnbull, who has encouraged this work and supported me throughout its completion. Thanks also to Amber Hughes for her patience, practicality and philosophical suggestions. This book would not be the same without the inspiration of your trust, your reading and your appreciation.

Foreword

John Fischetti

There are 68.5 million forcibly displaced people in the world.
 40 million of our fellow Earthlings are internally displaced, 25.4 million more are refugees and 3.1 million are asylum seekers. (https://www.unhcr.org/figures-at-a-glance.html)
 The number of refugees is the same population as the whole of Australia or the whole city of Shanghai. The diaspora facing the planet is shocking, made worse by war, famine, disease and political environments that marginalize the most vulnerable.
 In this book Maura takes on these issues straight away: *Chapter 1:* Many students are disadvantaged by the impact of neoliberal policies and purposes on education, but it may be students with refugee experiences who have the greatest need for educational experiences which exemplify pedagogical love and care and respect what it is to be human. The task of teachers and others who would engage in this teaching with love and care is made increasingly difficult by the standardization and quantification of their work. Accompanied by the stresses and pressures of the need to continually improve their productivity and demonstrate their efficiency, the notion of teaching as an act of love and caring may appear to many to be almost impossible. However, the negligence of authentic scholarship and the proliferation of values that erode society, community and sense of self to profit the privileged few may easily be considered as immoral acts against humanity.
 And, again in Chapter 8: Education in these contexts has looked backwards, not forwards, and, as such, is totally unprepared for the impact of authentic multiculturalism in which traditional and modern, diverse ways of knowing and doing are honoured and respected as legitimate epistemologies. It steadfastly ignores philosophies and knowledge which bring hope to the urgent task of educating students to cope with inevitable tensions of a 'multi- perspectival world' characterised by change, 'contradiction, chaos and complexity ' (Gidley, 2016 p. 112), which, while important all students, is urgent and critical for students with refugee and asylum seeker experiences whose ontologies already mirror the change 'contradiction,

chaos and complexity' of 'the multi-perspectival world' of which Gidley writes and which reflects the 'Postformal world' of Sardar (2010).

Although the following story is a bit of an urban legend, it may make a connection as to how to frame the education opportunity for students with refugee and asylum seeker experiences in Westernized status quo school systems. During the early days of personal computers most companies incorporated memory chips that were made in Japan. An American computer company issued a request in their contract for a large order of memory chips that asked the company to ensure for quality control of 90%--that is that 90% of the chips would work. The company that filled the request was confused by that stipulation and sent two boxes of chips to the US to complete the order. One box contained 100% working chips and a second box of 10% of the first order contained defective chips. The computer chip manufacturer's assumption was that they would always achieve 99.99% effectiveness in all of its products, not assume a predetermined number that just wouldn't work. Their only solution to satisfy the order was to deliberately ship defective chips separate from the ones that worked. Most Western schools operate on a philosophy of education that assists some of their students some of the time. For those vulnerable learners, this predetermined failure rate places anyone of difference, particularly learners with refugee and asylum seeker experiences, most at risk. The system assumes first language mastery, active parent engagement, access to resources to support learning and cultural capacity to know such things as holiday customs and certain "basics" only known to people from the region. Add to that the post traumatic nature of the refugee experience, particularly those from awful wars and famine, it is no wonder that Maura proposes a whole new vision for refugee education. It is a compelling history and call to action. It is important work for all of us in education. And given the world's current strife, will only be more important from here.

Professor John Fischetti
Pro Vice Chancellor
Faculty of Education and Arts
University of Newcastle, Australia
John is a global expert in school transformation, teacher education, and leadership for learning for all.

Introduction

This writing has been an incredible personal journey. Compelled by the need to write about an issue which is critical to a global audience, I do not seek to speak for the millions of refuge and asylum seekers who are compelled to place their children and young people in education systems that are increasingly inappropriate learning environments for many children and youth from multiple backgrounds and life experiences, including those with refugee and asylum seeker experiences. I write to open the dialogue, to focus the hearts and minds of everyone involved in education, to the stark realities that are so much part of everyday lives in westernized societies to be accepted without critical reflection and without attention to what it is to be human and humane. I hope, that as this book is read, that the readers can place the children and young people in their lives in the situation that faces the students who compelled me to write this work, and that they can place themselves in these communities. I also hope that some positive action, some constructive discourse and some restorative engagement can be prompted in educational contexts to create an increased sense of belonging, compassion and hope for all these students and their new futures.

Table of Contents

Acknowledgements vi

Foreword vii

Introduction ix

Chapter One: Power, Politics, People and Pedagogy 1

Chapter Two: Power: Discourses of Power 19

Chapter Three: Politics: Neoliberalism and Education 35

Chapter Four: People: Refugee status, Trauma and Loss 52

Chapter Five: People: Compassion and Beloning 69

Chapter Six: People: Schools as Safe Spaces 85

Chapter Seven: People: The School and Leadership 104

Chapter Eight: Pedagogy: Ways of Knowing and Doing 121

Chapter Nine: Pedagogy: Educating for Global Competence ... 140

Index 155

Chapter One: Power, Politics, People and Pedagogy

Introduction

The world is currently disrupted by famine, war, violence, and the predatory actions of people against each other. At the time of writing, nearly 66 million people, the largest number in history, are displaced from their homes and urgently in need of assistance from those who are more fortunate. Fifty five percent of these come from just three countries; Syria (5.5 million), Afghanistan (2.5 million) and South Sudan (1.4 million) http://www.unhcr.org/en-au/figures-at-a-glance.html). Almost three million of this number are temporarily placed in Turkey, one and a half million in Pakistan, almost one million in both Lebanon and the Islamic Republic of Iran, and eight hundred thousand in Ethiopia. There are twenty- two and a half million refugees. Over half of this number are under 18 years of age, all of whom have experienced atrocities associated with their refugee status. Refugees are those individuals who must flee their own countries for fear of prosecution as the result of their race, ethnicity, religion, nationality, political opinion, or membership of a specific social group (see http://www.unhcr.org/en-au/figures-at-a-glance.html). Despite their many differences, these individuals have several characteristics in common. These include an overwhelming sense of loss, emotional if not physical trauma and suffering, and the desperate journey to escape the familiar contexts in which they were previously domiciled. The details of these flights vary considerably. The impact on mental, emotional and physical wellbeing is universal, only varying in degree.

> Davidson, Murray, and Schweitzer (2008), found that refugee experiences result in poorer general health; poorer mental health including increased somatisation and dissociation; increased levels of psychological distress including susceptibility to posttraumatic stress disorder (PTSD), anxiety and depression; impairments in cognitive function; low perceptions of educational achievement and career aspirations; a lack of family cohesion and reduced feelings of belonging (in Sellars & Murphy, 2017:2).

These statistics, although confrontational, are hardly surprising. Many people are detained in rudimentary camps with few or no amenities, overcrowding and little chance of improving their circumstances independently. Although relief agencies and other groups often attempt to provide some educational experiences for youth, the lack of resources and transitory nature of these sites and their occupants make consistent, skilled support impossible. Education, if it exists for some youth at all, is invariably interrupted. The focus of this writing does not include the difficulties of educational provision for children and adults in such camps as it may be fraught with other contextual complications.

Several countries act as hosts to these camps and detention centres on a temporary basis, whilst other countries agree to accept an agreed quota of individuals in various categories each year. The latter include 'first world' countries; democratic, industrialized, capitalist countries which often have similar economic interests (see http://www.nationsonline.org/oneworld/third_world_countries.htm). Less than half of the displaced population is hosted by these countries. Seventeen percent are in Europe, sixteen percent in The Americas and eleven percent in Asia and the Pacific. It is in these locations that young people who are of appropriate age, are most likely to be compelled to participate in mandatory, mass education. Mass education universally is characterised by three core elements;

> '.. is institutionally chartered to be universal, standardized and rationalized....institutionalized at a very general collective level…is institutionally chartered to conduct the socialization of the individual as the central social unit…' (Boli, Ramirez, & Meyer, 1985: 148-149).

It is these contexts and their students with refugee experiences that are the focus of this work.

Mass Education in a Neoliberal Paradigm

The establishment of school systems and mandatory attendance for children and young people between certain ages is not new, nor is it confined to first world countries. Similar systems have been established in most parts of the world, differing only in the detail of how they are administered (Boli et al., 1985). As society changed in response to advancements in industry, technology, the economy and world affairs, so did the nature and characteristics of education (Tait, 2013). Currently, educational policies in capitalist countries are heavily influenced by the ideologies of various versions of neo liberal economic policies. The neo liberal policies of the 1980s, although differing in the detail, resulted in the break from the Keynesian post war policies which had led to the development of systems such as Swedish social democracy and the welfare provisions in the UK (Steger & Roy,

2010). The government controlled all the flow of money in and out of the country and high taxes on the wealthy and large corporate companies were used to pay for increased social services and higher wages for workers. Neoliberalist principles championed by Thatcher in the UK and Reagan in the USA focused on a very different paradigm indeed. The common foundations of all neoliberal policies that were implemented during that period were Deregulation, Liberalism and Privatization. During the 1990s Blair in the UK and Clinton in the USA, followed by many of their trading partners, took a more moderate approach and attempted to balance this free trade model (liberalism) with more sensitivity towards the community concerns and social responsibilities that were the results of the policies in the previous decade. Global financial crisis and the establishment of the World Trade Organisation have had some impact on the nature of neoliberalism in the twenty-first century, but the cornerstone of the ideology, free trade, remains (Steger & Roy, 2010), as does the impact of this economic rationalism (Pusey, 1991) on education.

Neoliberalism has redefined education itself in the twenty-first century. In its quest to create new markets where none previously existed and to expand the existing markets, neoliberalism has had a critical impact on educational policies and practices (Connell, 2013a; Ross, 2017) and shows little sign of abating (Wilkins, 2017). Once fully established, these market reforms began to exercise power in every sphere of public life, including schools and what is understood as educational reform. These were implemented mainly as the result of the privatization of many previously owed goods and services, the open trade agreements and the reconfiguration of workforce conditions; which changed not only the ways in which people worked in terms of casual, contract and part time employment, but also the opportunities for lowly paid trade occupations where wages paid by first world countries could not compete with that paid by other countries. The effect of this was increasingly felt by the working classes. Education became aligned increasingly with an industrial model, with the introduction of measurable outcomes and high levels of accountability, much of which is reminiscent of Foucault's panopticon theory of surveillance and monitoring (Foucault, 1977, 1979). Substantially increased funding for private schools, including religious systemic schools and independent schools, not only took much of the responsibility for educating specific groups of students away from public education systems, but led to increasing privatization of a mandatory public service as parents at distinct levels of socio economic status increasingly took advantage of a widening range of school choice. Providing society with choice is a cornerstone of neoliberal ideology and, as with other areas of public life, the promotion of school choice has been embraced by individuals who may benefit most from the neoliberal perspective of education (Angus, 2015).

However beneficial the notion of school choice appears to be on the surface, in this economic political model, school choice can serve to disrupt education and minimize the potential of all students to achieve at school. Based on economic principles, not on educational philosophies and accompanying theory, neoliberalist education stresses high levels of individualism, compliance for schools and students to attain outcomes that are benchmarked by neoliberal agenda which promote hegemonic values and market this as an acceptable and appropriate world view (Angus, 2015; Connell, 2013a, 2013b; Ross, 2017; Steger & Roy, 2010). As a result, poor student performance is considered to be the responsibility of individual schools and the product of economy driven political decision which have increasingly permeated educational systems. In response, many parents who have sufficient knowledge of how systems are being managed and have adequate income to choose, become concerned that their children achieve these benchmarks and perform well at school. In order to ensure this outcome, parents who are fiscally secure are increasingly seeking out the best schools in public systems and competing for places in schools in the private sector (Angus, 2015; Connell, 2013b). Market policies ensure, that even in school choice, parents become consumers. Neoliberal educational policies not only eliminate alternative educational views but classify society increasingly on cultural and economic capital (Bourdieu, 1986b, 1990; Bourdieu, Passeron, & Saint Martin, 1994). Students are classified, not on merit but on inherited status. Consequently, students from low socioeconomic backgrounds invariably attend public schools in their own socioeconomic settings. As will be discussed later, choice of school impacts heavily on individuals' sense of identity (Angus, 2015).

The Purpose of Education in a Neoliberal Paradigm

In congruence with educational policies which are developed according to economic principles, the purpose of education is reconceptualised to reflect these values and processes. The neoliberal ideology has a very distinct understanding of the purpose of schooling. Students are regarded as 'human capital' and are educated to have the skills and attitudes of a productive workforce (Gary, 2016). This is in contrast to previous sociological theories of schools as institutions for the reproduction of society, for example Bourdieu's understanding of purpose of education

(Bourdieu, 1986b, 1990; Bourdieu et al., 1994), and the use of institutional regulation, monitoring and conditioning to produce a subservient, passive society as in Foucault' theory of the Panopticon (Foucault, 1977, 1979). This is not to dismiss these theories as irrelevant to the neoliberal purpose of education, as has been indicated previously, the notion of capital is critical to the neoliberal educational endeavour, and Foucault's understanding of schools as institutions under regular surveillance and monitoring remain major themes in education dominated by neoliberal economic policies. Currently, there is considerable discussion about Bourdieu's notions of capital, most specifically the understanding of social capital (see, for example, Putnam, 2002; Putnam & Goss, 2002) and Foucault's Panopticism (Ball, 2012, 2013; Hope, 2013) and their relevance to the contemporary purpose of education. Both philosophies are discussed later in more detail as they are important in the interpretation of the neoliberal purpose of education and to the lived realities of students with refugee experiences in school systems of countries where this is the dominant political paradigm.

Productivity is foundational to the neoliberal notion of education. People have become increasingly productive through time as the result of the changing of society, increased technological advances, more powerful energy sources and more efficient production processes (Zhao, 2012). However, increased productivity is not a world- wide phenomenon. In the context of first world countries, it has produced better living conditions, better health options and longer working lives, and decreased opportunities for employment in many traditional occupations. Zhao (2012:66), discusses 'creating jobs, not finding jobs' as a perspective from which to view the future. This is entirely congruent with the neoliberal agenda of expanding existing markets and creating new ones, however, not entirely realistic given the limited curriculum, prescriptive pedagogies and ever increasing permeation of competition in neoliberal education systems which dominate first world countries (Ross, 2017) . A positive view of this paradigm is that education was created for the role that it now plays in preparing individuals by training them in languages and skills of society and then sorting them out into appropriate roles in that context. A more critical view is that the power that is exercised in this sorting process is dominated by those groups who are privileged in society, and that education is used as a tool to reinforce and reproduce the advantages of these groups only, to the exclusion of those who are not members (Connell, 2013a).

An equally important, but less discussed feature of neoliberal education philosophy in both its vision and purpose of education is the way in which it reduces the wholeness and complexity of human life to simply that of workers (Gary, 2016). Human beings are distinguished from other life forms by their capacities for reflection, exploration and investigation and other meaningful forms of leisure that are not just the state of not working, but that are rich non-work experiences that fulfil a deeply held human need and provide opportunities to develop another way of viewing the world. Gary (2016) particularly highlights that education in the neoliberal ideology not only lends itself to individuals increasingly identifying themselves in terms of work, but dehumanizes individuals. He argues that not only does it collapse what it is to be human into producers and consumers, but encourages people to live at a superficial level, that which is not to do with reason and intellectual activity, but is 'operating below the cognitive- reasoning register'; operating at the level of consumer desire. The most critical feature that Gary (2106) brings to the discussion about the neoliberal educational paradigm is that of quality of schooling. He states, 'the cerebral emphasis of modern schooling…is poorly equipped to guide us into an alternative way of being'. To engage with 'an alternative way of being', he recommends radical pedagogy, including a change of habitus (Bourdieu, 1986a). This assessment of the lack of scholarship in neoliberal educational frameworks is echoed by Ross (2017) who states 'when education is forced into the marketplace, the marketplace of ideas shuts down'. It is into this educational paradigm that students with refugee experiences are placed when being accepted into the so called 'developed' countries which embrace neoliberal ideology in any of its diverse manifestations.

Other Perspectives in the Purpose of Education

The neoliberal paradigm has not always dominated education. It is currently dominant because the economy is dominating neoliberal governments and not vice versa (Steger & Roy, 2010). Historically, there have been many theoretical perspectives on the purposes of education which reflect the changing nature of society and perceived needs. Dewey (1938) for example, observed that the primary purpose of education was not to prepare students for the future, but to help them live practically and sensibly in their own environments at that time, meaning that education was life at that time and to provide students, in an orderly manner, with the skills they needed to join society. These skills included a critical and enquiring mind and was articulated as 'social efficiency'. He was a very strong advocate of learning as experience and believed that the quality of the experiencer was paramount to learning. Quality learning experiences were those that combined theory and practice. Much later, Adler (1982) brought together major themes which had influenced education for some time. He presented three main objectives of education; to develop students as citizens, to promote individual holistic development and to prepare young people for work. Over a decade later, again in recognition of the changing nature of society, deMarrais and LeCompte (1995) indicated four main purposes of education; intellectual development of students, especially in literacy and numeracy, economic purposes, that is for reasons of employment, the development of social and moral responsibilities and, interestingly, a fourth purpose which had not previously garnered much public attention; education for political purposes, including the assimilation of migrant students. The degree to which this is possible is debatable, given the hegemonic principles upon which current neoliberal education systems are administered, monitored and evaluated.

There is hope, however. 'There are many things that can be done to mitigate the deleterious effects that neoliberalism has on education in North America and beyond' (Ross, 2017:4). While it is not possible for those directly involved in educational contexts to entirely transform the hegemonic foundations of these education systems, it is possible to develop attitudes and strategies that serve to empower all students for whom schooling is a disempowering experience, the most vulnerable of which are students with refugee experiences. One of the most basic and most human of the 'things' that can be done to 'mitigate' the impact of neoliberal policies on education is to recognize what it is to be human and to understand educating students as the 'whole child'.

The purpose of the first mass education system established in Prussia in the 18th century was holistic education which focused on the process of supporting increasingly mature levels of both cultural and personal growth (Gidley, 2016). Influenced by German and Swiss educational systems, it was an integrative initiative in that it focussed on the development of whole person. Sadly, this notion of education was eroded by the industrialized, more factory style model whose sole purpose was to provide workers for the immense factories that resulted from the British Industrial Revolution. Several independent, alternative models of education developed early in the twentieth century and reflected the educational ideals of people such as Montessori, Steiner and Dewey. Gidley (2016:135) speculated that all these educators were 'tapping into an important zeitgeist' or spirit of the times that was reacting against the utilitarian focus of contemporary mass education. While these theories had many individual characteristics, they also had many common features, including an emphasis on imagination and creativity, practical engagement, spirituality and many attributes of Postformal reasoning (Kincheloe & Steinberg, 1993), which will later be discussed in detail, but which essentially involve four pedagogical principles or values. These are love, life, wisdom and voice, much of which was absent from utilitarian agendas in education.

The next significant challenges to conventional, mass educational thinking came in the late 1960s and 1970s and reflected a new consciousness of the need to question the policies and practices of mainstream schooling amidst the background of youth protests and dissent around the issue of the involvement of capitalist countries in the Vietnam war. It was a period of alternative education, characterized by several new perspectives on how learning may be best achieved. Neill's Summerhill School (Neill, 1960),which advocated free schooling where adults supported learning but did not plan anything for the students to learn, the students determined this themselves, was one comment on the rigidity of the regular classrooms. Holt's (1964, 1970) critique of the school system and support of home schooling was another. Illich (1975) advocated strongly that schooling in economy based countries simply served to corrupt and institutionalize society and that, in order to deinstitutionalise society, education needed radical reform.

> Many students, especially those who are poor, intuitively know what the schools do for them. They school them to confuse process and substance. Once these become blurred, a new logic is assumed: the more treatment there is, the better are the results; or escalation leads to success. The pupil is thereby "schooled" to confuse teaching with learning, grade advancement with education, a diploma with competence, and fluency with the ability to say something new. His imagination is "schooled" to accept service in place of value. (Illich, 1975:9)

In place of tightly kept regimes and frameworks, he suggested networks of learners who could connect and provide genuine opportunities for each individual to engage with others for the purposes of learning, sharing and caring. It was also the period in which critical pedagogy was brought to public prominence as Freire (1970) highlighted the political nature of teaching and learning, perceiving that no educational process was neutral and advocating teacher awareness of their professional life as a series of political actions. Freire (1970) also focused on education for the poor, deploring the 'banking' model of education which not only led to the reproduction of unjust society, but which did not allow the underprivileged opportunities to engage in educational discourses that provided them with opportunities to improve their situation. Whilst all these 'alternative' educational ideas were highly critical of the traditional industrial model of schooling, it is in the work of Illich and Freire that notions of 'care' in educational interactions articulated for over half a century. Nearly half a century later, reforms in educational politics, policies and practices have been scant, despite decades of academic writing. These discourses included considerable attention being paid to the role of the teacher (see, for example, Poulou, 2005; Warner, 2006), the importance of school climate (see, for example, Cohen, 2006; Coladarci, 1992; Cotton, 1996; Loukas & Robinson, 2004), child care (see, for example, Fanning & Veale, 2004; Gerhardt, 2015), teaching as an act of caring (see, for example, Darder, 2009) and a philosophy of care (Noddings, 2012; 2005) being articulated as means by which students can be positively socialised into the constructs of tolerance, kindness and reciprocal, caring relationships.

Love and Care in Education

Darder (2009, 2017) in her discussion of the work and friendship that she shared with Freire, provided a definition of that surpasses the commonly held assumptions of the concept of love. She states,

> …is a political and radicalized form of love that is never about absolute consensus, or unconditional acceptance, or unceasing words of sweetness or endless streams of hugs and kisses. Instead it is a love that I experienced as unconstructed, rooted in a committed willingness to struggle persistently with purpose in our life and to intimately connect that purpose with what he called our 'true vocation' – to be human. (Darder, 2009:567)

Freirean philosophy demonstrated the ways in which the political, economic and social backgrounds of people served to explain the current social and economic inequity in the world. It illustrated how discrimination, injustice and capitalist agendas, such as those expressed in neo liberal influences in education, dehumanize people so that they have reduced capacity to act humanely in regards to themselves, others and the environment. His notion of teaching for love included tolerance and acceptance of diversity, of opposing perspectives and contrary views. Teaching as an act of love for Freire was not about being well meaning and inducting students into an acceptance of the social and moral inequities of traditional schooling. It was about teachers having a deep understanding of the negative impact of these educational systems on the students' capacities to develop the skills, confidence and competencies that were required for them to transform their worlds. To teach with love demanded that educators at all levels of school engage with issues of social justice and give marginalised students a voice in the educational context of privilege and hegemony.

Many of these themes are echoed in moral teaching from an ethic of care (Noddings, 2005, 2012) . This philosophy of teaching lacks the radical, political perspective of Freirean thinking, but it resonates the message of what it is to be human in the treatment of others in educational contexts. Noddings (2012) reflects on the importance of the human disposition to care and be cared for. Eschewing long, rational debates about the importance of care, Noddings posits that, as humans in the world, people have some experience of being cared for, and as such, can recognise and have the potential to engage with acts of caring for others. For Freirean scholars, Noddings' perceptions of this capacity for love of self, others and the world may be significantly diminished by the dehumanizing influences of poverty, discrimination and disempowerment; but the individuals for whom this philosophy is most critical are those who have not been discriminated against and are not battling poverty and disempowerment to the degree to which the people championed by Freire and the other critical pedagogues have. This is simply because to qualify to teach in schools in first world countries, it is necessary to engage with the characteristics of neoliberal influences in education. To become teachers, individuals have to successfully participate in the standardization, the competitive component, the dialogue and discourses of the privileged. The degree to which they personally invest in the systemic disadvantage of certain groups of students depends on their capacities to demonstrate moral leadership and reflect on their practice, critically evaluating it, both in terms of self-interest and their potential for service to others.

Noddings (2005, 2012) relied heavily on the very essence of what it is to be human to develop a powerful perspective from which professional decisions could be made, accountability criteria and professional responsibilities mediated and inclusive practices evolved. Her philosophy demands that the most caring and nurturing learning environment for students is a basic right for students and a professional priority for educators. Schools which embrace an ethic of care as a leadership principle do not confine their caring to the students themselves but evidence it in the ways the staff interact with each other and with the wider school and local communities. It was not dependent on rules and regulations for effective implementation, but rather gave precedence to the needs of individual students in their particular contexts. The purpose of educating from an ethic of care is to bring about effective, nurturing solutions for students which acknowledge their unique situations, issues and concerns. From this philosophical perspective, an ethic of care requires more than superficiality. It demands commitment to the lived reality of what education could be. The four constituent actions of an ethic of care are the demonstrated actions of caring relationships. Noddings termed this 'modelling'. It is lived praxis. As always, effective communication is critical in the development of trusting, caring relationships. Dialogue in the ethic of care facilitates deeper understanding of the perspectives and concerns of others, promotes caring and empowering solutions and allows for an analysis of the patterns of behaviours and responses that impact on the students, their caregivers and the wider community.

The strength of dialogue as articulated in this philosophy is both the acknowledgment of 'humanness' of all the participants and the dignity of difference and diversity.

Dialogue is also important to distinguish between the authenticity of the ethic of care and the virtue ethic. In this context the virtue ethic is the enactment of the choice to take decisions that are assessed by the teachers and educational systems as 'good' for the students. This frequently relates to practices and procedures which students dislike, are inappropriate for them as individuals or are simply a somewhat blind adherence to the status quo. Much of this notion relates to Freire's concerns for the role of teachers to show leadership in issues of social injustice and systemic unfairness. The underlying motivations for employing a virtue ethic may be dissimilar, but the outcomes are very similar in that students are disheartened, disempowered and frequently disengaged from their learning. Dialogue places students themselves in the discussion in the ethic of care. This dialogue helps teachers get to know their students better, develop a commonly interpreted framework for interactions and helps teachers assess how effective their caring has been. It is also the means by which different perspectives can be discussed and examined for rigour, different ways of knowing and doing can be explored and the channels through which students can examine issues that impact in their own lives and affect their beliefs, values, dispositions and attitudes.

The mutuality of the relationships of care that are foundational to this philosophy reiterate the Freirean mandate that people must empower themselves and participate actively in the process of transformation. In this instance, the cared for must also contribute to the acts of caring by becoming carers. This reciprocal dynamic may be the key to successfully building school community with shared values and respect for others. The contribution of the students in these caring educational environments supports the development of informed, caring and dignified communication with others and becomes part of the modelling principle, the lived acts of responding to being human and the capacities of humans to develop empathy, tolerance and respect; foundational attitudes and attributes of teaching for love and for care. Caring is not just to be read about, discussed or subtly mandated as part of a hidden curriculum (Giroux & Penna, 1979), it is practiced as collaborative, not competitive, learning. It is a daily, ongoing commitment to explicit, strategic pedagogical approaches for engaging students with each other in positive and mutually supportive interactions. The notion of practicing this dedication to caring for others also involved acts of care in the wider school community that had the potential to change lives for the better. In this manner, students were empowered, both by their altruistic acts of caring and by the responses they receive as a result. Noddings views this aspect of the ethic of care as a component of moral education which was not associated with the theories of moral development explored by the cognitive developmentalists (see, for example, Kohlberg, 1975). This concept of practice has the potential to be particularly powerful in empowering students. Education that empowers has capacity to transform.

The remaining principle of the ethics of care is confirmation. The ethic of care remains the only theory of moral education to include a principle such as this. It is best understood as the acts of affirming the best in someone by working with them to help them grow in the ways that they are striving for, in the ways that they value, and in the ways that are important to them. Confirming supports the educational notion of high expectations for all students, in which every learner is considered capable of expanding on their relative strengths. For this principle of confirmation to be authentic, it must be valued by both the teachers confirming the achievements and the students whose competencies are being valued and enriched. This process is often facilitated by the dialogue that enables teachers to get to know their students' goals and aspirations. In the action of confirming someone, it is important that the affirmation be intended to support the development of the student in becoming the best person they could possibly be. The continuity of dialogue and caring interactions that allow this trust to develop are an essential part of this process as establishing, developing, and maintaining the caring relationships. This is because the development of the trusting interactions and dialogue that enable true confirmation, takes time. This process may involve the continual practice of checking, assessing and evaluating values and goals. The trusting dialogues developed as part of this process may require critical reflection (Sellars, 2017) of decisions made by both students and teachers, the rationales that underpinned them and the alternative dialogues that could have been considered to support the students' striving to become the best humans they could become, empowered by their capacities to care.

Postformal Education

Gidley (2016) in her exploration of the political, socio- cultural, economic and historical impacts on educational theory and practices, returned to the notion of pedagogical love as the first of her core pedagogical values for her Postformal education framework, designed to effect radial change in the ways in which educational practice is conceived and conducted. She strongly stated that, 'this is the time to think deeply, feel intensely and have the courage to act' (Gidley, 2016:189). She recognised what is apparent on an everyday basis to many students in schools, that pedagogical love is the most important of the many characteristics that are absent in many current educational contexts. Asserting the central role of love in all spirituality and notions of caring, Gidley denounced the purposes and practices of current neoliberal education as damaging and promoting of 'callous values' (2016:190); a perspective explored earlier in this chapter. She cites the inevitable consequences of socializing young people into society without any recourse to love and care. Prominent amongst these consequences are the issues of mental health and the associated lack of belonging, connectedness and community, all of which are already significant concerns for students with refugee experiences and which underpin the many psychological and social reasons for the introduction of pedagogical love.

Gidley discussed this pedagogical love in three major themes. These were higher purpose, dialogical reasoning and integration. These are each unpacked in terms of Postformal Reasoning Qualities that relate to Spiritual Development, Contemplation and Compassion (Gidley, 2016). The higher purpose relates to the need to restrict self-interest, become less egocentric and be open to be inspired to a life purpose that relates contributing towards improving the life of others. This is a direct challenge to the egocentric, producer- consumer identity that neoliberal education agenda support in their various manifestations. For many individuals, self-interest does not need the encouragement of competition, success at the expense of others, indifference and the misappropriation of blame that is attributed to those in less fortunate circumstances; all of which are evidenced in the application of economic policy to the human interactions of education. The second reasoning quality relates to dialogical reasoning, which, unlike formal thinking, does not result in winners and losers. It is an interactive dialogue in which the views and opinions of others are respected and considered in the process of discovering decision-making in which all parties can experience successful outcomes. The final Postformal reasoning quality invited a more holistic view of what is considered educative in education systems. The discipline specific, specialized and fragmented ways of teaching and learning prevent an integrated approach which acknowledges the ways in which disciplines inform each other (see, for example, Sellars, 2018) and which compartmentalize knowledge, skills, concepts and capacities.

Not only does this inhibit students' capacities and opportunities to synthesize their learning and maximize their competencies, it does not reflect the authentic purpose of learning, which is to enhance individuals' lives and empower them to create the prospect of change and improvement. Gidley envisaged this integrated approach as more than content integration and connectedness. In describing the

Postformal reasoning quality she emphasised 'a systems approach' (Gidley, 2016) which implies the integration of all the components of a system. In the case of education, it would be evidenced as students and teachers working together to implement curriculum and evaluation, including on assessment. Ideally, students and teachers would be working together in a dialogical process to develop curriculum and evaluative procedures. This process would not have as its focus the conquering of an elitist, narrow selection of required knowledge, but the knowledge, skills and conceptual learning that would inform, empower and motivate students to engage with their relative strengths (see, for example, Sellars, 2008) and achieve the learning they value. The implications of this understanding of pedagogical love for students with refugee experiences and the interpolation of the remaining three pedagogical values developed by Gidley will be discussed in the detail of the following chapters as the focus of authentically educating these groups of young people and children is increasingly extrapolated. These theories of teaching as an act of love have the potential to make a difference as evidenced by Freire, Noddings and in Gidley's radical reconceptualising of education. They are each a human response to injustice and disempowerment created by self-interest at powerful levels in society. As the statistics show, the groups of people who have endured much of the suffering as the results of this self-interest and hegemony are those with refugee experiences, particularly the children and young people.

Conclusion

Many students are disadvantaged by the impact of neoliberal policies and purposes on education, but it may be students with refugee experiences who have the greatest need for educational experiences which exemplify pedagogical love and care, and respect what it is to be human. The task of teachers and others who would engage in this teaching with love and care is made increasingly difficult by the standardization and quantification of their work. Accompanied by the stresses and pressures of the need to continually improve their productivity and demonstrate their efficiency, the notion of teaching as an act of love and caring may appear to many to be almost impossible. However, the negligence of authentic scholarship and the proliferation of values that erode society, community and sense of self to profit the privileged few may easily be considered as immoral acts against humanity. This is because the values and purpose of neoliberal education systems socialize young people into perceptions of public life which is egocentric and materialistic. This is further disempowering and dehumanizing for students with refugee experiences who are already at risk, despite their many strengths. These considerations alone should make compelling reasons for educational policy makers, leaders and teachers to investigate the strategies that identify as educational actions of love and care. The development of more equitable, more inclusive societies depends on reconceptualising education and restoring trust to those who have undergone the most extreme dehumanizing experiences. To do this effectively, educationalists need understanding, strategies and skills which can be customized for their own contexts, under the framework of pedagogies of love and care. The following chapters are devoted to exploring the knowledge, concepts, theories and information that can make this a reality.

References

Adler, M. (1982). *The Paidea Proposal: An Educational Manifesto.*. New York: Collier Macmillan.
Angus, L. (2015). School Choice: Neoliberal Education Policy and Imagined Futures. *British Journal of Sociology of Education, 36*(3), 395-413.
Ball, S. J. (2012). *Foucault, Power, and Education* Retrieved from http://newcastle.eblib.com/patron/FullRecord.aspx?p=1101409
Ball, S. J. (2013). *Foucault and Education : Disciplines and Knowledge* Retrieved from http://newcastle.eblib.com/patron/FullRecord.aspx?p=1189375
Boli, J., Ramirez, & Meyer, J. (1985). Explaining the Origins and Expansion of Mass Education. *Comparative Education Review,, 29*(2), 145-170.
Bourdieu, P. (1986a). The Forms of Capital. In J. G. Richardson (Ed.), *Handbook of Theory and Research for the Theory of Education* (pp. 46-58). New York: Greenwood.
Bourdieu, P. (1986b). The Forms of Capital. In J. G. Richardson (Ed.), *The Handbook of Theory: Research for the Sociology of Education* (pp. 241-258). New York: Greenwood Press.
Bourdieu, P. (1990). *Reproduction in Education, Society, and Culture*. London: Sage.
Bourdieu, P., Passeron, J., & Saint Martin, M. (1994). *Academic Discourse: Linguistic Misunderstanding and Professorial Power* Cambridge: Polity Press.
Cohen, J. (2006). Social, Emotional, Ethical, and Academic Education: Creating a Climate for Learning, Participation in Democracy, and Well-Being. *Harvard Educational Review, 76*(2), 201.
Coladarci, T. (1992). Teachers' Sense of Efficacy and Commitment to Teaching. *The Journal of Experimental Education, 60*(4), 323-337.

Connell, R. (2013a). The Neoliberal Cascade and Education: An Essay on the Market Agenda and its Consequences. *Critical Studies in Education*, 54(2), 99-112.

Connell, R. (2013b). Why do Market 'Reforms' Persistently Increase Inequality? *Discourse: Studies in the Cultural Politics of Education*, 34(2), 279-285.

Cotton, K. (1996). *School Size, School Climate, and Student Performance.* Retrieved 30 November 2012 http://upstate.colgate.edu/pdf/Abt_merger/Cotton_1996_Size_Climate_Performance.pdf

Darder, A. (2009). Teaching as an Act of Love: Reflections on Paulo Freire and his Contributions to our Lives and our Work. In A. Darder, M. Baltodano, & R. Torres (Eds.), *The Critical Pedagogy Reader* (second ed.). New York: Routledge.

Darder, A. (2017). *Reinventing Paulo Freire: A Pedagogy of Love* . New York: Imprint Routledge

Davidson, G., Murray, K., & Schweitzer, R. (2008). Review of Refugee Mental Health Assessment: Best Practices and Recommendations. *Journal of Pacific Rim Psychology*, 4, 72-85.

deMarrais, K., & LeCompte, M. (1995). *The Way Schools Work: A Sociological Analysis of Education* (2nd ed.). White Plains, NY: Longman.

Dewey, J. (1938). *Experience and Education.* . New York: Simon and Schuster.

Fanning, B., & Veale, A. (2004). Child Poverty as Public Policy: Direct Provision and Asylum Seeker Children in the Republic of Ireland. *Child Care in Practice,* 10, 241-251.

Foucault, M. (1977). Panopticism (A. Sheridan, Trans.) *Discipline and Punish: The Birth of the Prison* (pp. 195-228). New York: Vintage Books.

Foucault, M. (1979). *Power, Truth, Strategy.* Sydney: Feral Publications.

Freire. (1970). *Pedagogy of the Oppressed.* New York: Continuum

Gary, K. (2016). Neoliberal Education for Work Versus Liberal Education for Leisure. *Studies in Philosophy and Education*, (October). Retrieved from doi:DOI: 10.1007/s11217-016-9545-0

Gerhardt, S. (2015). *Why Love Matters.* New York: Routledge.

Gidley, J. (2016). *Postformal Education: A Philosophy for Complex Futures.* Switzerland Springer International Publishing.

Giroux, H., & Penna, A. (1979). Social Education in the Classroom: The Dynamics of the Hidden Curriculum. *Theory and Research n Social Education,* VII(1), 20-42.

Holt, J. (1964). *How Children Fail.* New York: Pitman Publishing.

Holt, J. (1970). *How Children Learn.* Hammondsworth: Pelican.

Hope, A. (2013). Foucault, Panopticism and School Surveillance. In M. Murphy (Ed.), *Understanding Foucault, Habermas, Bourdieu and Derrida.* New York: Routledge.

Illich, I. (1975). *Deschooling Society.* London: Calder and Boyers.

Kincheloe, J., & Steinberg, S. (1993). A Tentative Description of Post- formal Thinking: The Critical Confrontation with Cognitive Theory. *Harvard Educational Review,* 63(3), 296-320.

Kohlberg, L. (1975). The Cognitive-Developmental Approach to Moral Education. *The Phi Delta Kappan,* 56(10), 670-677.

Loukas, A., & Robinson, S. (2004). Examining the Moderating Role of Perceived School Climate in Early Adolescent Adjustment. *Journal of Research on Adolescence,* 14(2), 209.

Neill, A. (1960). *Summerhill.* New York: Hart.

Noddings, N. (2005). *The Challenge to Care in Schools: An Alternative Approach to Education* (second ed.). New York: Teachers College Paress.

Noddings, N. (2012). *Philosophy of Education.* Boulder Coloradao: Westview Press.

Poulou, M. (2005). Educational Psychology within Teacher Education. *Teachers and Teaching,* 11(6), 555-574. doi:10.1080/13450600500293241

Pusey, M. (1991). *Economic Rationalism in Canberra.* Melboune: Cambridge University Press.

Putnam, R. (2002). *Democracies in the Flux: The Evolution of Social Capital in Comtemporary Society.* Oxford: Oxford University Press.

Putnam, R., & Goss, K. (2002). Introduction. In R. Putnam (Ed.), *Democracies in Flux: The Evolution of Social Capital in Contemporaty Society.* Oxford: Oxford University Press.

Ross, W. (2017) The Fear Created by Precarious Existence in The Neoliberal World Discourages Critical Thinking/Interviewer: M. ABDELMOUMEN. *American Herald Tribune.*

Sellars, M. (2008). *Using Students' Strengths to Support Learning Outcomes: A Study of the Development of Gardner's Intrapersonal Intelligence to Support Increased Academic Achievement for Primary School Students* Saarbrucken, 97: VDM Verlag.

Sellars, M. (2017). *Reflective Practce for Teachers* (second ed.). London: Dage.

Sellars, M. (Ed.) (2018). *Authentic Contexts of Numeracy: Making Meaning across the Curriculum.* Singapore: Springer.

Sellars, M., & Murphy, M. (2017). Becoming Australian: A Review of Southern Sudanese Students' Educational Experiences. *International Journal of Inclusive Educational Experiences,* 0(0,0), 1-20. Retrieved from doi: https://doi.org/10.1080/13603116.2017.1373308

Steger, M., & Roy, R. (2010). *Neoliberalism: A Very Short Introduction:* . New York: Oxford University Press.

Tait, G. (2013). *Making Sense of Mass Education.* Melbourne, Vic: Cambridge University Press.

Warner, D. (2006). *Schooling for the Knowledge Era.* Camberwell, Victoria: Australian Council for Education Research Press.

Wilkins, A. (2017). *School Governance: Redressing the Democratic Deficit.*

Zhao, Y. (2012). *World Class Learners.* Thousand Oaks Calif: Coewin.

Chapter Two: Power: Discourses of Power

Introduction

Individuals with refugee and asylum seeker backgrounds and experiences know about power. They have first -hand experiences of the abject terror and brutality of the powerful who physically and emotionally abused and oppressed them, denied them of their human rights and homelands and condemned them to contribute to the great diaspora in history (see http://www.unhcr.org/en-au/figures-at-a-glance.html). These manifestations of power are overtly brutal, flagrantly uncaring and indifferent to the human misery that is widely inflicted on others. They are also aware of the power of dominant cultural and social mores in the new homeland situations in which they are placed and of the exclusionary discourses and decision making that affect individuals, families and entire communities (Anders, 2012; Anders & Lester, 2015; Bevir, 1999). This chapter examines the discourses of power, epistemologies and societal control as manifested in the educational institutions of the western societies in which students with refugee and asylum seeker backgrounds are placed. This examination mainly focusses on aspects of the theoretical work of Foucault and reflects the implications of these discourses for individuals, families and entire communities.

Foucault: Discourse and Power

In current educational contexts, there appears to be an increased focus on the work of Foucault (Leask, 2012), with much of the discussion extrapolating Foucault's notion of institutional power (Foucault, 1977; 1991) and its capacity to regulate human behaviour and diminish the capacity of individuals for agency or personal intent. Tait (2013), comments on Foucault's work in education indicating,

> Rather than concentrating on issues of power and inequality, this paradigm focusses instead on the techniques and practices by which we are shaped as particular types of individual, and by which we have our conduct regulated (p.4).

While Foucault's work is often considered to be open to interpretation (Ball, 2012), his contribution to understanding the mechanisms of modern power play in educational contexts is important however, as much of what constitutes institutional power has the capacity to challenge, if not exclude, the possibility of authentic educational opportunities for many students with refugee and asylum seekers backgrounds. It also provides one avenue by which the structures, regulations and management systems that have become so integral to educational institutions as to become invisible and invincible to those who are the products and participants of them, can be critically examined and evaluated in relation to their stated purposes, to their officially articulated roles in societies and to their function as arbitrators of epistemologies and intelligences. In many ways, it appears that this endeavour reflects much of the entire purpose of Foucault's work.

In order to do this effectively, it is important to determine which interpretations of some of Foucault's key terms are most suitable for this purpose. For example, his use of discourse is not limited to the linguistic interchange that occurs. Rather, Foucault uses the term 'discourse' in a way that takes into consideration the context, the content and the power relations of any interaction. Weedon (1997), interprets Foucault's use of discourse as

> Ways of constituting knowledge, together with the social practices, forms of subjectivity and power relations which inhere in such knowledge's and relations between them. Discourses are more than ways of thinking and producing meaning. They constitute the 'nature' of the body, unconscious and conscious mind and emotional life of the subjects they seek to govern (p. 108).

This definition indicates the foundational understanding from which Foucault utilized his methodologies of archaeology and genealogy to investigate the means by which each historical period developed and legitimized select knowledge systems and beliefs as socially acceptable 'truths' whilst simultaneously ignoring or rejecting other 'epistemes' as lacking in value or acceptability. Weedon (1997), also provides a definition of power as conceptualized by Foucault, indicating that power is

> ...a dynamic of control and lack of control between discourses and the subjects, constituted by discourses, who are their agents. Power is exercised within discourses in the ways in which they constitute and govern individual subjects (p. 113).

Foucault dispels that idea that power is confined to specific persons, authoritative bodies or episodes in time (Foucault, 1991). He finds that power pervades as part of the fabric of society, part of the accepted 'truth' of any society, and that it is under constant change and renewal. He states, 'Power is everywhere' and 'comes from everywhere' (Foucault 1998: 63), it defines society and those who part of it.

He identifies different types of power, indicating that each can be asserted in multiple ways in society. He also recognises that different societies have different 'truths' which provide a mantle of cohesion and common understanding for those who belong to them. The two major types of power in that he proposes are dominant in western societies are juridical power and normative power. He theorizes that modern societies are largely disciplinary societies in which power is not generally exercised through force, as it was historically. Juridical power is defined by Foucault as power that is used by governments, institutions of law and generally political power. He states

> Power was exercised mainly as a means of deduction, a subtraction mechanism, a right to appropriate a portion of the wealth, a tax of products, goods and services, labor and blood levied on subjects......a right to seizure....it culminated in the privilege to seize hold of life in order to suppress it. (Foucault, 1998 p.136)

This is a type of power that prevents or prohibits certain behaviours in a society and imposes penalties or punishments for transgressions. Something is forfeited by the offender if this power is rebelled against, or the rules made by political institutions and governments are broken. This type of power is a 'top down' type of power which is applied to all individuals in society, although that results in some members of society having more power than others. Individuals lose power; in terms of something tangible and measurable; when juridical power is operationalized against them for transgressions.

Foucault describes the other aspect of power that co exists with juridical power in western societies. In a comparison of the sovereign power that historically ruled populations and had the right of life and death over the subjects of those societies (right of death), he discusses the 'transition' of the nature of this power to the new order (power over life). He argues,

> But a power whose task is to take charge of life needs continuous regulatory and corrective mechanisms. It is no longer a matter of bringing death into play in the field of sovereignty, but of distributing the living in the domain of value and utility. Such a power has to qualify, measure, appraise, and hierarchize, rather than display itself in its murderous splendor; it does not have to draw the line that separates the enemies of the sovereign from his obedient subjects; it effects distributions around the norm. I do not mean to say that the law fades into the background or that the institutions of justice tend to disappear, but rather that the law operates more and more as a norm, and that the judicial institution is increasingly incorporated into a continuum of apparatuses (medical, administrative, and so on) whose functions are for the most part regulatory. A normalizing society is the historical outcome of a technology of power centered on life. (Foucault, 1978 p.144).

Foucault views normative power as positive power that seeks to improve and empower the lives of individuals and society as a whole. He is very clear that dwelling exclusively on the deductive power of the juridical neglects the positive potential of normalizing power to be productive, to increase the capacities of individuals and entire populations. He states,

> We must cease once and for all to describe the effects of power in negative terms: it 'excludes', it 'represses', it 'censors', it 'abstracts', it 'masks', it 'conceals'. In fact power produces; it produces reality; it produces domains of objects and rituals of truth. The individual and the knowledge that may be gained of him belong to this production' (Foucault 1991: 194).

Normative power is not located in formal government institutions. There are no laws that can be studied. Social norms are located in unofficial institutions and are formed by opinion, much of which may be based on the knowledge that is available from scientific expertise and is judged to be the most appropriate, preferred customs and practices of the society. Transgressions against social norms do not attract juridical penalty but various forms of reactions from other members of society who deem the transgression to be against the interests of others in their society. These reactions generally comprise of negative reinforcement, whereas the adherence to societal norms elicit reactions that are considered to be positive reinforcement. This power is everywhere in society and can be exercised by all members of society who consider themselves to be within the parameters of the 'norm' in that they are reflecting the consensus of what is considered to be normal behaviours and attitudes in the society to which they belong. Individuals are 'normalized' by one of the two types of normative power; disciplinary power. This power is the means by which individuals maximize their capacities and enhance their integration in society by viewing their bodies as 'a machine'(Foucault, 1978 p.139) which can be regulated and trained to be a productive and compliant member of society. This disciplinary power is enforced through surveillance, which is extrapolated in detail in his earlier work (Michel Foucault, 1991) where he analyses the prison system and the education system as examples of this model of panoptic surveillance. The regulatory force at work in this model is the self. Individuals know there is a possibility, but not a certainty of being observed all the time, and consequently, they regulate their own behaviours so that if, at any time, they are under surveillance, they are seen to be adhering to the internalized social norms.

The other type of normalizing power is known as biopower, which is focussed on the normalization of entire populations. Biopower aims to do this by establishing 'norms' using the bell curve. In order to achieve this, government and other bodies collect statistics and data pertaining to every aspect of life (and death) that is pertinent to the population. Every facet of life is placed under surveillance with the aim of establishing the 'norm' and identifying anything that doesn't fit on the curve. Everything needs to fit on the various scale, measures, charts and tests so that every aspect of people can be measured as a mathematical abstraction at the level of the population. This is all done to ensure the health and wellbeing of the people in the society. Resistance to biopower is more difficult than, for example, civil disobedience is to juridical power. In order to resist biopower, it needs to be disrupted from within as the normative disciplines are empowered by repetition. Butler (2001), discusses the difficulty of identifying exactly what Foucault means when he discusses resistance by critique. She concludes that it is the response to a 'tear' in fabric of knowledge that is presented as truth. Foucault (1987) himself suggested that critique and resistance of the 'norms' of biopower is about not being governed quite as much; about minor disruptions and not rejection or subversion of the entire system of power, which he concluded was not just a necessary but productive aspect of society.

Foucault: Knowledge and Education

Challenging the commonly accepted adage that 'knowledge is power', Foucault focusses on the relationship between power and knowledge from a different perspective, conceptualizing their relationship as a dynamic association, not one that is statically dependent one on the other. He proposes that the powerful are the individuals who construct knowledge from their 'expertise;', and that the relationship between power and knowledge are so intricately entwined as to be considered seamless, thus creating the notion of 'power/knowledge'. Mills (2003), describes this construct.

> Foucault characterizes power/knowledge as an abstract force which determines what will be known, rather than assuming that individual thinkers develop ideas and knowledge (p.70).

Consequently, in each historical era, what is considered relevant and valued as socially constructed knowledge is then disseminated, regulated and validated through the external institutions of power, currently the prisons, hospitals and schools (Foucault, 1977). While much of the Foucauldian analysis undertaken by educationalists appears to have focussed on the negative nuances associated with normative power (Ball, 2012; Leask, 2012), Panopticism as applied to mandatory schooling and the certainty of disempowerment. Leask (2012) notes;

> Using Foucault, or his toolbox, to understand education would thus seem a decidedly fraught affair: the more that oppressive power-structures are exposed, the less possibility there is for any kind of self-originating ethical intention on the part of teachers or students (p. 58)

This perspective presents educational contexts as those which are totally dominated by carceral constraints, by authorities whose singular aim is to 'supervise, transform, correct, improve' (Foucault, 1979, pp. 302–3). Consequently, in this perspective, the classroom becomes the domain in which publicly accepted values and protocols are enforced in a similar fashion to the ways in which these are enacted in other institutional environments. They are...

> ...subject to a whole micro-penality of time (lateness, absences, interruptions of tasks), of activity (inattention, negligence, lack of zeal), of behaviour (impoliteness, disobedience), of speech (idle chatter, insolence), of the body ('incorrect' attitudes, irregular gestures, lack of cleanliness), of sexuality (impurity, indecency) ... (Foucault, 1979, p. 178).

Whilst there may be particular aspects of these measures of disciplinary power that remain embedded in homeland educational contexts of students with refugee and asylum seeker backgrounds as repressive power exercised as physical punishment, for the majority, disciplinary power is self-regulated in deference to possibility of being observed, and in deference to 'norms' that are accepted as the everyday behaviours, interactions and customary practices in any particular educational context. These 'norms' are not arbitrary but are determined by the mechanisms of the 'biopower' that is identified by Foucault. The means by which these 'norms' are translated into everyday practices and procedures that are taken for granted as 'the way that things are done'. This process is achieved in schools by means of mandatory documentation. These national and regional laws, curriculum content and detail and policy papers which combine both aspects of power; juridical and normative; in order to regulate and record behaviours, ensure conformity to the 'norms' and monitor every aspect of student identity that is considered, by the manufactures of these documents, to be necessary to the sustained efforts of the systems. In this manner, data and statistics are available for the perpetuation of norms and also for the identification of trends which may be considered to be deleterious to society in general.

Racism and exclusion

Foucault did not use the term racism in its current meanings of either devaluing others by engaging with negative stereotypes or xenophobia which results in domination or of believing that 'self' is superior and therefore rejecting others by exclusion. He used the term in a way that excluded any notion of opinion. In his later work Foucault frequently engaged with the notion of governmentality (Lemke, 2000) which appeared to extend and reframe his concept of biopower. While Foucault did not ever explain the exact relationship between governmentality and biopower or biopolitics, governmentality does appear to include the conception that, not only did authorities gather statistics and data to monitor populations and to improve their circumstances, but that they did so with another purpose in mind. Linked with neo political regimes, Foucault (2003) stated

> The specificity of modern racism, or what gives it its specificity, is not bound up with mentalities, ideologies, or the lies of power. It is bound up with the technique of power, with the technology of power. ...The juxtaposition of – or the way biopower functions through - the old sovereign power of life and death implies the workings, the introduction and activation, of racism. And it is, I think, here that we find the actual roots of racism (p. 258).

This new idea of modern racism is also intrinsically linked with construct of governmentality. Foucault describes this as,

> The ensemble formed by the institutions, procedures, analysis and reflections, the calculations and tactics that allow the exercise of this very specific, albeit complex form of power, which has as its target population, its principle form of knowledge political economy, as its essential technological means apparatuses of security (1991 p. 102).

This definition may, on the surface, present a relatively abstract view of governmentality. However, the means of governance that he describes is currently observed to be status quo in western industrialised countries. This has powerful implications for the inclusion, wellbeing and future prospects of whole categories or groups of populations in these societies.

Rasmussen (2011), explains this writing of Foucault's as 'flexible technology of power that entails a new and novel form of government (p. 40). This new and novel form of government was able therefore to differentiate between those individuals who were to be invested in and those who were not- leaving those who were not to metaphorically 'die' in that they were not deemed to be members of society who merited access to resources and benefits that that would facilitate maximum human functioning as part of society. It appears to Foucault that the role of some of the medical sciences changed from one of nurturing and healing to censorship in order to protect society from any abnormalities (Foucault, 1987). Ball (2012), in his work on the history of British education as perceived through a Foucauldian analysis, gives detailed descriptions of the laws which prevented some individuals, at various times throughout history, from participating in education because of their perceived disability; intellectual or physical. In Foucauldian terms, these individuals were not to be invested in as part of society.

What implications are there for students with refugee and asylum seeker backgrounds?

This brief analysis of some of the key characteristics that Foucault suggest need to be investigated in western societies indicates that, in order to make an authentically humanitarian gesture towards entire populations of society some serious consideration needs to be concentrated on issues that these new members of society cannot raise as a matter of priority. These issues include matters that are decided at various levels of authority and expertise that hold the knowledge power balance, the aims and purposes of governmentality and who is be invested in and who is left to 'die' and the extent to which new arrivals within these circumstances will ever be able to engage in powerful discourse. These concerns do not only have long term impact on the individuals who are identified as those with refugee or asylum seeker experiences, but on the fabric of the societies into which these communities are settled, and on the minutiae of the daily lives of these students in schools.

The very means by which individuals and specific populations are classified and differentiated in these societies provides not only identifiers which determine those with some common experiences of refugees from those with asylum seeker backgrounds. These identifiers are used, not only establish the *ascribed* (Watters, 2007 p.7) status of these individuals, and the legal implications for both groups of people, they are also used to categorize those which may be classed as students and those who are not, a situation which may determine the future prospects of many young people whose statistical information is vague, unable to be processed or simply not known at all. Additionally, much of the data gathering so important to Foucault's notion of governmentality, its apparatus and purposes may also have little or no relevance in the countries where many of refugee and asylum seekers originated.

Watters (2007 p.7) notes that particularly pertinent to the categorization process is the notion of chronological age, with Western perspectives of childhood identifying this group as between 0 – 17 years of age. This is a particularly sensitive assessment for many students with refugee experiences and asylum seeker backgrounds because, not only may statistical information be unavailable, irrelevant to them socially and culturally or completely unknown, young people may appear considerably more mature and hence older than their Western counterparts as the consequence of their experiences, additional responsibilities and obligations; both to themselves and others. Failing to identify within the 0-17 age range impacts considerably, not only on their educational opportunities, but also on their access to health and welfare support and to programs focussed on enabling successful integration which are primarily developed for those identified as students. This initial classification process continues to impact on the level of schooling that identified students are allowed be enrolled in, irrespective of their multiple, diverse educational experiences and academic prowess.

This aspect of governmentality that pervades what may otherwise be considered educational opportunities for self-improvement, socialization and academic growth frequently results in students with refugee and asylum seeker backgrounds being placed in inappropriate classroom contexts relative to their understandings of Western school systems, their operations and procedures, and, importantly, the epistemological foundations of these institutions which are regarded as 'truth' and which exclude all other epistemologies as without value or currency. Issues which have critical impact on the capacities of students with refugee and asylum seeker backgrounds are not limited to notions of childhood or age. For those who are admitted to the educational institutions, there may be expectations from some cultural groups that their children and young people be placed in the contexts where they are most likely to develop basic competencies that are decisive in terms of potential future success, irrespective of the student's age and with reference to their background of formal schooling, interrupted schooling or perhaps no previous experience of schooling at all (Brown, Miller, & Mitchell, 2006; Dooley, 2009, 2012; Emert, 2014; McWilliams & Bonet, 2016; E. Miller, Ziaian, & Esterman, 2018; J. Miller, 2009). The 'norms' of classification that are applied to Western schooling processes and procedures preclude any other than age- based criteria. Consequently, many students in these groups have their educational prospects marred by the lack of *skills*, knowledge and capacities that are 'taken for granted' as foundational competencies for future learning in their new homelands.

For students who have the *ascribed* classification of refugee or asylum seeker, there may be another classification applied; that of students at risk; which in itself is used as an identification mechanism in the Foucauldian notion of 'othering' or practices of subdividing within technologies of government. This practice is present in the power/knowledge paradigm discussed by Foucault (1998) and the colonialism of Said (1978). When a population is 'othered' it serves to prioritise any of their perceived weaknesses and strengthen the sense of power of those doing the *othering*. When this is used as mechanism by governments or authorities, it serves to ensure the hierarchy of these bodies and reinforce their position in this order of power. This 'othering' leads to the perspective that students with refugee and asylum seeker backgrounds are 'problems' that need to be addressed in a particular, specific manner by policymakers and 'micromanaged' by teachers (Watters, 2007 p.126). This perspective of this population of students in western classrooms typically leads to three major discursive domains focussing on child development, trauma, risk and resilience, the normative basis and evaluative criteria of which are exclusively based in western perspectives, ideologies and theory and formulated in the context of institutional parameters and procedures with little concern or consideration of cultural difference.

This exclusive perspective on universalized child development processes infused with western cultural norms not only has the effect of classifying students with refugee and asylum seeker backgrounds with the consequence of setting them outside the norm, but of concealing important issues that are related to social power, culture and identity. This absolute confidence of the western perspective of child development is challenged by LeVine (2010 p. 31), who notes in his commentary on theories of child development developed using observations from American clinical practice;

> …..other non-pathological variants of childhood social development are possible in cultures with differing developmental goals. In this instance, the psychiatric theory ignored or underestimated the plasticity of human social and emotional development and claimed, in effect, that deviation from American standards of child rearing would lead to psychopathology, a claim that cannot survive empirical scrutiny of in diverse cultures. The evidence we have so far indicates that, on the contrary, there are multiple pathways……..to healthy or at least non-pathological psychic conditions in adulthood.

The implications technologies of power which are manifested as school routines and strictures and of a western model of 'optimal' child development being utilized to address the perceived problems of a Burundian family settled in an American town becomes clear in the narrative of Anders and Lester (2014). They describe how Burundian students in an elementary school are forbidden to speak their heritage (first) language, how they are isolated from their siblings and not permitted to visit each other during school hours or speak to each other if they pass in the hallway. Silent, single file constitutes a regulatory passage to and from class and to and from lunch. There is no collaboration permitted in classroom activities; each student is expected to work alone. Amid this administrative, controlling interaction, one Burundian child (Spiderman) becomes depressed, his teacher has low expectations for him despite his academic achievements, indicating a lack of intention to consider him worth investing in. Amongst all this authoritative power and micromanaging, the reasons Anders and Lester describe their work as "Specifically, we detail the power non-Native, whitestream, racist institutions deploy to do harm" (Anders & Lester, 2014 p.169) becomes apparent.

In discussing the 'depth and layers of suffering' that these students endured as the result of resettlement circumstances, the authors began to question their own perspectives of inequity were allowing them to develop any real understanding of the suffering of these students in the research context. They write;

> As Farmer (2005) has noted, the denial of the real origins of suffering "serves the interest of the powerful" (p. 17). There were feelings we had about our own experience in the process that seemed untranslatable, and there were issues we wanted to address that were not neatly tied to data points. Our interpretations of the non-Native, whitestream, and racist institutional norms that school and health professionals reproduced to maintain authority and power in the school and in the only health system to which Spiderman and his family had access revealed unadulterated condemnation (Grande, 2004; Urrieta, 2005 in Anders & Lester 2014 p.171).

While Foucault (1991) urges a positive perspective on the potential of power in his later work on governmentality, this narrative is a wretched example of much of what he perceives institutional power in society to represent in his earlier works (Foucault, 1977). The senseless imposition of petty, inhumane and uncaring rules, routines and discourses designed to dehumanize and 'normalize' in the institutional context of the educational professionals is only surpassed by the resultant medical treatment of Spiderman. His depression was diagnosed and treated with drugs intended, not for children, but for adult psychosis and schizophrenia. His parents were excluded from the Foucauldian discourse which determined this outcome. Spiderman was threatened with school penalties for his subsequent sleepiness in class.

In an attempt to understand the situation with the medication prescribed and the side effects this was causing more fully, Spiderman's parents and the researchers of this study endeavoured to engage in dialogue with both school and health professionals. Their enquiries resulted in the many mechanisms of power being engaged by both cohorts of 'experts', ultimately revealing, in this instance, the powerlessness of the parents and those who supported them in the face of those who wielded institutional power and authority. Spiderman's parents were issued with an ultimatum; cease all contact with the researchers or seek support independently. Out of fear and lack of resources, they chose the former. It would appear, in this instance, that Foucault's (1997) concern that branches of the medical professional had changed their role of healing to one of oppression and censorship to avert any societal contact with those outside of the 'norm' is credible. The issue that is most alarming in this narrative, however, is the notion that all of these actions were viewed as acceptable by individuals who worked as part of these systems. Leask (2012) comments;

> Teachers are, in essence, 'technicians of behaviour', or 'engineers of conduct' (Foucault, 1979, p. 294), who have absorbed (or, rather, are formed by) a set of disciplinary norms which they, in turn, impose upon their charges. ……… Furthermore, and perhaps more importantly, education would also seem to be a core element in the production of *us* (p.60).

In this instance, it is difficult to defend the ways in which these teachers and health professionals 'have been formed' and have imposed their 'disciplinary norms' and power play upon those in their *care*. Campbell (2007), notes that because education is such a value laden profession, teachers may become 'desensitized' to their own behaviours. These ' behaviours may include engaging in actions which are unfair, patronizing, bullying or arrogant and those considered to be basically immoral (Sellars, 2017 p. 36). Farmer (2005 p. 28), notes, 'Structural violence takes its toll in ways that seem to defy explanation'. In this case, the structural violence is operationalized through the school, viewed by Tait (2013) as being primarily about regulation and inculcation and not, as commonly viewed, as predominantly concerned with educating students to maximize their potential. He notes (2013, p. 91) 'if you want to understand how we govern contemporary societies, the first place to look is the school', a perspective that is validated by the very nature of compulsory schooling, enrolment ages, curricula and other authoritarian aspects previously discussed. Indeed, the school remains as an institution which reflects Foucault's earliest notions of power structures.

> Foucault (1995) recognised that power is exercised and operates in all directions rather than from the top down. Our education system, however, tends to a post war perspective of top down totalitarian power: education is 'done' to children. Foucault was concerned with places where the recipients, perhaps 'clients' in modern parlance, have little to say in what happens to them. This is a good description of most schools, where students have no real control over the curriculum, teaching, learning or organizational systems (Harber, 2002) in (Watson, Emery, Bayliss, Boushel, & McInnes, 2012 p. 133).

While Foucault's (1995) also present power as a relationship dynamic in which the power of those in authority is necessarily accepted by those upon whom the power is exercised. It appears that in the case of Spiderman and his parents, the capacity to resist this authoritarian power was not able to be realized, as his parents obviously felt that they were not in any position to 'push back' at the agents of power. Given their position in society and in the school, it appears that they felt that they could not engage in any further investigation of Spiderman's case. The totalitarian power of school provides potent imperative to meet the standards of the 'norm' and engage in institutional surveillance, monitoring and evaluative techniques, overriding any 'self -originating ethical intention' (I. Leask, 2012 p. 58) on the part of these professionals. It also erodes any positive disposition they may have towards developing a mutually beneficial symbiotic relationship, critical to the success of students with refugee and asylum seeker backgrounds (Wilkinson & Langat, 2012).

Conclusion

This discussion of power from a Foucauldian perspective served to illustrate the ways in which power operates, not only at levels of authority, but in the minutiae of everyday lives and interactions. It examines how power can be used in schools to mould and regulate individuals in the institutions, both students and staff, to accept and imitate the 'norms' of any society as 'truth' and the single, acceptable manner by which these 'norms' are maintained, despite their constant redefinition and renewal. It also presents the notion of 'discourse' as more than words and conceptual ideas and indicates how power relationships are demonstrated and reinforced in these communications. Importantly, it presents the symbiotic relationship between power and knowledge and the impact that may have on those with lesser power, their epistemological beliefs and their subsequent aspirations of success and acceptance as partners in decision making that pertains to their wellbeing. In developing his unique perspectives on aspects of societal development and on his interpretation of the operations of diverse forms of power, Foucault explains how societies have been woven together, often unconsciously and unsuspectingly, by their very participation and acceptance of societal expectations, and how this impacts on individuals or communities in societies who are 'othered' or seen as inferior. Many of the students with refugee and asylum seeker backgrounds are viewed as inferior in western educational institutions for a number of reasons, but essentially, this deficit perspective originates in the narrowness of the definitions of 'knowledge' determined by the powerful and the perceived lack of power possessed by those who have been '*ascribed*' refugee and asylum seeker status.

It is certainly sensible to argue that this Foucauldian analysis of power as demonstrated in western societies and its institutions are inflicted on all students and not exclusively those with refugee or asylum seeker backgrounds. However, the responsibility of educating large numbers of students with backgrounds of loss, trauma, violence and dispossession in western educational systems has done nothing if not highlight the precarious state of schooling and its intractability with regards to procedural and regulatory regimes, use of administrative power to examine and exclude and narrowness of worldview. These students, amongst all the students who suffer from educational institutionalism and who do not feel they have sufficient power to challenge authority, deserve to be invested in, to be nurtured and to be provided with an education that reflects their own hope, courage and humanity. In order to achieve this, educational reforms that are authentic, far reaching and cognisant of what is it to be human in the 21st century with core values of 'love, life, wisdom and voice (Gidley, 2016) provide a way forward.

As Foucault identifies power as belonging to everyone and as pervading every aspect of life, despite the insidious nature of administrative power, the concerns of restructuring education should not only be directed to the decision-makers, the policymakers, the statisticians or the educators, but to all the participants in school communities and those who support them. As societies are increasingly micromanaged by structures of governmentality, the support systems that are available for these students and communities need not only to provide education that supports 'Wisdom as waking up to multiplicity (Gidley, 2016 p.232)', but one that celebrates, not stifles, human potential for complexity of thought and a fully integrated self (Gidley, 2008). For societies who accept students of refugee and asylum seeker students and their communities, new 'norms' need to emerge, most especially those in relation to epistemologies and ontologies; 'norms' that challenge the core of neoliberal thought and practice.

References

Anders, A. (2012). Lessons From a Postcritical Ethnography, Burundian Children With Refugee Status, and Their Teachers. *Theory Into Practice, 51*, 99-106.

Anders, A., & Lester, J. (2015). Navigating Authoritarian Power in the United States: Families With Refugee Status and Allegorical Representation. *Cultural Studies ↔ Critical Methodologies, 15*(3), 169-179.

Ball, S. J. (2012). *Foucault, Power, and Education*. In. Retrieved from http://newcastle.eblib.com/patron/FullRecord.aspx?p=1101409

Bevir, M. (1999). Foucault, Power and Institutions. *Political Studies, XLVII*, 345-359.

Brown, J., Miller, J., & Mitchell, J. (2006). Interrupted Schooling and the Acquisition of Literacy: Experiences of Sudanese Refugees in Victorian Secondary Schools. *Australian Journal of Language and Literacy, 29*(2), 150-162.

Butler, J. (2001). What is Critique? An Essay on Foucault's Virtue. *European Institute for Progressive Cultural Policies*. Retrieved from http://eipcp.net/transversal/0806/butler/en

Campbell, E. (2007). *The Ethical Teacher*. New York: Open University Press.

Dooley, K. (2009). Re-thinking Pedagogy for Middle School Students with Little, No or Severely Interrupted Schooling. *English Teaching: Practice & Critique (University of Waikato), 8*(1), 5-19.

Dooley, K. (2012). Positioning Refugee Students as Intellectual Class Members. In F. McCarthy & M. Vickers (Eds.), *Immigrant students: Achieving Equity in Education* (pp. 3-20). Charlotte, NC: Information Age Publishing, Inc.

Emert, T. (2014). "Hear a Story, Tell a Story, Teach a Story": Digital Narratives and Refugee Middle Schoolers. *Voices From the Middle, 21*(4), 33-39.

Farmer, P. (2005). *Pathologies of Power: Health, Human Rights and the New War on the Poor*. Berkley: University of California Press.

Foucault, M. (1977). Panopticism (A. Sheridan, Trans.). In *Discipline and Punish: The Birth of the Prison* (pp. 195-228). New York: Vintage Books.

Foucault, M. (1978). *The History of Sexuality* (Vol. 1). New York: Pantheon Booka.

Foucault, M. (1987). The Ethic of the Care for the Self as a Practice of Freedom: An Interview with Michael Foucault on 20th January 1984. In J. W. Bernauer & D. M. Rasmussen (Eds.), *The Final Foucault*. Cambridge, Mass.: MIT Press.

Foucault, M. (1991). *Discipline and Punish: The Birth of aPprison*. . London: Penguin.

Foucault, M. (1991). Governmentality. In B. Burchell, G. Gordon, & B. Miller (Eds.), *The Foucault Effect: Studies in Governmentality*. Chicago: Chicago University Press.

Foucault, M. (1998). *The History of Sexuality: The Will to Knowledge*. London: Penguin.

Foucault, M. (2003). Society Must Be Defended' (D. Macey, Trans.). In *Lectures at the Colle¤ge de France 1975^1976,* . New York: Picador.

Gidley, J. (2008). Beyond Homogenisation of Global Education: Do Alternative Pedagogies such as Steiner Education have anything to offer an Emergent Globalising World? In S. Inayatullah, M. Bussey, & I. Milojevic (Eds.), *Alternative Educational Futures: Pedagogies for an Emergent World* (pp. 253-268). Rotterdam, Netherlands: Sense Publications.

Gidley, J. (2016). *Postformal Education: A Philosophy for Complex Futures*. Switzerland: Springer.

Leask, I. (2012). Beyond Subjection: Notes on the Later Foucault and Education. *Educational Philosophy and Theory, 44*(sup1), 57-73. doi:10.1111/j.1469-5812.2011.00774.x

Lemke, T. (2000). *Foucault, Governmentality, and Critique*. Paper presented at the Rethinking Marxism Conference,, University of Amherst (MA). http://www.thomaslemke web.de/engl.%20texte/Foucault,%20Governmentality,%20and%20Critique%20IV.pdf

LeVine, R. (2010). Cultural Influences on Parenting and Child Development. In C. Worthman, P. Plotsky, D. Schechter, & C. Coummings (Eds.), *Formative Experiences: The Interaction of Caregiving, Culture and Developmental Psychobiology*. New York: Cambridge University Press.

McWilliams, J. A., & Bonet, S. W. (2016). Continuums of Precarity: Refugee Youth Transitions in American High Schools. *International Journal of Lifelong Education, 35*(2), 153-170. doi:10.1080/02601370.2016.1164468

Miller, E., Ziaian, T., & Esterman, A. (2018). Australian School Practices and the Education Experiences of Students with a Refugee Background: A Review of the Literature. *International Journal of Inclusive Education, 22*(4), 339-359. doi:10.1080/13603116.2017.1365955

Miller, J. (2009). Teaching Refugee Learners with Interrupted Education in Science: Vocabulary, Literacy and Pedagogy. *International Journal of Science Education, 31*(4), 571-592. doi:10.1080/09500690701744611

Mills, S. (2003). *Michel Foucault*. London: Routledge.

Rasmussen, K. (2011). Foucault's Genealogy of Racism. *Theory, Culture & Society,* (5), 34-51. Retrieved from doi:DOI: 10.1177/0263276411410448

Said, E. (1978). Introduction. *Orientalism* (8 ed.). New York: Vintage Books.

Sellars, M. (2017). *Reflective Practice for Teachers* (2nd ed.). London: Sage.

Tait, G. (2013). *Making sense of Mass Education*. Melbourne: Cambridge University Press.

Watson, D., Emery, C., Bayliss, P., Boushel, M., & McInnes, K. (2012). *Children's Social and Emotional Wellbeing in Schools*. Bristol, UK: The Policy Press.

Watters, C. (2007). *Refugee Children: Towards the Next Horizon* (1 ed.). Florence: Taylor and Francis.

Weedon, C. (1997). *Feminist Practice and Poststructural theory* (Second Ed.). Maldon MA: Blackwell.

Wilkinson, J., & Langat, K. (2012). Exploring Educators' Practices for African Students from Refugee Backgrounds in an Australian Regional High School *The Australasian Review Of African Studies, 33*(2), 158-177.

Chapter Three: Politics: Neoliberalism and Education

Introduction

The developed world is currently in the grip of a neo liberal paradigm. Neoliberalism is a theoretical model, an economic policy and a political perspective. If neoliberalism was to be crudely described as 'the survival of the fittest' then it would appear that students of refugee and asylum seeker experiences would have all the necessary qualifications and characteristics to be successful in these environments and societies. Unfortunately, this is not the case, and the challenges of this paradigm are made expressly clear in the ways in which they are operationalized in education. Whilst it is not uncommon that politics and political interest are reflected in educational policies, the contributions and prioritizing concerns of neoliberal thought are particularly disadvantageous for those who are already considered to be underprivileged in society, including those students who have been ascribed refugee and asylum seeker status. This chapter explores the ways in which neoliberalism reaches every corner of educational endeavour, and interrogates the manner in which it has changed the nature of teaching and learning interactions, of what means to be a teacher and what it means to be 'educated' in this political and economic paradigm.

Neoliberal Foundations

In the most simple and concise terms, the notion of neoliberalism is based in a nineteenth century notion of classical liberalism, which evolved from the humanist school of thought. This was is a philosophical and ethical idea which focused on rationality, and the capacity of humans to be responsible for their own lives and actions (Steger & Roy). This theory was extended into financial policies following the economic theories of Adam Smith, an eighteenth - century philosopher and economist who proposed that free trade would bring prosperity to all involved and encouraged importing and exporting as a means of trade expansion. A practice that remains a cornerstone of economic policies in current practice. By the late nineteenth century, the neoclassical libertarians advocated for minimal inference by the state in matters of trade, with some notable exceptions, believing it promoted democracy and increased personal freedom. Because of the diverse forms of classical liberalism, democracy and freedom which were not necessarily included in their policies. Liberal policies and perceptions changed again in the first decades of the twentieth century with widespread criticisms of classical libertarian claims from notable philosophers including Dewey and Hayek (Koopman, 2009). It is from the theoretical frameworks of these diverse understandings of liberalism, notably classical liberalism, from which the many faces of current neoliberal activities in western countries have evolved. The term appears to be represented negatively by any number of scholars from diverse disciplines commenting on various aspects of society, for example;

> The word describes what many perceive of as the lamentable spread of capitalism and consumerism, as well as the equally deplorable demolition of the proactive welfare state (Bourdieu 1998; 1998a; 2001; Chomsky 1999; Touraine 2001; Harvey 2005; Hermansen 2005; Saad-Filho and Johnston 2005; Hagen 2006; Plehwe et al. 2006) (Thorsen, 2009 p. 4).

Whilst this discussion focusses primarily on the impact of political decision making and policies on education and its implications for students with refugee and asylum seeker experiences, it is impossible to interrogate this aspect of modern life in resettlement countries as if it were an island, free from any of the other impacts of neoliberalism. The societal demand for information and technology, and the expertise in utilizing these effectively is reflected in educational policy and practice, not to enhance the lives of students and maximize their capacities, nor simply to support the economy. It is utilized as a form of social control which sets standards and 'norms' and which serves to discard members of society who do not conform to these values. Atasay (2014), notes

> In economies that are highly dependent on information and technology, the market logic of sustaining the availability and the high quality of technically skilled labor or individuals educated for the 21st century, has established itself as a fundamental factor of production and a social goal of post-industrial societies that strives for affluence and increased welfare. Education is therefore increasingly marketed towards that end. On the other hand, aligning education and learning with the neoliberal economy is not merely a material economic incentive to remain productive and efficient. This paper will argue that the human capital framework of post-industrial relations of production is also part and parcel of a neoliberal discourse of social control aimed at cultivating social subjectivities that align their conduct with competitive economic sensibilities (Olssen, 2006). Moreover, social welfare agenda of neoliberal reforms are embedded in a competitive regime of "free" consumer subjects, who are mobilized

under the "free-market" machine that selectively works as a social discipline and disposing mechanism to cripple populations that do not identify with neoliberal market principles (p. 172).

Members of society, therefore, are 'polarized' by neoliberal policies. There are sections of society who benefit from market agenda and those who do not. Societies are encouraged dismiss the homeless, the poorly paid and other disadvantaged groups as non – functional members of society who are 'lesser' human beings than those who benefit from market agenda; in schools and in trade. The manner in which neoliberal accountancy uses the information provided by statistic gathering in its immigration policies to separate those who are acceptable (i.e. useful to the economy) and those who are not (Lehman, Annisette, & Agyemang, 2016) validates Foucault's (Foucault, Senallart, Burchell, & College de France, 2008) claim that there was nothing laissez – faire about this complex form of governmentality, it is about ultimate surveillance. Neoliberal dedication to 'free trade' marketing as opposed to 'fair trade' (Koopman, 2009), marketing is also worth ethical scrutiny. "Walk Free Foundation."), estimated that there are 40.5 million people forced into modern slavery worldwide. Many of these are children engaged in forced labour. Through the chain of supply that is facilitated by large global companies, the products of slave labour reach societies in all parts of the world and connects each consumer to the global issue of contemporary slavery. Amongst the products of slave labour are some of the commodities considered to be rudimentary aspects of everyday life in developed countries. Farmer (2005), noted that,

> Working in contemporary Haiti, where in recent decades political violence has been added to the worst poverty in the hemisphere, one learns a great deal about suffering........The biggest problem, of course, is unimaginable poverty, as a long succession of dictatorial governments has been more engaged in pillaging than in protecting the rights of workers, even on paper. As Eduardo Galeano noted in 1973, at the height of the Duvalier dictatorship, "The wages Haiti requires by law belong in the department of science fiction: actual wages on coffee plantations vary from $.07 to $.15 a day." In some senses, the situation has worsened since. (p. 30).

However, these issues of trade practice may largely be overlooked as topics for public scrutiny as engaging in critical thinking in neoliberal societies is considered very dangerous business (Abdelmoumen, 2017).

Neoliberalism and Education

Schools are acknowledged to be the major centre of acculturation for young people (Hamilton & Moore, 2004; Stewart, 2011). They are expected to convey the culture, social expectations and behaviours of the societies in which they are placed, in addition to other functions attributed to them which may include monitoring and surveillance (Foucault, 1977), reproduction of social class by means of fiscal abundance (Connell, 1982) or the stratification of society by identification of various types of 'capital'(Bourdieu, 1986, 1990), although there are some who question the very purpose of education in neoliberal societies (see, for example, Biesta, 2015). An understanding of the educational system and the ways in which it impacts on families and communities that include young children, students and youth with refugee and asylum seeker experiences is critical to their potential to develop positive attitudes and affirmative intercultural interactions in order to enable successful integration and a sense of 'belonging' (Stewart, 2011). This is not only because children of all ages spend more time in institutions that ever before (Watson, Ermery, Bayliss, Boushel, & McInnes, 2012), but because it helps develop an awareness of the ways in which one stage of schooling facilitates success in the next, a progression that may not be the experience of these populations, especially in the context of early childhood education.

Schools frequently act as the 'gatekeepers' to other learning opportunities and prospective occupations by the implementation of the evaluative practices that are deemed appropriate for the societies in which they are placed. They are generally part of a system, the policies, characteristics and policies of which are implemented as mandatory curricula, processes and procedures. In the instance of western education systems, these are based on the political expediencies of neoliberalism or economic rationalism, the latter being indicative of the

> ...reduction in spending by the state on such things as education, health and social welfare and the delivery of the whole or part of these services by the private sector (Wadham, Pudsey, & Boyd, 2007 p. 55).

This economic perspective may give choice of schooling and associated services, but in relation to the majority of families and communities of students with refugee and asylum seeker experiences, the 'user pays' utilization of services provided by the private sector is not an option. For them, and for many other students, inadequately funded public schools and associated services are their only opportunity of complying with the law of mandatory schooling and accessing the allied health services that support educators.

Perhaps a powerful way in which to express the impact of neoliberal policies on the possibilities of authentic education is to draw an analogy with the account of the MacDonaldisation of French haute cuisine described by Fantasia (2010), a theme that is also investigated in the context of globalization and education by Gidley (2016) and Wadham et al. (2007) . Fantasia states,

> What has distinguished industrial cuisine (and its various affiliated institutions) from *haute cuisine* (and its cult of artisanship) is that the industrial is governed by the principles and rules of the economic field. Its standards uphold the values of profit maximization, standardization, high volume production, technological innovation, speed and efficiency; whereas *haute cuisine* has been governed by the logic and values of art and artisanship, with a fidelity to traditional practice, to the fabrication of unique creations, to complex and sophisticated technique, aesthetic refinement, low volume production, formal training the consumption of time etc. one extols the quantity of production, the other the quality of creation; the one is led by the managerial skills of the *chef d'enterprise,* the other by the virtuosity of the *chef d'cuisine* (p. 39).

Much of the power and control that neoliberal politics exerts over educational matters is achieved by the strictures of its 'audit' culture and agendas of accountability (Biesta, 2015; Black & Wiliam, 2005; Darling- Hammond, 2004; de Lissovey, 2013; Susan Groundwater-Smith & Nicole Mockler, 2009; Lipman, 2009) exercise throughout the system. Biesta (2014), reports succinctly on exactly how this process is implemented and how, from policy to pupil, no aspect of education is left unaffected by its insidious influence. He states,

> Now that governments in many countries have established a strong grip on schools through a combination of curriculum prescription, testing, inspection, measurement and league tables, they are turning their attention to teacher education in order to establish total control over the educational system (p. 121).

The ways in this 'total control' are established are also investigated by Ball (2016b) who identifies three 'technologies' that are being used by neoliberal governments to change the ways in which education is experienced. He nominates these as 'Market, Management and Performance (p. 1). Arguing that neoliberalism in education has done much to change the way in which individuals value themselves and others, he echoes the concerns of Atasay (2014) regarding the ways in which neoliberal education is changing society and its interrelationships. He seeks to alert educationalists, teachers in particular about the totality of the impact of seeming small, innocuous changes to policy and practice that, when viewed in total, constitute a threat to the ways in which educators have traditionally engaged in their professional work. He explores the market impact of the privatization of much of schooling, either by supporting choice in private schools or permitting various other bodies to have a substantial say in the running of schools. Irrespective of the opportunity of these organizations and private schools to make profit, both these types of privatization have the result of changing the status of schooling from a service to a commodity, which in turn, influenced the ethical and moral considerations of those associated with this privatization measures. This is exacerbated by the changes in the ways school leadership is articulated. School management, as viewed by Ball, is now the position of activating change, not just in the way things are done, but in the ways that an educated person is to be defined, in the understanding of what it is to teach and learn and in what it is considered to be teacher's work. His most critical comment is reserved for what he terms as 'performativity', which, in essence, can be the interpreted as the ultimate insult to education and those who are dedicated to its aims of, professionalism, ethics and integrity. He states,

> Performativity is a term I use in a particular way – not just to refer to systems of performance management or the deployment of performance indicators but rather to the complex and powerful relationships between such indicators and management systems and teacher identity and professionalism (Ball, 2003, 2008, 2012). In one simple sense professionalism is the enemy of performance. While professionalism, as I see it, rests upon judgment related to principles, set within the context of practice, systems of performativity seek to pre-empt and displace judgment and de-contextualize practice with a form of responsiveness to external drivers: ……. More and more in education, and other parts of the public sector, our days are numbered – literally – and those numbers are collated and monitored ever more closely and carefully. Performativity is a technology that relates effort, values, purposes and self-understanding directly to measures and comparisons of output. Indeed, within the rigours and disciplines of performativity we are required to spend increasing amounts of our time in making ourselves accountable, reporting on what we do, rather than doing it. Forms, grids, databases, reviews and audits are daily more a part of our practice. Furthermore, they do not simply report our practice: they inform, construct and drive our practice. Our sense of what is right is challenged by what is necessary or, more precisely, what is measured (p. 7-8).

A return to the concerns of Biesta (2014), provides an opportunity to more fully understand the concerns about teacher education that are explored here by Ball (2016). Neoliberal policy has influenced the very human interaction that occurs in the teaching and learning relationship for students in schools. It requires pre- service and in-service teachers to change their perceptions of teachers' work as a 'caring' profession and necessitates them to re- evaluate themselves and their work in terms of productivity. This not only impacts negatively on the capacities of teachers to reflect on their work, to develop teacher judgment and to engage in the ongoing process of reconceptualising their identities as teachers, it downgrades teachers' potential to make a difference to their students' learning. The crisis of conscience around teacher preparation and teacher professional learning in neoliberal educational contexts has attracted considerable concern from those who understand the capacities of teachers to interpret any mandatory documentation in ways that are personally meaningful and that support the learning of their students (see, for example, Bolkan, 2015; Cetin-Dindar, 2016; Evans & Tribble, 1986; Noble, 2002, 2004; Sellars, 2014; Tomlinson, 2000).

> Educational endeavour, which had previously been focused on the promotion of social equity and on preparing young people for work in societies that retained many of the characteristics of the industrial era, became increasingly viewed as a means by which national economic viability and social stability could be sustained (Brown & Lauder, 1996). These circumstances resulted in massive changes to approaches in educational governance, which has subsequently resulted in change to professional practice. Formerly a relatively autonomous profession, with agency to implement various basic curricula through any number of personally meaningful pedagogical practices, teachers and student teachers have now found themselves in a culture of unprecedented and increasingly intensive external audit and supervision (Sellars, 2017 p.27).

Teacher preparation that focusses on developing skills for pre-service teachers so that a primary part of their work demands that they understand diverse learners, their various motivations and ways of making meaning and they engage in facilitating students' identities as competent learners as a priority in their professional work. Teacher preparation that is dictated by the governing authorities and governed, regulated and supervised by its agents not only restricts personal scholarship, choice and creativity in practice, but lends itself to being corrupted by industrial principles of economic efficiencies, production quotas, benchmarking and ubiquitous practices, producing at best, trained technicians and at worst, 'tick a box' teachers.

Angus (2007), amongst others concerned about teacher education in the current political climate (see, for example, Clark, 1988; Darling-Hammond, 2010; Darling-Hammond, Chung, & Frelow, 2002; Evertson, Hawley, & Zlotnik, 1985; Goodwin, 2010; Hatton & Smith, 1995), asks the pertinent question; does current teacher preparation prepare competent technicians or informed players? Some answers may lie in the interpretation of the requirement of teacher standards, another nod to the industrialized notion of schooling, which has been welcomed and promoted by some but approached more cautiously by others who (see, for example, Apple, 2001; Darling-Hammond, 2004; 1999; Darling-Hammond & Wise, 1985; Evans, 2008; Groundwater-Smith & Mockler, 2009; Sachs, 2003; Schuck, Gordon, & Buchanan, 2008; Thiessen, 2000).

Whilst standards for professional occupations are often a positive indication of a high level of expertise maintained by the members of the profession in question, in the case of teaching, it can be argued that professional standards for teachers is itself an oxymoron. Every professional organization that develops standards for its members does so in collaboration with its members and implements these under the guidance of democratically elected member of the profession. They take into account that what is considered to be professional practice is culturally and geographically mediated (Helsby, 1996; Holroyd, 2000). This is not the case for teaching standards, which are designed to be applied to teachers in diverse contexts across entire nations. Consequently, the development of common policies, agendas in new managerialism, and a shift in financial responsibilities accompanied by strict accountability may lead, in some contexts, to a decrease in professionalism.(Day & Smethem, 2009). Sachs (2003), indicates that this situation results from local social, political and economic factors.

In a return to the analogy with the industrialized cuisine and haute cuisine, it becomes apparent that the entire teaching 'industry' in neoliberal public -school systems and other which are funded by governments, is one that boosts economy in all aspects of the educational field and maximizes profit making by outsourcing many of its responsibilities to private providers. It further embraces an industrial model by standardizing teaching and learning, teacher education, curriculum and policy documents. In this type of benchmarking of what is to be taught, when it is to be taught and what is to be considered valuable, neoliberal governments take control of the epistemological foundations of societies in much the same way as Foucault had envisaged when he discussed the power/knowledge interpolation (Mills, 2003). The high -volume production characteristic of industrialised cuisine is reflected in the education practices which are dominant in neoliberal classrooms to give an impression of efficiency. These include one size fits all pedagogies of transmission (Haberman, 2010), universal testing (Gardner, 2000c), teaching to the test (Abrams, Pedulla, & Madaus, 2003),(and publicly glorifying the results) and discriminating against those areas of knowledge and wisdom that cannot be assessed by standardized testing (Zhao, 2016). In this way, speed and technological advances are postured as the major traits and most highly prized components of modern societies and of educational prowess. Gidley (2008), considers,

> One of the greatest obstacles to creating learning societies for the future is the model Of Western culture- and, by default, the model of education – that is being promoted by globalization (p. 247).

Models of education that may be considered to be the haute cuisine of schooling are those which respect diversity and a multiplicity of perspectives, in addition to the holistic development of students as humans. This requires, not a focus on so called 'value free' rapid technological change but a change of ideology (Lanning,

1994). This ideology would need to include the notion that teaching is a value laden, interactive, art form (Shulman, 1983), not a technical appointment, that the tradition role of 'caring' in schools (Noddings, 2005, 2012) is a vital component of developing the cognitive, emotional, social, physical and spiritual attributes of all children and young people. To do this authentically, educators have to invest time and creativity in their professional work. Students must be educated in environments where their needs as individual learners can be met and where concepts, knowledge and skills that are not instantly measurable in standardized procedures are valued and respected for their capacity to contribute to improving the human condition. The increased workload experienced by teachers in neoliberal educational contexts is largely administrative (Darling-Hammond, 2009; Groundwater-Smith & Mockler, 2009), and does little to contribute to the overall quality of the teaching and learning interactions that contribute to their own professional learning as reflective experiences and to the overall wellbeing of a diverse student cohort. This can be summed up in a comment by Shulman, (1983, p. 488) that

> it is 'ludicrous' to try and dictate how teachers should best respond when policy and practice are so often the antithesis of each other. Indeed, creative and effective ways of responding to students' needs is often to be found by engaging in critical professional discourse, the capacity for which is an essential component of transformative education (Sellars, 2017 p. 30).

The ways in which educational reforms in a variety of neoliberal policies and contexts have been undertaken, bear no relationship to transformative practices, incorporating, as common themes, the five following components;

– They are proposed because governments believe that by intervening to change the conditions under which students learn, they can accelerate improvements, raise standards of achievements and somehow increase economic competitiveness
– They address implicit worries of governments concerning perceived fragmentation of personal and social values in a society
– They challenge teachers' existing practices, resulting in at least temporary destabilization
– They result in an increased workload for teachers; and
– They do not always pay attention to teachers' identities – arguably central to motivational efficacy, commitment, job satisfaction and effectiveness (Day & Smethem, 2009 p. 3).

What implications are there for students with refugee and asylum seeker backgrounds?

One of the most critical disadvantages for these populations of students is the ways in which they are perceived as students in neoliberal education. As many students with refugee and asylum seeker background do not speak the language of the majority cultures into which they were placed, they are immediately susceptible to perceived as 'deficit'. This has considerable consequences for both their teachers and the students themselves (see, for example, Bigelow, 2010; Bigelow & Tarone, 2004; Brown, Miller, & Mitchell, 2006; Chan & Dally, 2001; Creagh, 2016; Dooley & Thangaperumal, 2011; Gee, 1989; Hammond, 2008; Matthews, 2008; McCarty, Watahomigie, & Dien, 2004; Miller, 2009). In many countries of settlement, the neoliberal education policies place students who are English Language Learners (ELLS) and have refugee and asylum seeker backgrounds in language intervention programs. In almost all instances, these programs reflect the neoliberal ideals of efficiency, productivity and sustained measurement. In many cases the language programs were originally designed for populations with very different educational backgrounds to those of refugee and asylum seeker students. These is particularly apparent when the students have little experience of print materials or have a background of oracy (Sellars & Murphy, 2018). These programs frequently have an overall concentration on grammar and vocabulary, to the detriment of the cultural and social values and the nuances of language in different situations (Ajayi, 2009; Karen Dooley, 2009a; Luke, Dooley, & Woods, 2011; McCarty et al., 2004). The programs are most frequently implemented in language centres and as withdrawal programs in schools, the latter of which frequently serves to identify students of refugee and asylum seeker backgrounds as deficit (Alford, 2014), limits their in class interactions with peers and teachers and may promote additional problems in potentially exclusive and hostile learning environments (Campbell Iii, 2017; Essomba, 2017; Riggs & Due, 2011).

The ways in which neoliberal education systems position students with refugee and asylum seeker backgrounds is not entirely due to public or school perceptions of these populations. The stresses of the economies of time and 'performativity' (Ball, 2016a) have created the new teaching and learning dynamic that Ball presents. Teachers do not have time to prioritize their students' individual needs in their pursuit of results, benchmarking, accreditation and meeting and maintaining standards (Dooley, 2009b; Naidoo, 2009) . Whilst this is pertinent to all learners and their situations, for students with refugee and asylum seeker experiences, it is exacerbated by the circumstances under which they are admitted to educational institutions in their new homelands with neoliberal government policies impacting on education. They enter schools with little or no continuity of schooling, limited language competencies to facilitate interactions and support learning in classrooms and slight, if any respect for their knowledge, skills and tenacity. They are expected to compete, with native language speakers who have had ongoing experience of various social and cultural norms, regular schooling and a sense of belonging, in the programs of assessment, measurement and standardization that are characteristic of neoliberal education systems. The impact of the restructuring of education to a more economically focussed agenda impacts on all students, but the issue identified by Ball is the most critical and dehumanizing for those in education who need, and deserve, to be recognised and valued as human. Ball states,

> I will consider neoliberalism mainly with a lower-case n rather than a capital N. That is, rather than the economy and economic policy, I will discuss interpersonal relations, identity and subjectivity, how we value ourselves and value others, how we think about what we do, and why we do it. That is, I want to address neoliberalism 'in here' – in the head, the heart and the soul – rather than 'out there' in politics and the economy…(Ball, 2016 p. 1-2).

This comment reflects the stark reality of neoliberal education systems which value only the statistically useful, the economically viable and those who play to rules of competition, efficiency and survival of the fittest. The heart of teaching, the very human interactions of nurture, of caring and supporting all learners as individuals of difference who have a right to learn equally effectively, is subsumed in the layers of accountability, in the narrow epistemological focus and in the merchant mentality of balancing the books, interrogating test results and anxiously perusing the leader boards. In many theories of child development, authentic education and student emotional and social wellbeing, teaching and learning environments such as these would be condemned as unsuitable ecosystems for children and young people. As such, they are totally inadequate setting in which to support students who have suffered the trauma and loss of refugee and asylum seeker experiences.

Conclusion

This chapter sought to identify the key principles of neoliberalism in contemporary societies which become new homelands to students with refugee and asylum seeker experiences and to their communities. It glanced briefly at the historical precedents of this political and economic theory and practice and the means by which it makes modern consumer societies compliant in practices associated with modern slavery and international market forces which discriminate against fair trade and equitable opportunity. It attempted to provide some insight into the subtle, incremental manner in which this political and economic perspective had redefined education and the nature of teaching and learning, by using these institutional places of learning as constantly supervised, monitored 'sorting' mechanisms by which students are graded and identified as economically useful to society or to be discarded. A discussion of the changing roles of teachers in this neoliberal model revealed that the major foci of their work has changed. They are increasingly employed in measuring, standardizing and complying with mandatory curriculum and other documentation, including excessive record keeping. Typically, all of this 'performativity' serves to distract and to minimize the time and energy traditionally devoted to student nurture and wellbeing, meeting the learning needs of diverse student population and undertaking what have been understood as traditional teacher professional responsibilities. It is in this educational environment that students who have experienced and survived unimaginable trauma and loss are facing new, uncertain challenges and futures.

References

Abdelmoumen, M. (2017, August 10th). Dr Wayne Ross: The Fear Created by Precarious Existence in The Neoliberal World Discourages Critical Thinking:. *American Herald Tribune*. Retrieved from http://ahtribune.com/indepth/1833-wayne-ross.html

Abrams, L. M., Pedulla, J. J., & Madaus, G. F. (2003). Views from the Classroom: Teachers' Opinions of Statewide Testing Programs. *Theory Into Practice, 42*(1), 18-29. doi:10.1207/s15430421tip4201_4

Ajayi, L. (2009). ESL Theory- Practice Dynamics: the Difficulty of Integrating Sociocultural Perspectives into Pedagogical Practice. *Foreign Language Annals, 41*(4), 639-659.

Alford, J. H. (2014). "Well, hang on, they're actually much better than that!": Disrupting Dominant Discourses of Deficit about English Language Learners in Senior High School English. *English Teaching: Practice & Critique (University of Waikato), 13*(3), 71-88.

Angus, L. (2007). Globalisation and the Reshaping of Teacher Professional Culture : Do we Train Competent Technicians or Informed Players in the Policy Process? In T. Townsend & R. Iates (Eds.), *Handbook of Teacher Education: Globalisation, Professionalism and Standards in Times of Change*. Dordrecht, The Netherlands: Springer.

Apple, M. (2001). Markets, Standards, Teaching, and Teacher Education. *Journal of Teacher Education, 52*(3), 182-196. doi:10.1177/0022487101052003002

Atasay, E. (2014). Neoliberal Multiculturalism embedded in Social Justice Education: Commodification of Multicultural Education for the 21st Century. *Journal for Critical Education Policy Studies (JCEPS), 12*(3), 171-204.

Ball, S. (2016). Neoliberal Education: Confronting the Slouching Beast. *Policy Futires in Education, 0*(0), 1-4. Retrieved from doi:DOI: 10.1177/1478210316664259

Biesta, G. (2014). *The Beautiful Risk of Education*. Boulder. : Paradigm Publishers.

Biesta, G. (2015). What is Education for? On Good Education, Teacher Judgement, and Educational Professionalism. *European Journal of Education, 50*(1), 75-87. doi: 10.1111/ejed.12109

Bigelow. (2010). Orality and Literacy within the Somali Diaspora. *Language Learning, 60*, 25-57.

Bigelow, M., & Tarone, E. (2004). The Role of Literacy Level in Second Language Acquisition: Doesn't who we study determine what we know? *TESOL Quarterly, 38*(4), 689-700.

Black, P., & Wiliam, D. (2005). Lessons from Around the World: How Policies, Politics and Cultures Constrain and Afford Assessment Practices. *Curriculum Journal, 16*(2), 249-261. doi:10.1080/09585170500136218

Bolkan, S. (2015). Intellectually Stimulating Students' Intrinsic Motivation: The Mediating Influence of Affective Learning and Student Engagement. *Communication Reports, 28*(2), 80-91. doi: 10.1080/08934215.2014.962752

Bourdieu, P. (1986). The Forms of Capital. In J. G. Richardson (Ed.), *The Handbook of Theory: Research for the Sociology of Education* (pp. 241-258). New York: Greenwood Press.

Bourdieu, P. (1990). *Reproduction in Education, Society, and Culture*. London: Sage.

Brown, J., Miller, J., & Mitchell, J. (2006). Interrupted Schooling and the Acquisition of Literacy: Experiences of Sudanese refugees in Victorian Secondary Schools. *Australian Journal of Language and Literacy, 29*(2), 150-162.

Campbell, J. A. (2017). Attitudes towards Refugee Education and its link to Xenophobia in the United States. *Intercultural Education, 28*(5), 474-479. doi:10.1080/14675986.2017.1336374

Cetin-Dindar, A. (2016). Student Motivation in Constructivist Learning Environments. *Eurasia Journal of Mathematics, Science & Technology Education, 12*(2), 233-247. doi: 10.12973/eurasia.2016.1399a

Chan, L. K. S., & Dally, K. (2001). Learning Disabilities and Literacy & Numeracy Development. *Australian Journal of Learning Disabilities, 6*(1), 12-19. doi:10.1080/19404150109546652

Clark, C. (1988). Asking the Right Questions about Teacher Preparation: Contributions of Research on TeacherThinking. *Educational Researcher, 17*(2), 5-12.

Connell, R. (1982). *Making the Difference:Schools, Families and Social Division*. Sydney: Allen & Unwin.

Creagh, S. (2016). 'Language Background Other Than English': a problem NAPLaN test Category for Australian Students of Refugee Background. *Race Ethnicity and Education, 19*(2), 252-273. doi:10.1080/13613324.2013.843521

Darling- Hammond, L. (2004). Standards, Accountability, and School Reform. . *Teachers College Record, 106*(6), 1047-1058.

Darling-Hammond, L. (1999). *Reshaping Teacher Policy, Preparation and Practice: Influences on the National Board for Teaching Professional Standards*. Washington, DC: AACTE Publications.

Darling-Hammond, L. (2009). Teaching and Educational Transformation: Second International Handbook of Educational Change. In A. Hargreaves, A. Lieberman, M. Fullan, & D. Hopkins (Eds.), *Teaching and Educational Transformation:* (Vol. 23, pp. 505-520). Netherlands: Springer

Darling-Hammond, L. (2010). Teacher Education and the American Future. *Journal of Teacher Education, 61*(1-2), 35-47. doi:10.1177/0022487109348024

Darling-Hammond, L., Chung, R., & Frelow, F. (2002). Variation in Teacher Preparation. *Journal of Teacher Education, 53*(4), 286-302. doi:10.1177/0022487102053004002

Darling-Hammond, L., & Wise, A. (1985). Beyond Standardization: State Standards and School Improvement. *The Elementary School Journal, 85*(3), 315-336.

Day, C., & Smethem, L. (2009). The Effects of Reform: Have Teachers really Lost their Sense of Professionalism? *Journal of Educational Change, 10*(2), 141-157. doi:10.1007/s10833-009-9110-5

de Lissovey, N. (2013). Pedagogy of the Impossible: Neoliberalisom and the Ideology of Accountability. *Policy Futires in Education, 11*(4), 423-435. doi:http://dx,doi.org/10.2304/pfie.2013.11.4.423

Dooley, K. (2009a). Intercultural Conversation: Building Understanding Together. *Journal of Adolescent & Adult Literacy, 52*(6), 497-506.

Dooley, K. (2009b). Re-thinking Pedagogy for Middle School Students with Little, No or Severely Interrupted Schooling. *English Teaching: Practice & Critique (University of Waikato), 8*(1), 5-19.

Dooley, K., & Thangaperumal, P. (2011). Pedagogy and Participation: Literacy Education for Low Literate Refugee Students of African Origin in a Western School System. *Language and Education, 25*(5), 385-397.

Essomba, M. À. (2017). The Right to Education of Children and Youngsters from Refugee Families in Europe. *Intercultural Education, 28*(2), 206-218. doi:10.1080/14675986.2017.1308659

Evans, E. D., & Tribble, M. (1986). Perceived Teaching Problems, Self-Efficacy, and Commitment to Teaching among Preservice Teachers. *The Journal of Educational Research, 80*(2), 81-85.

Evans, L. (2008). Professionalism, Professionality and the Development of Education Professionals. *British Journal of Educational Studies, 56*(1), 20-38.

Evertson, C., Hawley, W., & Zlotnik, M. (1985). Making a Difference in Educational Quality Through Teacher Education. *Journal of Teacher Education, 36*(3), 2-12. doi:10.1177/002248718503600302

Fantasia, R. (2010). 'Cooking the Books'of the French Gastronomic field. In E. Silva & A. Warde (Eds.), *Cultural analysis and Bourdieu's Legacy: Settling Accounts and Developing Alternaticves*. Albington, Oxen: Routledge.

Farmer, P. (2005). *Pathologies of Power: Health, Human Rights and the New War on the Poor*. Berkley: University of California Press.

Foucault, M. (1977). Panopticism (A. Sheridan, Trans.). In *Discipline and Punish: The Birth of thePrison* (pp. 195-228). New York: Vintage Books.

Foucault, M., Senallart, M., Burchell, G., & College de France. (2008). *The Birth of Biopolitics: Lectures at the Collège de France, 1978-79.* . Basingstoke, England: Palgrave Macmillan.

Gardner, H. (2000c). *The Disciplined Mind: Beyond Facts and Standardized Tests, The K-12 Education Every Child Deserves.* New York: Penguin Books.

Gee, J. (1989). What is Literacy? *Journal of Education, 171*(1), 18-25.

Gidley, J. (2008). Beyond Homogenisation of Global Education: Do Alternative Pedagogies such as Steiner Education have Anything to Offer an Emergent Globalising World? In S. Inayatullah, M. Bussey, & I. Milojevic (Eds.), *Alternative Educational Futures: Pedagogies for an Emergent World* (pp. 253-268). Rotterdam, Netherlands: Sense Publications.

Gidley, J. (2016). *Postformal Education: A Philosophy for Complex Futures*. Switzerland: Springer.

Goodwin, A. (2010). Globalization and the Preparation of Quality Teachers: Rethinking Knowledge Domains for Teaching. *Teaching Education, 21*(1), 19-32.

Groundwater-Smith, S., & Mockler, N. (2009). What Learning Community? A Knotty Problem. Teacher Professional Learning in an Age of Compliance. In (Vol. 2, pp. 101-111): Springer Netherlands.

Groundwater-Smith, S., & Mockler, N. (2009). Who Pays the Piper? Agendas, Priorities and Accountabilities. Teacher Professional Learning in an Age of Compliance. In (Vol. 2, pp. 93-100): Springer Netherlands.

Haberman, M. (2010). 11 Consequences of Failing to Address the 'Pedagogy of Poverty'. *Kappan Classic, 92*(2), 45. Retrieved from kappanmagazine.org website: kappanmagazine.org

Hamilton, R., & Moore, D. (2004). *Educational Interverntions for Refugee Children: Theoretical perspectives on best practice*. Abibgton, Oxen: Routledge.

Hammond, J. (2008). Intellectual Challenge and ESL Students: Implications of Quality Teaching Initiatives. *Australian Journal of Language and Literacy, 31*(2), 128-154.

Hatton, N., & Smith, D. (1995). Reflection in Teacher Education: Towards Definition and Implementation. *Teaching and Teacher Education, 11*(1), 33-49. doi:10.1016/0742-051x(94)00012-u

Helsby, G. (1996). Defining and Developing Professionalism in English Secondary Schools. *Journal of Education for Teaching, 22*(2), 135-148.

Holroyd, C. (2000). Are Assessors Professional? Student Assessment and the Professionalism of Academics. *Active Learning in Higher Education, 1*(1), 28-44.

Koopman, K. (2009). Morals and Markets: Liberal Democracy Through Dewey and Hayek. *The Journal of Speculative Philosophy, New Series,, 23*(3), 151-179. Retrieved from doi:10.1353/jsp.0.0083

Lanning, R. (1994). Education and Everyday Life: An Argument against "Educational Futures". *Canadian Journal of Education / Revue canadienne de l'éducation, 19*(4), 464-478.

Lehman, C., Annisette, M., & Agyemang. (2016). Immigration and Neoliberalism: Three Cases and Counter Accounts. *Accounting, Auditing & Accountability Journal,, 20*(1), 43-79.

Lipman, P. (2009). Beyond Accountability. In A. Darder, M. Baltodamao, & R. Torres (Eds.), *The Critical Pedagogy Reader* (2nd ed.). Abingdon, Oxen: Routledge.

Luke, A., Dooley, K., & Woods, A. (2011). Comprehension and Content: Planning Literacy in Low Socioeconomic and Culturally Diverse Schools. *The Australian Educational Researcher, 38*(2), 149-166. doi:10.1007/s13384-011-0021-0

Matthews, J. (2008). Schooling and Settlement: Refugee Education in Australia. *International Studies in Sociology of Education, 18*(1), 31-45. doi:10.1080/09620210802195947

McCarty, T. L., Watahomigie, L. J., & Dien, T. (2004). *Sociocultural Contexts of Language and Literacy*. Retrieved from http://newcastle.eblib.com/patron/FullRecord.aspx?p=238935

Miller, J. (2009). Teaching Refugee Learners with Interrupted Education in Science: Vocabulary, Literacy and Pedagogy. *International Journal of Science Education, 31*(4), 571-592. doi:10.1080/09500690701744611

Mills, S. (2003). *Michel Foucault*. London: Routledge.

Naidoo, L. (2009). Developing Social Inclusion through After-school Homework Tutoring: A Study of African Refugee Students in Greater Western Sydney. *British Journal of Sociology of Education, 30*(3), 261-273. doi:10.1080/01425690902812547

Noble, T. (2002). Blooming with Multiple Intelligences. A Planning Tool for Curriculum Differentiation. *Learning Matters, 7*(3).

Noble, T. (2004). Integrating the Revised Bloom's Taxonomy with Multiple Intelligences: A Planning Tool for Curriculum Differentiation. *Teachers College Record, 106*(1), 193-211.

Noddings, N. (2005). *The Challenge to Care in Schools;An Alternative Approach to Education* (2nd ed.). New York: Teachers College Press.

Noddings, N. (2012). *The Philosophy of Education*. Boulder Colorado: Westview Press.

Riggs, D., & Due, C. (2011). (Un)common ground?: English Language Acquisition and Experiences of Exclusion amongst New Arrival Students in South Australian Primary Schools. *Global Studies in Cultue and Power, 18*(3), 273-290.

Sachs, J. (2003). Teacher Professional Standards: Controlling or Developing Teaching? *Teachers and Teaching, 9*(2), 175-186. doi:10.1080/13540600309373

Schuck, S., Gordon, S., & Buchanan, J. (2008). What are We Missing Here? Problematising Wisdoms on Teaching Quality and Professionalism in Higher Education. *Teaching in Higher Education, 13*(5), 537-547.

Sellars, M. (2014). Skills and Strategies for Differentiation. In *Reflective Practice for Teachers* (pp. 225-247). London: Sage.

Sellars, M. (2017). *Reflective Practice for Teachers* (2nd ed.). London: Sage.

Sellars, M., & Murphy, H. (2018). Becoming Australian: A Review of Southern Sudanese Students' Educational Experiences. *International Journal of Inclusive Education, 22*, 490-509.

Shulman, L. (1983). Autonomy and Obligation. In L. Shulman & G. Sykes (Eds.), *Handbook of Teaching and Policy*. New York: Longman.

Steger, M., & Roy, R. (2010). *Neoliberalism: A Very Short Introduction:* . New York: Oxford University Press.

Stewart, J. (2011). *Supporting Refugee Children: Strategies for Educators*. Ontario Canada: University of Toronto Press.

Thiessen, D. (2000). A Skillful Start to a Teaching Career: A Matter of Developing Impactful Behaviors, Reflective Practices, or Professional Knowledge? *International Journal of Educational Research, 33*, 515-537.

Thorsen, D. (2009). *The Neoliberal Challenge*. Department of Political Science. University of Oslo. Retrieved from http://folk.uio.no/daget/neoliberalism2.pdf

Tomlinson, C. (2000). Differentiation of Instruction in the Elementary Grades. *Eric Digest*. Retrieved from http://ecap.crc.illinois.edu/eecearchive/digests/2000/tomlin00.pdf

Wadham, B., Pudsey, J., & Boyd, R. (2007). *Culture and Education*. Frenchs Forest, NSW: Pearson Education Australia.

Walk Free Foundation. Retrieved from https://www.walkfreefoundation.org/understand/

Watson, B., Ermery, C., Bayliss, P., Boushel, M., & McInnes, K. (Eds.). (2012). *Children's Social and Emotional wellbeing in schools*. Bristol, UK: The Policy Press.

Zhao, Y. (2016). Shifting the Paradigm: Assessing What Matters. In Y. Zhao (Ed.), *Counting what Counts: Reframing Education Outcomes* (pp. 169-180). Bloomington, IL: Solution Tree Press.

Chapter Four: People: Refugee status, Trauma and Loss

Introduction

This chapter takes a closer look at refugee and asylum seeker status. It also discusses the ways in which an understanding of the nature and extent of refugee experiences of trauma and loss can be established in the literature and research perspectives of the first world cultural contexts in which these students are settled. This is an important distinction as suffering and loss are culturally mediated Frater-Mathieson (2004); (Watters, 2007), as are the ways in which the resultant symptoms and psychological experiences are interpreted and interventions determined. This detailed analysis from the literature and theoretical frameworks is not intended to present a deficient, hopeless, or totally dependent representation of these populations, but to examine, the urgency with which educational practices need to be reformed to meet the needs of these students and to engage with pedagogies of love and care, including compassion, for all these students irrespective of cultural social and individual differences. Declarations from the United Nations, supported by researchers and experts in the associated areas of forced migration and refugee experiences, clinicians, psychologists and support services indicate that the essential nature of authentic education is critical for the psychological wellbeing of these populations (McBrien, 2005; McBrien & Ford, 2012). This presents considerable challenges to the current foundations and purposes of education as articulated by neoliberal governments.

Refugee and Asylum Seeker Status

The classification of these populations, despite the onerous nature of labelling groups of individuals, allows some understanding of the distinctions made amongst and within students with refugee experiences, their families, and wider communities. Refugees are defined as individuals who have been granted this status by the United Nations or some other country.

- They are outside their own country
- Have a well-founded fear of persecution due to his/ her race, religion, nationality, member of a particular social group or political opinion, and are
- Unable or unwilling to return. (http://www.roads-to-refuge.com.au/whois/whois_definitions.html)

Unlike migrants, who voluntarily leave their country in search of a better life elsewhere, refugees are forced migrants and are the most vulnerable of these populations (Berry, 1997; Berry, Phinney, Sam, & Vedder, 2006; Berry, 2009; Berry, Horenczyk, & Kwak, 2006; Doná & Berry, 1994; Ogbu, 1995a, 1995b). There are several reasons for this vulnerability, most of which relate to lack of choice. These populations have little or no control over their displacement and subsequent departure of their homeland. They have few opportunities to return, if they wished to do so and they have very little input into the whereabouts of their final destinations. This results in considerable hardship, disempowerment, disadvantage, and a sense of helplessness about their own futures and that of their children (http://www.roads-to-refuge.com.au/resources/transcripts/transcript-who-is-a-refugee.html, http://www.unhcr.org/).

Asylum seekers are individuals who have left their countries under duress or fear from prosecution and are yet to be granted asylum in another country. Approximately one million individuals a year seek asylum. This population is frequently subsumed into the group of refugees after they have been granted asylum, although in times of mass evacuation of countries when it is not possible to interview asylum seekers individually, they are included as 'prima facie' refugees (http://www.unhcr.org/en-au/asylum-seekers.html, http://www.unhcr.org/). For the purposes of this writing, students with refugee experiences will include the children and young people of individuals who are seeking, or have been granted asylum. While it is acknowledged that the characteristics of these populations may differ, much of the trauma, the distress, and the need for pedagogies of love and care is common to both. Consequently, this chapter also validates why pedagogies of love and care are vital for the emotional, social, and academic growth of these students, despite the very mention of the word *love* challenging the foundations of the audit based culture that economic influences have imposed on educational endeavours.

Love, Care and Compassion

Gidley (2016:194) expressed this succinctly 'it is not hard to imagine that words like *love* are likely to create what MacLure calls '*ontological panic*' amongst the educational audit police'. A similar response may be made to the notion of compassion, which, in this context, is discussed in terms of being *human* (Hume, in Pinson, Arnot, & Candappa, 2010). There have been many philosophical debates over the centuries regarding the exact nature and source of compassion, its role in society, its capacity to undertake the task of bringing a dimension of morality to individuals and societies and its part in determining the appropriate responses of those involved in education to groups and individuals who may be deserving of compassionate understanding (Pinson et al., 2010). In an attempt to establish how the component of compassion can be assimilated into the notion of pedagogies of love and care, these philosophical reflections provide ways in which to understand how the educational paradigms of school systems influenced by the purposes and ideologies of an economic agenda can fail to acknowledge basic human reactions to students and communities with refugee experiences.

In highly competitive, individualistic, academic environments the degree of self-interest is high and dominates what it means to be successful (Connell, 2013a, 2013b; Vickers & McCarthy, 2010). Additionally, in Rousseau's (Pinson et al., 2010) notion of compassion, it was predicated not only by the individual, but by the acknowledgement of community. In communities where students with refugee experiences are not included and are not considered to be part of the community, compassionate responses may be disparaged or not engaged with at all. Compassionate individuals need to have the capacity to remove the barriers of difference and identify themselves with those who are suffering. The impact of homogeneity, in addition to the standardization of pedagogies, assessment and standards itself, promotes self-interest at system, school and individual levels of participation and commitment to educational endeavours as part of the neoliberal notion of the rivalry required to support the 'free market' principle (Connell, 2013a; Gary, 2016; Steger & Roy, 2010).

This, in turn, has the capacity to desensitize those involved in education to the point where individuals who are in any way different, or have diverse needs, do not have the attributes to authentically belong to that community and are therefore not regarded compassionately. Rousseau's theory of compassion serves to highlight the importance of perceptions of belonging, not only for those seeking to belong, but for those in the community to which newcomers seek to belong. It also heightens sensitivity towards the overriding significance of self- interest and its potential to dominate societal norms and notions of humanity and resultant quality of interactions. Indeed, self – interest is a trademark of neoliberal governments their associated policies when applied to education and other services. Most prominently discussed in terms of the costs and demands on services that communities with refugee experiences inflict on their host nations (Stewart, 2011; Watters, 2007), self-interest has even replaced the 'hate and ignorance' discussions of the historical slave trade in America and the associated inhuman practices and rituals which, for many, were acceptable social norms (Kendi, 2016).

Nussbaum (in Pinson et al., 2010:27) brought together hotly contended theories around the notion of compassion by detailing three 'cognitive judgements' which elicit compassionate emotions. She described these as:

– An appraisal of the 'size' of suffering of another- making a judgement that the suffering is serious
– The belief that the person does not deserve the suffering, that it is not his or her fault, or that the suffering is disproportionate in relation to the blame, and
– The judgement of one's own vulnerability and possibility of being in the other's position

Nussbaum also argued that social and moral judgements of compassion need to be based on the understanding that those who are suffering still have agency and that the condition from which they suffer is temporary and the result of specific circumstances. This notion resonates with Freire (1970), who constantly affirmed the capacity of those who are marginalized, discriminated against and dehumanised, act positively on their own behalf and to retain their sense of agency.

This capacity for agency, however, is easily diminished in the face of the ever-changing policies in countries that have a growing tendency to place economic profit before human compassion (Sivanandan in Pinson et al., 2010; Watters, 2007). As the numbers of people with refugee experiences rapidly grow, the rights and conditions under which these populations are accepted into many first world countries are continually changing, frequently to the detriment of those seeking new homelands and indicating significant political shifts (Pinson et al., 2010). In their discussion of the economics of belonging and compassion in the UK for example, Pinson, Arnot and Candappa (2010) elaborate on the debate about the capacity and willingness of nation states to deliver the universal human rights that were promised to refugees and asylum seekers. They report that the closure of borders and vigorous application of new restrictions in the face of the increased numbers of those needing aid and new homelands is purportedly to reassure the safety and security of British citizens by exercising their power to close borders and introduce new laws and regulations regarding immigration. These actions, and similar steps taken in other countries and presented to citizens via various media outlets, represent another appeal to the self-interests of those in charge. Frequently it serves to support social norms and conditions which reinforce the notion that these populations do not belong, cannot be identified with, and therefore do not need compassion. Bauman (in Pinson et al., 2010:207) sums up that governments seek to:

> …..unload part of the accumulated anxiety…..by demonstrating their energy and determination in the war against foreign job seeking and other alien gate crashers, the intruders into once clean and quite orderly and familiar native backyards.

These factors, whilst at first glance, have little to do with educating students with refugee experiences may have a considerable impact on communities, including the children and young people. The tightening of regulations and governing policies not only create prolonged periods in transitory camps and detention centres, which are often themselves sites of exploitation, abuse, and emotional damage, but they influence the ways in which some sections of the host communities respond to those with refugee backgrounds who are accepted into these new homelands. Potentially included in those influenced negatively are the perceptions of those who would be employers, neighbours, teachers, and classmates (Stewart, 2011), all of whom need to develop a deep understanding of the types and impacts of the trauma, loss and grief experienced by these populations.

Trauma, Loss, and Grief

Displacement itself is a significantly traumatic experience, causing, as it does, the loss of the sense of 'belonging'. Displacement 'dismantles the emotional, spiritual and physical connections with place' (Frater-Mathieson, 2004:12). This is a major contributor to poor health in general and mental health in particular. The impact of displacement alone is frequently underestimated as a significant source of trauma and loss. Much of this may be caused by misinformation and generally uniformed statements about the capacity of children to be resilient, the ability of young children to remember loss and trauma and the notion that once they are resettled all will be well again. The definition and understanding of resilience of students with refugee experience is important to recognize, but it is also critical to understand that all students with refugee experiences have suffered trauma, that even resilient children need support, that not all students should be pathologized as mentally at risk, nor should it be assumed that the impact of trauma with be immediately apparent (Frater-Mathieson, 2004; Sellars & Murphy, 2017; Stewart, 2011). The effects of trauma may last a lifetime for some children and young people and only become apparent at different stages of their lives (Frater-Mathieson, 2004; Steele, Silove, Phan, & Bauman, 2002; Stewart, 2011). Very typical reactions include anxiety, fear, mood swings and irrational behaviours.

The impact of childhood and adolescent trauma, described as developmental trauma, is an important aspect of attempting to understand the situation of students with refugee and asylum seeker status. Typically, students are placed in classes with teachers who lack professional learning regarding the specific ways in which trauma can impact on children and young people. De Bellis (2010), indicates that there are five major ways in which the brain and body respond to an infinite number of stressors. Firstly, 'dysfunctional and traumatized interpersonal relationships (p. 391), including those with family or with the wider society to which they belong. These cause disturbing and stressful memories. Secondly, these stressors in childhood cause mistrust and a lack of faith in those in authority. De Bellis comments that the influence of these stressors is difficult to heal and requires lengthy support in order to desensitize these individuals to distrust and regain the capacity for these students to trust and have empathy for others. It also has been found that the impact of these same stressors is more detrimental in the developmental stages of life than in adulthood. This is because in childhood they are believed to alter the biological stress symptoms and subsequently, negatively impact on brain development. Intense fear or anxiety stimulates the release of chemicals in the brain which cause recognisable physical symptoms of fear, including 'tachycardia, hypertension, increased metabolic rate, hypervigilance, and increased levels of stress chemicals, including catecholamine (p. 392-393)'. Prolonged exposure to these stressors produces increased levels of stress chemical which interfere with healthy brain development and have the potential to increase the chances of psychopathology.

The impact of developmental trauma on brain development is influenced heavily by individual differences and environmental factors. The fourth principle of developmental traumatology indicates that type and frequency of the stressors, the genetic and cultural factors that may provide resistance to combat impact of these stressors and the stage of development associate with the timing of the stressors are all instrumental in determining the possibility of reversing the influences of these stressors. De Bellis writes,

> Birth to adulthood is marked by progressive physical, behavioural, cognitive and emotional development, with changes in brain maturation paralleling these stages. Biological stress response systems are interconnected at many levels to coordinate an individual's responses and

> adaptations to acute and chronic environmental stressors, and these interconnections influence brain development. In the developing brain, elevated levels of catecholamine and cortisol may lead to adverse brain development through a variety of mechanisms……...As puberty begins, white cortical matter is maturing, particularly in the prefrontal areas of the brain, which house executive functions, planning, moral decisions and problem -solving. Subcortical areas of the brain linked to emotion, including the amygdala, are also nearing maturity, As connections of inhibitory neurons from prefrontal areas to the amygdala mature, the to control thought and impulses develops (DeBellis, 2010 p. 394-395).

The fifth principle of developmental traumatology is the appearance of post-traumatic stress disorder in children and young people. These are frequently manifested as anxiety attacks, nightmares, poor concentration and hypervigilance.

A fuller clinical analysis of the symptoms of trauma for these children and young people are readily available in various medical and psychological writings. However, Blackwell and Melzak (2000), for example, discussed these impacts of trauma as exhibited by the behaviours of students with refugee and asylum seeker experiences in school contexts. They describe how these behaviours may present as extreme reactions to everyday events and how these may prevent students from participating fully in the educational experiences of schooling. Ehntholt, Smith, and Yule (2005) also discussed these behaviours, indicating frameworks for school based interventions designed to support these students and facilitate improved participation in the learning process. Hart (2009) described in some detail the factors which may impact negatively on the efforts of students with refugee experiences to take full advantage of educational opportunities. He prioritized the need for programs that improved the potential for emotional and mental wellbeing and described interventions that, under the supervision of a specialist clinician, could be implemented productively by adults who were not experts in mental health support, recommending that these types of specifically designed programs offer ongoing, consistently implemented avenues for schools to promote improved mental and emotional health for their students with refugee experiences. Many of these program would involve participation in cognitive behaviour therapy, string social support systems and rely on the normal maturation process of the brain (De Bellis, 2010 p. 394). Copping and Shakespeare-Finch (2010) also discussed the need for trauma services. They explored the different cultural perspectives and practices that were required to support those with refugee experiences and highlighted the need to develop more diverse, inclusive support systems for these populations. Cultural, social and individual differences in students with refugee experiences rendered some populations more susceptible to prolonged post traumatic stresses and specific programs are required to support those at further risk of emotional and mental ill health (Schweitzer, Melville, Steele, & Lacherez, 2006; Stewart, 2011).

Bryant-Davis (2005a, 2005b) focussed on the impact of interpersonal trauma and the devastating impact this could have on self-identity. The healthy development of the brain, especially in the years after puberty, supports internal regulation and standards of behaviours. Individual who develop healthy brains during this critical period have a sense of self and identity, understand the motivations of others and develop cognitive skills in abstraction, amongst other self-regulating capacities. Self- identity is globally understood to be dependent on the care giver's responses, which not only promote secure attachment to the caregiver but builds the child's sense of integrity (Bornstein, 2010). Interpersonal trauma, including the emotional, mental, and physical impact of observing and experiencing abuse inflicted by people on others, including rape, torture and disclination, racism and lack of acceptance, have negative impacts on the healthy development of self-identity and on the brain itself, especially in childhood and adolescence (De Bellis, 2010). Bryant-Davies (2005) reflected that many students with refugee and asylum seeker experiences survive the initial traumas and loss only to find ongoing stresses and trauma in their new homelands as they struggle to cope with these experiences, which not only brings fresh hurt but further damages perceptions of self and positive identity formation. The results of which are frequently expressed as negative and intense reactions of anger. Bryant-Davies noted that society in general responds differently and less positively to those who react to the inhumane treatment they have undergone with anger and offered a reminder that beneath this anger is the hidden world of sadness, tears, suffering and loss. He advocated, therefore, for interventions that have to capacity to facilitate 'transition in positive self-identity' (Bryant-Davis, 2005a:176), a recommendation which would require the participation of entire communities as social support, and one which is particularly important for school communities in neoliberal education.

Children and young people are also highly influenced by the levels of stress and distress experienced by their parents and caregivers (see, for example, Stewart, 2011:105-108), known as intergenerational transmission of trauma (Schechter, 2010). Schechter states,

> Posttraumatic stress disorder (PDST) and commonly comorbid psychopathology associated with the intergenerational transmission of violent trauma (i.e. dissociative, somatoform, affective, personality and substance abuse disorders) are serious public health problems....However, the specific psychological mechanisms by which.........are transmitted remain largely unknown (p. 256).

Schechter continues, however, to recount the success of a culturally sensitive mental health intervention in a case which had previously been misunderstood by North

American health authorities, and its impact which endured, with support and positive reinforcement interactions, for some years. While acknowledging that each case is unique and thus there are no general guidelines for supporting students who are experiencing the effects of intergenerational transmission of violent trauma, it is an important aspect of acknowledging the circumstances which influence the healthy development of students with refugee and asylum seeker backgrounds. This is because the traumatic nature of interpersonal relationships that these students experience in their everyday interactions with those who suffered the initial traumatic events has the same impacts on the brain development and other aspects of student development as those described by De Bellis (2010) in the context of developmental trauma experienced first-hand. The result is that, in addition to their own traumas and anxieties, students with refugee and asylum seeker backgrounds may become and stay, increasingly at risk (Hamilton & Moore, 2004). This may be as the direct result of witnessing the suffering of their parents and caregivers or indirectly as the result of the deterioration of the adults' capacities to provide the standard of parenting and care that they previously maintained (Bornstein, 2010; Hamilton & Moore, 2004; Stewart, 2011). In many cases of this type there is an 'adultization' of these students as they increasingly become more adult like, take family responsibilities, become carers for those who in other circumstances would be caring for them and lose their childlike nature.

There are also other circumstances that appear contradictory. Stewart (2011), for example, found a dichotomy between students who did not appear to have any issues at all at school and at the support systems which were established to aid. She initially harboured doubts, considering perhaps that their resilience and endurance somehow allowed them to remain immune to the deep-seated traumas and distress that school and system authorities assumed would impact negatively on their capacities to live relatively normal lives. In this population, settling in Canada from sub Saharan Africa, what she discovered were personal stories of unconscionable terror, loss, and abuse. Many of the students interviewed by Stewart had not previously revealed their circumstances of forced migration and the horrors they had suffered. What she found, under the surface of their everyday lives in their new homeland, were significant cases of poor mental health, post-traumatic stress syndrome and unresolved grief for the families the students had lost or been forced to leave behind in their homelands. Loss of their homes and homeland itself was also the source of much grief and sadness.

Despite their human capacities for incredible resilience and hope and their appreciation of their new homeland, many students were, at a less superficial level, suffering from deep psychological issues and concerns, both for their own stories and those of their parents, particularly their mothers, who, in many cases, were attempting to raise their children and face new challenges alone. In some cases, the symptoms of this group of students' psychological trauma did not become evident until as much as two years later. These differences and diverse ways of coping with the experiences of forced migration, trans migration and post migration are very real and reflect the multiplicity of human resources and the wide range of coping strategies that individuals depend on to make meaning from even the most horrendous of experiences. This poses challenges for educators who must revaluate students' needs for support services and mitigate the impact of deep psychological issues in a system that is inflexible, economically driven and which values economy and efficiency in all aspects of teachers' professional work, and in the functions of the allied health support systems.

To provide an overall picture of the diversity of impacts these experiences have on students with refugee and asylum seeker experiences at various developmental stages of their growth, it can be useful to understand the possible influences of childhood experiences on future development into adulthood, including the development of sustained resilience. This is not to suggest that the only influences on development in adulthood are early childhood experiences, although how the child copes with these certainly appears to impact on how individuals live their lives (Eastmond in Watters, 2007). Any discussion of the ways these experiences prevail on students' lives is not intended to provide a fixed, linear explanation or sequence of events that Eastmond (in Watters, 2007:24) describes as the 'refugee curve' to explain the trauma, loss and grief that children with refugee experiences may suffer during migration, trans migration and post migration. It is an attempt to illustrate the interaction and the mutual impact of individuals and their environments and the extremely diverse personal capacities of some students to the possible consequences of abrupt, enforced change to this relationship. The discussion of resilience that follows is a view that presents students with refugee experiences as active respondents, not passive victims of the external events that have bearing on their lives. It stresses their capacity for human agency in making meaning in their lives without trivializing or neglecting the experiences of trauma, loss and grief (Plummer in Watters, 2007:25).

Resilience

There is a great deal written about resilience in the context of students with refugee experiences (see, for example, Hamilton & Moore, 2004) and this process of positive adaptation in the face of difficulties has been extensively used in policy and support documents that focus on the provision of support for these students. Watters (2007) discussed the current tendency to use resilience in many of these documents in a merely tokenistic manner and suggested that rather than use this term to pathologize these populations, a new paradigm needed to be developed, one in which some students with refugee experiences and asylum seeker experiences are perceived as 'models' of resilience, given their capacities to adapt positively to the situations which are the result of major trauma and loss. Cicchetti (2010) indicates that resilience is,

> conceptualised as an individual's capacity for adapting successfully and functioning competently, despite experiencing chronic stress or adversity following exposure to prolonged or severe trauma (p. 251).

He confirms that, whilst empirical research is being undertaken to detect the psychosocial determinants of resilience, these are only in their initial stages, dues to the complexity of the construct and the need to somehow correlate the findings of a multi- level, interdisciplinary approach. Amongst the fields of investigation, are genetics, psychophysiology, neuroendocrinology, and emotion regulatory processes. The complexity with which resilience is viewed medically eliminates many of the simplistic programs that are operationalised in educational settings to 'promote resilience' for students with refugee and asylum seeker experiences as the traumas may be too widespread in nature, too traumatic and too frequently experienced. However, Richter (2010), states;

> …..despite the string influences of material circumstances in early life, research on resilience across a variety of cultures indicates the presence of three potentially powerful counter forces; warm responsive caregiving in the early years, meaningful family and social relationships and opportunities to learn and succeed (p. 531).

As many students with refugee and asylum seeker experiences arrive in new homelands without their primary caregivers, this presents a considerable challenge for educators who attempt to make opportunities for education available to them. Typically, many students in these populations have lost close family members to war and its attendant atrocities. This places somewhat exclusive responsibilities on schools and other organizations to provide the social and learning contexts in which these students may have opportunities to develop some degree of resilience, to adapt and function 'normally' in their new settlement societies. To achieve this, those with whom refugee and asylum seeker students interact in their social and academic environments must engage them with deep respect for their suffering, traumatic experiences and feelings of loss and displacement, in addition to an over-riding priority to employ an ethic of care (Noddings, 2005, 2012). These educational and social aspirations are not evidenced as characteristics of neoliberalized educational concerns, goals or aspirations and it remains to be seen how these shortcomings effect the students as citizens in a globalized world.

It could be conceded that educational policy makers are cognisant of this 'nurturing' role that is incumbent on their institutions and have made attempts to deflect the responsibilities into a nebulous context of societies in general. Masten and Powell (in Watters, 2007:130-131 emphasis in original) indicated that resilience could be defined as 'an inference about a person's life that requires *two fundamental judgements* 1) that the person is 'doing okay' and 2) that there is now or has been significant risk or adversity to overcome'. Policies and documents that have used this type of definition are aimed at improving the *environment* of the students, through engagement with good schools, active club teams and social activity membership and the provision of resources such as libraries, health care services, safe neighbourhoods, and other community facilities. Many of these environments operate as institutions, and as such, may operate with the Foucauldian notions of power, uniformity in practices and expectations and epistemology (Foucault, 1977, 1979).

The challenges presented by all aspects of Western societies are articulated by Stewart (2011), who conceptualized four major areas of challenge for these students. She identified these as Economic, Psychosocial, Environmental, and Educational, adding that, in her Canadian study, ' the issue of racism and discrimination was largely a problem in all facets of the ecological systems' that constituted the fabric of neoliberal societies (Stewart, 2011:126). Watters (2007) also questioned the quality of experiences that these environments may be able to offer students with refugee experiences. He explored several aspects of these types of 'ecological' decisions aimed at supporting these populations. Schools with 'good' results or reputations may not be ideal environments for these students if they are made to feel incompetent, deficit or are bullied because they are different. Schools which engage with pedagogies of love and care are not regularly amongst the criteria considered by neoliberal education authorities which are based in principals of productivity and human capital. Communities, clubs, and associations may accept membership of these students but neglect them in ways that exclude them from full participation as they too are often institutionalized by rules regulations and conditions of belonging. The perceptions that these populations develop over time in their interactions with others are easily internalized and impact on self – identity (Bryant-Davis, 2005a, 2005b), which, depending on the nature of these perceptions may support the continued development of the characteristics of resilience, or have the opposite outcome.

Capacities for resilience can be developed or destroyed, which has critical implications for educators. It is not a characteristic that individuals have or not. Stewart (2011:239) discusses 'protective factors' which support individuals when they are faced with significant difficulty or adversity. She indicates, in an addition to the broad principles articulated by Richter 2010), that these factors- these coping skills- are not the same for everyone and have varying degrees of strength or impact. Not only is resilience an individual construct, it is not present in the same degree in every adverse situation that an individual may encounter (Hamilton & Moore, 2004). Consequently, it is possible to support resilience development as a generalized capacity; and many programs have been developed for that purpose for use in general school contexts with all students (see, for example, McGrath & Noble, 2003; Stewart, 2011), but it should be anticipated that the impact may not be as positive for some students as for others. Despite this situation, some studies have pointed to characteristics that have the potential to support students with refugee experiences, many of which require students to have complex cognitive capacities. For example, Apfel and Simon (in Watters, 2007:132) found in a psychoanalytical study of Israeli and Palestinian students with refugee and asylum seeker experiences, that the characteristics of 'resourcefulness, curiosity, intellectual mastery, capacity to conceptualize and generalize knowledge, flexibility in emotional experiences, autobiographical memory, life goals, altruism and moral determination' supported the development of resilience. This may be a sound finding for that specific group of students, but no detail about their previous schooling, circumstances of status, age, gender or other demographic or transitional information was available to determine the generalizability of these findings, although these complex cognitive capacities could certainly be considered to be a firm foundation for resilience building in most circumstances.

The overall understanding of resilience, its complexity and supports depend significantly on the capacity of individuals to adapt a positive perspective. Hamilton and Moore (2004) place this perspective in the educational context, by linking resilience to an acknowledgement of existing strengths and resources and by indicating that individual student characteristics are variables that educators need to account for in their planning to secure positive outcomes for these students.

A perspective that is typically dismissed in the efficiencies and economies of neoliberal school systems. They dismiss the popular but erroneous attitudes that young students will just forget their trauma and that 'resilient' students will continue to cope successfully without support. Their comments reflect their awareness of the impact of developmental trauma theory and support their determination that children's losses are more closely interpolated with their environments and their stage of development than are those experienced by adults. All students with refugee and asylum seeker experiences need to have new environments in which to interact optimistically. School communities have a vital role in developing the types of environments which are positive, that support students' strengths and which have educators who have the professional interests and capacities to engage with this student population humanely. To achieve this, school leaders and their staffs need to engage the entire community in 'reflective conversations' that develop 'collective consciousness' (Seymour, 2004:28) of the urgency of working towards pedagogies of love and care. However, the problematic nature of many schools and associated support and social systems which are highly competitive, rigid, prescriptive, and standardized is apparent. Many of the environmental recommendations that are made for students with refugee and asylum seeker experiences not only discourage many of the traits that contribute to healthy degrees of resilience, they have the potential to create dependent, passive individuals who are stripped of any autonomy and of their sense of agency, in much the same way as adults with refugee and asylum seeker experiences are 'overly protected' in some new 'homelands' and denied any real control over their lives.

Conclusion

This chapter clarified what it means to have refugee and asylum seeker status. It briefly examined the meaning of compassion, love and care in relation to neoliberal societies and their educational institutions and policies that impact on the acceptance of individuals with refugee status and asylum seeker status into their societies. It stresses the understanding that those who are suffering the effects of trauma and loss still have agency, but that the increase in the numbers entangled in the global diaspora is resulting in the revision of policies and restrictions that affect those with refugee and asylum seeker status, decreasing their capacities for agency.

It explored in some depth the ways in which developmental trauma relating to interpersonal interactions has the capacity to impact on the cognitive and emotional growth in children and young people and analyses the potential of educational institutions to undertake their societal role in mediating these influences and promoting the development of healthy psychological development and resilience. The challenges presented to educational institutions in neoliberal contexts revolve around responsibilities of developing learning contexts based on care, acceptance and belonging as primary characteristics in schools that are measured by their efficiency, their economies, their dedication to standardized testing and their commitment to students as human capital.

References

Berry, J. (1997). Immigration, Acculturation, and Adaptation. *Applied Psychology: An International Review, 46*(1), 5-68.

Berry, J., Phinney, J., Sam, D., & Vedder, P. (2006). Immigrant Youth: Acculturation, Identity, and Adaptation. *Applied Psychology: An International Review, 55*(3), 303-332.

Berry, J. W. (2009). A Critique of Critical Acculturation. *International Journal of Intercultural Relations, 33*(5), 361-371. doi:10.1016/j.ijintrel.2009.06.003

Berry, J. W., Horenczyk, G., & Kwak, K. (2006). *Immigrant Youth in Cultural Transition: Acculturation, Identity, and Adaptation Across National Contexts*. In. Retrieved from http://newcastle.eblib.com/patron/FullRecord.aspx?p=331698

Blackwell, D., & Melzak, S. (2000). *Far from the Battle but Still at War: Troubled Refugee Children in School*. London: Child Psychotherapy Trust.

Bornstein, M. (2010). From Measurement to Meaning in Caregiving and Culture. In C. Worthman, P. Plotsky, D. Schechter, & C. Cummings (Eds.), *Formative Experiences: The Interaction of Caregiving, Culture and Developmental Psychobiology*. New York: Cambridge University Press.

Bryant-Davis, T. (2005a). Afterword. In *Thriving in the Wake of Trauma* (pp. 173-181). Conneticut: Praeger.

Bryant-Davis, T. (2005b). Introduction. In *Thriving in the wake of trauma* (pp. 1-11). Conneticut: Praeger.

Cicchetti, D. (2010). Commentary: Infant Abuse in Rhesus Macaques. In C. Worthman, P. Plotsky, D. Schechter, & C. Cummings (Eds.), *Formative Experiences: The Interaction of Caregiving, Culture and Psychobiology* New York: Cambrindge University Press.

Connell, R. (2013a). The Neoliberal Cascade and Education: An Essay on the Market Agenda and its Consequences. *Critical Studies in Education, 54*(2), 99-112.

Connell, R. (2013b). Why do Market 'Reforms' Persistently Increase Inequality? *Discourse: Studies in the Cultural Politics of Education, 34*(2), 279-285.

Copping, A., & Shakespeare-Finch, J. (2010). Towards a Culturally Appropriate Mental Health System: Sudanese-Australians' Experience with Trauma. *Journal of Pacific Rim Psychology, 4*, 53-60.

De Bellis, M. (2010). Developmental Traumatology: A Commentary on the Factors for Risk and Resiliency in the Case of an Adolescent Javanese Boy. In C. Worthman, P. Plotsky, D. Schechter, & C. Cummings (Eds.), *Formative Experiences: The Interaction of Caring, Culture and Developmental Psychbiology*. New York: Cambridge University Press.

Doná, G., & Berry, J. W. (1994). Acculturation Attitudes and Acculturative Stress of Central American Refugees. *International Journal of Psychology, 29*(1), 57-70.

Ehntholt, K., Smith, P., & Yule, W. (2005). School-based Cognitive-behavioural Therapy Group Intervention for Refugee Children who have Experienced War-related Trauma. *Clinical Child Psychology and Psychiatry, 10*(2), 235-250.

Foucault, M. (1977). Panopticism (A. Sheridan, Trans.). In *Discipline and Punish: The Birth of the Prison* (pp. 195-228). New York: Vintage Books.

Foucault, M. (1979). *Power, Truth, Strategy*. Sydney: Feral Publications.

Frater-Mathieson, K. (2004). Refugee Trauma, Loss and Grief: Implications for Intervention. In R. Hamilton & D. Moore (Eds.), *Educational Interventions for Refugee Children*. New York: Routledge.

Freire. (1970). *Pedagogy of the Oppressed*. New York: Continuum

Gary, K. (2016). Neoliberal Education for Work Versus Liberal Education for Leisure. *Studies in Philosophy and Education,* (October). Retrieved from doi:DOI: 10.1007/s11217-016-9545-0

Gidley, J. (2016). *Postformal Education: A Philosophy for Complex Futures*. Switzerland: Springer.

Hamilton, R., & Moore, D. (2004). *Educational Interverntions for Refugee Children: Theoretical Perspectives on Best Practice*. Abibgton, Oxen: Routledge.

Hart, R. (2009). Child Refugees, Trauma and Education: Interactionist Considerations on Social and Emotional Needs and Development. *Educational Psychology in Practice, 25*(4), 351-368. doi:10.1080/02667360903315172

Kendi, I. (2016). *Stamped from the Beginning: The Definitive History of Racist Ideas in America*. New York: Nation Books.

McBrien, J. L. (2005). Educational Needs and Barriers for Refugee Students in the US: A Review of the Literature. *Review of Educational Research, 75*(3), 329-364.

McBrien, J. L., & Ford, J. (2012). Serving the Needs of Refugee Children and Families through a Culturally Appropriate Liaison Service. In F. McCarthy & M. Vickers (Eds.), *Refugee and Immigrant students: Acheiving Equity in Education* (pp. 107-126). Charlotte, NC: Information Age Publishing, Inc.

McGrath, H., & Noble, T. (2003). *Bounce Back! Classroom Resiliency Program*. Sydney: Pearson Education.

Noddings, N. (2005). *The Challenge to Care in Schools; An Alternative Approach to Education* (2nd ed.). New York: Teachers College Press.
Noddings, N. (2012). *The Philosophy of Education*. Boulder Colorado: Westview Press.
Ogbu, J. (1995a). Cultural Problems in Minority Education: Their Interpretations and Consequences- Part two- The Case Studies. *The Urban Review, 27*, 271-297.
Ogbu, J. (1995b). Cultural Problems in Minority Education: Their Interpretations and Consequences-Part one: Theoretical Background. *The Urban Review, 27*, 189-205.
Pinson, H., Arnot, M., & Candappa, M. (2010). *Education, Asylum and the "Non-Citizen' Child: The Politics of Compassion and Belonging*. Basingstoke, UK: Palgrave Macmillan.
Richter, L. (2010). Global Prespectives on the Well Being of Children. In C. Worthman, P. Plotsky, D. Schechter, & C. Cummings (Eds.), *Formative Experiences: the Interactions of Caregiving, Culture and Developmental Psychobioology*. New York: Cambridge University Press.
Schechter, D. (2010). Multigenerational Ataques de Nervios in a Dominician American Family: A Form of Intergenerational Tramsmission of Violent Trauma. In C. Worthman, P. Plotsky, D. Schechter, & C. Cummings (Eds.), *Formative Experiences: The Interaction of Caregiving, Culture and Developmental Psychobiology*. New York: Cambridge University Press.
Schweitzer, R., Melville, F., Steele, Z., & Lacherez, P. (2006). Trauma, Post-migration Living Difficulties, and Social Support as Predictors of Psychological Adjustment in Resettled Sudanese Refugees. *Australian and New Zealand Journal of Psychiatry,, 40*(179-187).
Sellars, M., & Murphy, M. (2017). Becoming Australian: A Review of Southern Sudanese Students' Educational Experiences. *International Journal of Inclusive Educational Experiences, 0*(0,0), 1-20. Retrieved from doi:https://doi.org/10.1080/13603116.2017.1373308
Seymour, M. (2004). *Educating for Humanity*. Boulder, Colorado: Paradigm Books.
Steele, Z., Silove, D., Phan, T., & Bauman, A. (2002). Long Term Effect of Psychological Trauma on the Mental Health of Vietnamese Refugees Settled in Australia: A Population Based Study. *The Lancet, 360*(1056-1061).
Steger, M., & Roy, R. (2010). *Neoliberalism: A Very Short Introduction:* . New York: Oxford University Press.
Stewart, J. (2011). *Supporting Refugee Children: Strategies for Educators*. Ontario Canada: University of Toronto Press.
Vickers, M. H., & McCarthy, F. E. (2010). Repositioning Rrefugee Students from the Margins to the Centre of Teachers' work. *International Journal of Diversity in Organisations, Communities & Nations, 10*(2), 199-210.
Watters, C. (2007). *Refugee children: Towards the Next Horizon* (1 ed.). Florence: Taylor and Francis.

Chapter Five: People: Compassion and Belonging

Introduction

This chapter introduces the current perspectives of neoliberal policymakers and populations regarding refugee and asylum seekers, including the students. It discusses some of the most politically sensitive and divisive issues of these contemporary societies (Dagg & Haugaard, 2016; Saltsman, 2014) and their regulations regarding stateless and status-less individuals. These including exclusion by detention (Pinson, Arnot, & Candappa, 2010) , vilification, dehumanizing (Bleiker, Campbell, Hutchison, & Nicholson, 2013; Hickerson & Dunsmore, 2016) and scaremongering (Greussing & Boomgaarden, 2017) by the popular media, 'othering' by communities in their new homelands and the defence of non -acceptance (Tarumoto, 2019). It considers of the impact of these factors on the refugee and asylum seeker students and their schooling. Dubbed as the 'human waste of globalization' (Bauman, 2004 p. 76), these displaced peoples challenge the societies of their new destinations to act towards them with human compassion. For many, this is a challenge that will not be met; an analysis of society using Bourdieu may indicate why this could easily be the case if school is considered to be the institution of societal production and reproduction.

Policymakers

Throughout the twentieth century, displaced persons and those who sought asylum were accepted and integrated into what are now identified as neoliberal, western societies. In comparison to the magnitude of the current diaspora, the numbers of those seeking a new homeland were relatively small. Pinson et al. (2010) provide a comprehensive, detailed analysis of the impact of the unrest and many civil conflicts that erupted after the end of the Cold War, resulting in an increased number of individuals seeking refugee status and asylum and a subsequent revision of policies and restrictions by many western states (Watters, 2007). The beginning of the twenty-first century and the decades that are following are currently witnessing a substantial increase in internally displaced persons (40 million), refugees (25.4 million) asylum seeker numbers (3.1 million) and stateless people (10 million) , the majority of whom are resettled in neighbouring countries (United Nations High Commission for Refugees, 2019). Eighty five percent of host countries are developing countries, which challenges many populist notions regarding the potential of the remaining 15% of these populations to 'overrun' the more highly developed western nations. Despite this, the responses of neoliberal governments to this crisis reflect a growing unwillingness to define and recognise their responsibilities towards these people, indicating that their reluctance is not essentially about numbers of refugee and asylum seeker communities, but about public issues regarding

> ... the physical and symbolic boundaries of the nation state, its identity and the legitimacy of preserving the concept in an age characterized by the fluidity of migration. In the context of liberal democratic states.........the topic creates major tensions within the logic of political and human rights (Pinson et al., 2010 p.10).

Much of this tension is created around major themes; the definitions of what constitutes valid reasons for forced migration and therefore genuine refugee status and the conditions and choices around forced migration, with this only being legitimized in many cases if there was no choice but to flee the original homeland. These debates include, as always in neoliberal discourses , who deserves to supported, permitted sanctuary and protection, who are 'undeserving' and who should be assigned to the 'human waste heap' described by Bauman (2004). These debates include considerations of the economies of accepting those with no legal rights to claim citizenship, but who do seek access to the wealthier societies of neoliberal states (Eastmond, 2011), and assessment, according to the logics of the government, to ascertain if those who seek citizenship are to be considered an economic asset or liability (Pinson et al., 2010; Watters, 2007). So, for neoliberal states, the global crossing of borders is viewed as highly desirable for products and goods, capital and profits in the interests of free trade, as it is 'a positive integrative force.......(facilitating) the intensification of economic and cultural interdependability.....(which) .. has the potential to contribute to international political solidarity (Brah et al., 1999 in Pinson et al., 2010 p. 13), but decisions regarding human migration and mobile citizenship are not viewed as nearly so desirable, depending on the local climate and public perceptions of those who seek to enter (Hattam & Every, 2010). Bauman (2004 p.9) identifies this situation as one of the major tensions around globalization. He states, 'power in the form of capital, and particularly financial capital, flows while politics remains tied to the ground bearing all the constraints imposed by its local character'. Nonetheless, the tightening of regulations and reworking of policies in the face of increased numbers of refugee and asylum- seeking individuals have not only revealed the agenda of the individuals and groups who make these, but have created a number of difficulties in the public perceptions of the nature and intentions of these populations, all of which served to engender mistrust and establish practices of exclusion, not compassion.

The notion of compassion has been long associated with controversy and discussion. It has been explored in western philosophy as a component of moral judgement, a natural disposition and an emotional aspect of moral philosophy. It has been explored as the natural desire to relieve the suffering of others, and is conceptualized as not only an individual trait but on that can be associated with communities and societies in general (Pinson & Arnot, 2010; Pinson et al., 2010; Williams, 2008). Of particular importance in this context is the understanding of the vital role compassion can play in establishing contexts of social justice. Williams (2008), states

> It is in this respect that the virtue of compassion might be located as a – if not *the* – cardinal virtue of humanistic models of community and social health. Compassion is that disposition or way-of-being that is most fundamentally other-regarding – always interpersonal, always involving a regard for the good of the other (Blum, 1980). It expands the boundaries of the self rather than tightening or strengthening them (see Nussbaum, 2001: 300). In this view, we might regard compassion as the vital conative force (i.e. that which directs and impels action) underlying the struggle for social justice. Compassion informs and, in fact, makes possible our awareness of suffering as an impediment to sentient well-being and flourishing and is thus crucial to a moral psychology of non-harm and benevolence – one by which we refuse to add suffering to the world and, positively, are inclined to remedy existing suffering wherever possible. Compassion might thus be understood as the moral foundation of social justice, with social justice promoted by and perpetuated through a collective value framework informed by an awareness of interconnectedness, sensitivity to the needs and interests of others, and rooted in the principle that 'the highest moral prescription is for humanity as a whole' (Kurtz, 1969: 9) (p. 7-8).

Williams (2008) further explains that it is in the ways that individuals and collective groups are valued, both by themselves and others, that they are able to overcome any obstacles to this essentially interpersonal capacity. Reiterating the three principals of compassion as articulated by Nussbaum (2001) and echoing the importance of care as conceived by Noddings (2005, 2012), Williams continues to explain that it is not necessary to evaluate or judge the ways in which the suffering came about in order to be compassionate, but warned that engaging in assessments and moral appraisals of the circumstances of the suffering may impact on individual and collective capacities to act compassionately. His comments on the impact of economic, neoliberal societies and the rise of individualism, which have all but destroyed the notion of community, have considerable consequences for the third of Nussbaum's cognitive judgements regarding the development of compassionate emotions, the first being the deliberations regarding the seriousness of the suffering, the second founded in the belief that the suffering is not the responsibility of the suffering themselves or that is extreme in relation to the actions of the sufferer. The third, critical judgement requires individuals and societies to acknowledge a sense of community with the sufferers. It is contingent on the capacity of others to see likenesses and similarities between themselves and the suffering. It is in this cognitive judgement that the multiple barriers, the degrees and types of social difference, impair the capacities of some sections of society or its members to identity with those who are suffering, to weaken their sense of vulnerability; to authentically and emotionally *step into the shoes* of the suffering members of humanity and to acknowledge that they also could be in that position.

> Evaluations of likeness and difference are often made on the basis of class, race, religion and other social markers that create both possibilities for similarity and prospects for judgments of difference (e.g. Fiske, 2004). While similarities may encourage us to be more sympathetic to, and thus more compassionate toward, the plight of others, social markers tend to be far more consequential in their reinforcement of difference (e.g. Beck, 1999). By virtue of the diversity that characterizes most contemporary western societies, differences are likely to be more readily available for appraisal than are similarities. Consequently, common social markers 'prove recalcitrant to the imagination' (Nussbaum, 2001) and are thus better regarded as social barriers to compassion than as grounds for compassionate awareness..............Where boundaries are strongest – where in-groups are most visibly demarcated from out-groups – is within those social systems built upon hierarchical privileging, whereby groups define themselves not only against others, but as superior (Nussbaum, 2001). Compassion must overcome not only constructions of group boundaries, but also boundaries of privilege – the other is both *different from* and *inferior to* (Williams, 2008 p.12).

In this way, many of the circumstances that created the suffering and victimization for refuge and asylum seeker communities in their original homelands; ethnicity, race, religion, poverty and other social characteristics; may return to impact on their potential to thrive and to belong in their new homelands. The probability of this occurring is highest in white, neoliberal, developed countries where the impact of difference is most influential (Bal, 2014).

The politics of belonging (Pinson et al., 2010) make it clear that belonging is not simply membership of a group or society, like compassion, it stresses the affective component, which constructs such as citizenship and associates do not. In order to be considered as an individual who 'belongs' positive reciprocal relationships must exist, the individuals must actually not just be identified by others as belonging but they must feel themselves that they belong. The politics of belonging do not only determine who belongs and how they achieve this 'belonging', but also to how different times and contexts, in addition to the characteristics of the persons who seek to belong, influence the negotiations that are undertaken by those seeking to belong. The site of immigration policies and border protection personnel are the typical environments in which the politics of belonging are most readily observed. Indeed, the various agencies employed to by nation states and neoliberal governments are frequently observed to be treating the same communities of asylum seeker and refugee communities differently, and in a contradictory manner at various levels of national, state, local and institutional administration (Hunpage & Marston, 2006). The politics of belonging necessitate the nation state and neoliberal societies to define, through the immigration policies, their physical boundaries, their political identities and demonstrate their commitment to social justice, compassion and tolerance (Pinson et al., 2010). Too often, these policies serve to identify asylum seeker and refugee individuals as criminals, terrorists or scroungers (Gatt, 2011; Pinson et al., 2010; Saltman & Means; Schubert & Wurf, 2014; Stewart, 2011; Watt, 2012; Watters, 2007).

There are two major avenues by which public opinion regarding refugee and asylum seekers are demonized. One is a direct governmental action which serves to automatically differentiate these populations from mainstream societies and at best, discourage compassion and empathy, at worst, dehumanize and distance from the 'normal' populace. The other is by using various forms of media influence to portray these populations as threats to society and its customary ways of life. Government policies that mandate dispersal of communities not only exclude and 'other' families and their children, they typically cause additional emotion stress as family and community networks, including access to their heritage language speakers, are considered pivotal to the mental health and wellbeing of these groups in society (Block, Cross, Riggs, & Gibbs, 2014; Hope, 2011; Massing, Kirova, & Hennig, 2013; Matthews, 2008; Miller, Thomas, & Fruechtenicht, 2014). Failure to disperse frequently impacted negatively on the groups' support systems and they typically lived in extreme poverty in densely populated city areas (Pinson & Arnot, 2007; Pinson et al., 2010). While dispersal policies mediated the impact of refugee and asylum seeker communities on education, health and support services, the impacts were not necessarily conducive to situations of belonging (Watters, 2007). The more extreme government policies and actions are an extremely shameful example of deliberate, prolonged erosion of human rights, which have called for a review of border policies in this era of globalization (Gerrard, 2017). The persistent, policed detention of large groups of men women and children who had already undergone significant suffering, trauma and loss provides evidence of neoliberal perspectives of compassion and belonging. Despite declarations of maintaining national security, isolating potential terrorists and identifying 'fake' asylum seekers, detention centres have been found to exercise rather arbitrary regulations, provide only prison like conditions and neglect not only the human rights of detainees, but their health, wellbeing and educational opportunities. In a discussion of detention centres in one neoliberal society, Pinson et al. (2010) write,

> Cole (2003) criticized the logic behind the detention of families, arguing that they are the least likely to abscond and mostly comply with the restrictions imposed upon them by immigration agencies because they have children. She adds, 'it must therefore be assumed…..this [detention policy] was intended to demonstrate that the government was not going to let even compassion stand in the way of a need to take a tough line with asylum seekers (p. 63).

Despite many concerns about the detention of children, neoliberal governments across the globe appear determined to subject those seeking a new homeland inside their borders to further hardship and indignities at the very least. Using blatant policy measures and inciting much public acceptance and approval of these through the popular media, neoliberal governments are dismissing compassion and belonging for the most ignoble of reasons; that of self- interest (Kendi, 2017).

Explicitly or covertly, these governments utilize the tabloid press and other media to influence public opinion about refugee and asylum seeker populations, typically by inflated the numbers of people seeking support, dehumanizing them and giving the public the impression that they were about to be literally invaded by millions and thousands of displaced individuals, when, in fact, the overwhelming majority (85%) of those depicted as fleeing from war, violence and persecution were resettled in developing countries. The use of derogatory terms that explicitly implied those seeking refuge or asylum were undesirable individuals was persistent and inflammatory. A typical example was an analysis of the UK press over two months in 2004. Pinson et al. (2010) report,

> The ICAR (2004:35) study also found out that the most commonly used terms in tabloid headlines about asylum seekers were 'arrested', 'jailed' and guilty. Words frequently used were 'bogus', 'false', 'illegal', 'failed' and 'rejected'. Other widely used terms in newspapers were 'scrounger', fraudster', 'sponger', robbing the system', 'burden/strain on resources', 'illegal working', 'cheap labour', 'cash in hand' 'black economy', 'criminal',' criminal violent', 'arrested, jailed, guilty', mob, horde, riot, rampage, disorder', 'a threat, a worry, and to be feared'. In contrast, the words 'genuine', 'real', 'successful', did not appear even once in headlines in the two- month period (p. 47).

The impact of this and later studies of media influence on public perceptions of refugee and asylum seeker populations (for example see Greussing & Boomgaarden, 2017 who found that both tabloid and quality press used similar frameworks at the height of the crisis in Europe; Nolan, Farquharson, Politoff, & Marjibanks, 2011) play a huge part in determining the ease with which individuals are able to integrate into the communities of their resettlement homelands (Alencar, 2018). The political responsibilities of considering the human response these populations appear missing in various reports of media research. For example, Bleiker et al. (2013) report on the dehumanizing effect of media images of refugee and asylum seekers with blurred faces which showed no facial features at all and Hickerson and Dunsmore (2016), reporting on Refugee Day media coverage in the US found that

> ...for US communities, refugees are salient as recipients of individual compassion, their worthiness vouchsafed by their industriousness or exotic charm. As represented in the coverage, communities relate chiefly to refugees through fun and family events (p. 435).

The media stereotyping continues (see, for erxample Watt, 2012), but there are isolated pockets of media usage to promote more positive and productive interactions with refugee and asylum seeking communities. For example, Bennett (2018), describes one of the ways in which media can be used to 'push back' against these negative and destructive perspectives of refugees and asylum seekers. Films were made on various devices including mobile phones, at considerable potential risk to the refugees and asylum seekers who were the filmmakers themselves. These films captured the journeys and harsh conditions that were experienced as part of the exodus from their original homelands and serve to inform the public about the true nature of refugee and asylum seeker experiences. Dunkerly-Bean, Bean, and Alnajjar (2014) also used film media to facilitate middle schoolers understanding of asylum and the interrelatedness of this to the broader notion of human rights and Emert (2013), used media to support the academic literacy skills of boys with refugee experiences from Africa and Asia. Sadly, reports of this nature are typically not read by the general populace and so the media continues to play a role in demonizing those with refugee and asylum seeker experiences, instead of using their vast influence and audiences to engender national support for compassion and belonging.

What implications are there for students with refugee and asylum seeker experiences?

Self-interest, profit, competition, individualism and blame are characteristics of neoliberal policy and education. Neoliberal education, like neoliberal politics serves to fracture society, polarize communities and inducts students in educational spaces in which they are taught, not to develop respect and accommodate diversity and difference but to concentrate on themselves and personal achievements. They are not provided with curriculum documents which predispose them to sympathy and care for community, or typically, learning environments which actively promote wellbeing of others and society (Hargrave, 2003). Neoliberal education also places an undue focus on the 'knowledge economy' as it serves their market mentality very well. However, as employment in the 'intelligence' sector does not compete with the sheer number of workers required in the service industries for example, indications are that the potential of the knowledge economy has been overstated. This may be because the more sophisticated, highly skilled occupations do not demand huge numbers of people to sustain their growth and advancement (Wadham, Pudsey, & Boyd, 2007). The culture of is also perpetuated by the individualistic nature of education and its means of measuring success. This not only assumes that all students have the same starting point but also that all students have to do to succeed is to work harder. In this way, individual success is not attributed to the system and the ways in which it positions students, nor the expertise and expectations of teachers, but rather with the student themselves, and implicitly, those students who do not succeed are have themselves to blame. This has the potential to have considerable impact on the potential of refugee and asylum seeker students to succeed in these systems. This understanding of power at micro and macro levels of education is further explored the work of Bourdieu (1990), which is widely used to explain the ways in which schools operate to perpetuate social inequality (Ferfolja, Diaz, & Ullman, 2018) and to alienate and disenfranchise students who do not have the necessary capital and habitus as required to be accepted and to belong to the 'field' of neoliberal schooling.

Bourdieu (1977, 1986, 1990; Bourdieu, Passeron, & Saint Martin, 1994) theorised that power was not ubiquitous, as Foucault had proposed (Foucault, 1979a, 1979b), but was culturally and symbolically created by the societal norms and mores of the society in which individuals exist. He discusses his social theory in terms of capital, habitus and field. Capital is identified in many forms, all of which contribute to symbolic capital as a means of ensuring privilege or power in their social field (for example, education). Human capital is not confined to economic capital, as monetary wealth may not guarantee acceptance in some social fields, it includes what Bourdieu describes as cultural and social capital. Cultural capital is arguably the most important capital in neoliberal education. It includes knowledge, skills, family backgrounds and tastes, linguistic capital. So cultural capital is accumulated by individuals at various levels of society, including personal characteristic of speech and linguistic register (Bernstein, 1990), academic qualifications and what are considered to be 'superior' types of activities such as perhaps an understanding and knowledge of classical music and opera, the ballet and established literature. According to Bourdieu, cultural capital is used to impose what one group considers to be 'best' and desirable on other groups in society as acts of what he describes as symbolic violence. He indicates that school curriculum and assessment practices are to be perceived as cultural capital in that they reflect the epistemologies of those who design these documents, determine what knowledge is worth knowing and designate those who do not reflect this knowledge in narrowly defined testing regimes as 'underachieving learners' according to the standards they have set using their own values and belief systems. Social capital may be about monetary wealth, prestige, property and position but that is not always the case. The networks and connections that individuals have as family tradition, acquaintances, memberships to elite social groups and institutions may easily outweigh the monetary wealth of individual and result in increased social capital simply because of their acceptance into the sections of society with most power and influence. Social and cultural capital as symbolic capital are frequently the determinants of who is educated at schools with restricted enrolment, highly qualified staff and limitless resources. In these environments mere monetary capital is not sufficient as symbolic capital for acceptance as these students without the cultural and social capital do not have the habitus to be accepted and to belong.

Habitus is understood to be the socially mediated dispositions, social practices and predispositions that are embedded into an individual's conscious and unconscious as a result of the interplay between an individual's free will and the social structures over an extended period if time. Habitus is not merely 'habit' as the name may suggest, but is an enduring and reproductive incorporation of ' a system of schemes for generating and perceiving practices (Bourdieu, 1990 p. 87). It is an important construct in Bourdieu's theory of society, particularly educational contexts, which he defines as a social field. The players in the educational field are members of the societies who are impacted upon by the policies and media representations that give refugee and asylum seekers their identities, however misleading. They are encouraged to develop habitus that protect and defend the privilege that so many of them rely on for the position in the field and for their symbolic capital. For many, this precludes a tendency towards compassion and belonging and promotes dispositions that do not allow them to overlook any differences of race, culture, social status and religion and to focus instead on the characteristics of what it is to be human and to undergo such experiences themselves (Williams, 2008)

Individuals may belong or enter more than one social field simultaneously in the course of their everyday lives. Acceptance in these fields, which include institutions, relationships, cultural and social practices; anywhere that social structures reflect cultural practices, is dependent on both capital and habitus. Identifying all these interfaces as potential sites for power struggles, Bourdieu posits that those who construct the field also have the most power within it. In educational contexts, those who determine the scope and definition of the nature of education, particularly public education, have advantages in that determine the 'rules of the game' in the types of the various capital they have accumulated, in their habitus, in the form of the knowledge and dispositions they possess as a result of their position to access and manage capital as symbolic capital and in the field. The power that these individuals have in determining the parameters, values and epistemologies of the institutional social field of education itself can only be a reflection of their habitus and their symbolic capital. For many students, including those with refugee and asylum seeker backgrounds, neoliberal education is an act of symbolic violence mediated only by those in the field whose habitus is informed by a sense of morality, emotional intelligence and ethical conviction and by the autonomy of the students themselves.

While habitus is not fixed and can change in relation to challenging social conditions, situations in which individuals question their beliefs and assumptions and times of collective disruption, the assertion by Bourdieu that habitus is unconsciously formed and reformed has been challenged as a dismissal 'of conscious calculation' which 'empties ordinary cognition of its conscious elements.......he overstates his case that cognitive structures are not forms of consciousness but dispositions of the body (Noble & Watkins, 2003 p. 529 in Reay, 2010 p. 81). This may be a pertinent observation for students of refugee and asylum seeker experiences who find themselves struggling to be accepted when placed in the unfamiliar field of neoliberal schooling and its attendant policies and practices. They may be in situations where they consciously and deliberately generate new dispositions and perceptions in order to develop the habitus required for acceptance and a developing sense of belonging.

Sayer (2010 p. 93), also discusses the limitations of Bourdieu's notion of habitus with regard to the lack of consideration given to emotional responses, their influences on behaviours and their connection to habitus, all of which are vital considerations for the development of compassion. He indicates that emotions are

> ....cognitive and evaluative, indeed essential elements of intelligence (Naussbaum, 2001: 3). They are strongly related to our nature as dependent and vulnerable beings. They are *about* something, particularly things that are important to our wellbeing and which we value and

yet are not fully within our control……..Emotions are highly discriminating, evaluative commentaries on our wellbeing or ill being in the physical world (for example pleasure in warmth); in our practical dealings with the world (for example, the frustration of failing to execute some task successfully); and in the social- psychological world (for example self-esteem or shame) (Archer. 2000; Nussbaum, 2001 in Sayer, 2010 p.94).

He attributes Bourdieu's neglect of emotions and of the role of personal, ethical responses and disinterested motivations to Bourdieu's 'power- based model of social life and…….'hermeneutics of suspicion (Sayer, 2010 p 95), a perspective which underpins Bourdieu's understanding of all human action as indicated by Navarro,

> Bourdieu, on the other hand, claims that all actions in any sphere of human interaction are fundamentally 'interested' (even solidarity) whether they are directed towards material or symbolic items. He proposes a science of social practices that posits as a premise (not as a hypothesis) that all practices are oriented towards the maximisation of material or symbolic results, that is, mainly interest-motivated. His starting point is, therefore, an acceptance of two basic principles of human behaviour. First, drawing on Weber (but expanding his scope), Bourdieu argues that all actions by individuals in social arrangements are interest-driven, regardless of the specificities of a given concrete context. As a result of this first premise, he maintains that while self-interest is the driving force of human behaviour, the final result is that social struggles are the main facet of social arrangements in any specific field, because individuals try to maximise their gains and accumulate resources under different forms of capital (economic, social, cultural, symbolic). The historical outcome of this persistent search for accumulation of resources is to entrench hierarchies that in their turn require a permanent vigilance to legitimise these social differences – hence a continuous effort to keep 'misrecognition' about the origins of these asymmetries. This is the reason why Bourdieu's theory is essentially political and deals with power relations as its core objective. (Navarrao, 2006 p 14).

While this may be a reflection of the individualistic characteristics so prevalent in neoliberal societies and education policies, endorsed by immigrant policy makers and their associated procedures for dealing with refugee and asylum seeker communities and by the popular media, Sayer insists that it is of

> ….enormous normative importance that people can also value others and their conduct in terms of their goodness and propriety, often regardless of their self- interest and sometimes in ways that do not match the inclinations of their habitus (2010, p. 95).

In other words, without a sense of moral and ethical conduct as a regular part of societal engagement, societies are in grave danger of initiating and perpetuating deliberate acts that result in harm and injustice. In considering the current situation faced by many students with refugee and asylum seeker experiences, it would appear that both aspects of habitus are important. Without the ethical consideration for action that are explored by Sayer, individuals would be entirely consumed by the concerns of accumulating the various forms of capital that allow them to have the access and acceptance into the various fields in which they wish to function with a sense of belonging, in this case, school contexts.

To recognise the emotional component of habitus is to acknowledge the opportunity for compassion and belonging, which relate to the emotional lives of the individuals under consideration. It is also important to be considered in Bourdieu's theory of the means by which schools replicate the 'status quo' of societies. They do this using the capital, habitus and power invested by those who create the field. In these cases they are the purveyors of competition, economic rationalism and self-interest as an overarching priority. How then, do these policy makers accommodate students with the least capital; cultural, social and economic; and the least habitus for acceptance into this educational field? More importantly, how can these students experience a sense of compassion for their situation and belonging in these schools? Ironically, Bourdieu (1990) insists that, despite his theory of social reproduction and the prominent role that schooling plays in this paradigm, this is neither a deterministic nor simple process. He recognises, as does Foucault (2003), that individuals have agency and autonomy. In education the reproductive function of schooling is mediated by many factors, including characteristics that are local, contextual and historical.

Consequently, much relies on the capacities of those at the micro level of schooling to develop their person sense of ethical and moral behaviour and engage in conscious reflection in the face of challenging social situations in order to reform their habitus, consider what is it is to be humanly compassionate and be sensitive to their sense of ethical and moral behaviours in order to authentically support students with refugee and asylum seeker experiences. The degree to which this acceptance and support can be realized depends not only on the demands and constraints of the educational systems and schools in which these students are placed but also on the perceptions and dispositions of individual teachers with regard to social, physical, racial and gendered difference, whether experienced as conscious or unconscious; and the impact of these perceptions and dispositions on their interactions with students (Travis, Kraehe, Hood, & Lewis, 2018)

Conclusion

It is apparent that those at the macro level of governments and policy makers do not wish to engage with the emotional constructs of compassion and belonging when presented with situations which require decisions to decisions to be made about prioritizing economic rationalist principles as expressed in various neoliberal models of government or remain true to promises of receiving and accepting people in most need of compassion and belonging. It is apparent where the priorities of neoliberal societies lie, in actions that are faithful to the capitalist underpinning of their market policies. It is not suggested that there is a deliberate attempt on the behalf of policymakers and systems directors to act unjustly towards any groups of students, but it is the combined action of all the 'players' in the field that contributes to the reproduction of society; 'the overall pattern of social, economic, political and cultural difference, differentiation and distinction (Wadham et al., 2007 p. 338)'. An analysis of society in Bourdieun terms indicated how refugee and asylum seeker students may be placed in terms of habitus and capital in relation to the field of education and concluded that in modern societies, the recognition of emotional life and the actions of moral, ethical consciousness are as important considerations in determining habitus as those Bourdieu claimed were unconscious and self-serving.

Attitudes to refugee and asylum seekers have undergone some transformations at the level of policy and the attendant procedures. These, combined with the influence of the media, have served to dehumanize these refugee and asylum seeker populations to the point of attributing blame for their precarious situations. It is then left to those at local levels of schooling to engage with these communities and their children as students; children, young people and humans with emotional lives and academic potential. This is simply because it is impossible to engage in authentic educational practice without being confronted by the human faces of these students and their communities. The important issues to investigate for those students and their communities who are granted settlement rights, despite the rigours of detention, dispersion and other exclusionary practices, are the characteristics of safe educational places for these children and young people; spaces where compassion and belonging are the cornerstones of student wellbeing.

References

Alencar, A. (2018). Refugee Integration and Social Media: A Local and Experiential Perspective. *Information, Communication & Society, 21*(11), 1588-1603. doi:10.1080/1369118X.2017.1340500

Bal, A. (2014). Becoming In/competent Learners in the United States: Refugee Students' Academic Identities in the Figured World of Difference. *International Multilingual Research Journal, 8*(4), 271-290. doi: 10.1080/19313152.2014.952056

Bauman, Z. (2004). *Wasted Lives: Modernity and its Outcasts*. Oxford. UK: Blackwell Publishing Ltd.

Bennett, B. (2018). Becoming Refugees: Exodus and Contemporary Mediations of the Refugee Crisis. *Transnational Cinemas, 9*(1), 13-30. doi:10.1080/20403526.2018.1471181

Bernstein, B. (1990). *Class, Codes and Control*. London: Routledge.

Bleiker, R., Campbell, D., Hutchison, E., & Nicholson, X. (2013). The Visual Dehumanisation of Refugees. *Australian Journal of Political Science, 48*(4), 398-416. doi:10.1080/10361146.2013.840769

Block, K., Cross, S., Riggs, E., & Gibbs, L. (2014). Supporting Schools to Create an Inclusive Environment for Refugee Students. *International Journal of Inclusive Education, 18*(12), 1337-1355. doi:10.1080/13603116.2014.899636

Bourdieu, P. (1977). *Outline of a Theory of Practice*. Cambridge UK: Cambridge University Press.

Bourdieu, P. (1986). The Forms of Capital. In J. G. Richardson (Ed.), *The Handbook of Theory: Research for the Sociology of Education* (pp. 241-258). New York: Greenwood Press.

Bourdieu, P. (1990). *Reproduction in Education, Society, and Culture*. London: Sage.

Bourdieu, P., Passeron, J., & Saint Martin, M. (1994). *Academic Discourse: Linguistic Misunderstanding and Professorial Power* Cambridge: Polity Press.

Dagg, J., & Haugaard, M. (2016). The Performance of Subject Positions, Power, and Identity: A Case of Refugee Recognition. *European Journal of Cultural and Political Sociology, 3*(4), 392-425. doi:10.1080/23254823.2016.1202524

Dunkerly-Bean, J., Bean, T., & Alnajjar, K. (2014). Seeking Asylum. *Journal of Adolescent & Adult Literacy, 58*(3), 230-241. doi:10.1002/jaal.349

Eastmond, M. (2011). Egalitarian Ambitions, Constructions of Difference: The Paradoxes of Refugee Integration in Sweden. *Journal of Ethnic and Migration Studies, 37*(2), 277-295. doi:10.1080/1369183X.2010.521323

Emert, T. (2013). 'The Transpoemations Project': Digital Storytelling, Contemporary Poetry, and Refugee Boys. *Intercultural Education, 24*(4), 355-365. doi:10.1080/14675986.2013.809245

Ferfolja, T., Diaz, C. J., & Ullman, J. (2018). *Understanding Sociological Theory foe Educational Practices* (2nd Ed.). Melbourne Victoria: Cambridge University Press.

Foucault, M. (1979a). *Discipline and Punish*. Harmondsworth: Peregrine.

Foucault, M. (1979b). *Power, Truth, Strategy*. Sydney: Feral Publications.
Foucault, M. (2003). Society Must Be Defended' (D. Macey, Trans.). In *Lectures at the College de France 1975-1976*, . New York: Picador.
Gatt, K. (2011). Sudanese Refugees in Victoria: An Analysis of their Treatment by the Australian Govenment. *International Journal of Comparative and Applied Criminal Justice, 35*(3), 207-219.
Gerrard, J. (2017). The Refugee Crisis, Non-citizens, Border Politics and Education. *Discourse: Studies in the Cultural Politics of Education, 38*(6), 880-891. doi:10.1080/01596306.2016.1227959
Greussing, E., & Boomgaarden, H. G. (2017). Shifting the Refugee Narrative? An Automated Frame Analysis of Europe's 2015 Refugee Crisis. *Journal of Ethnic and Migration Studies, 43*(11), 1749-1774. doi:10.1080/1369183X.2017.1282813
Hargrave, A. (2003). *Teaching in the Knowledge Society: Education in the Age of Insecurity*. England: Open University Press.
Hattam, R., & Every, D. (2010). Teaching in Fractured Classrooms: Refugee Education, Public Culture, Community and Ethics. *Race Ethnicity and Education, 13*(4), 409-424. doi:10.1080/13613324.2010.488918
Hickerson, A., & Dunsmore, K. (2016). Locating Refugees. *Journalism Practice, 10*(3), 424-438. doi:10.1080/17512786.2015.1025417
Hope, J. (2011). New Insights into Family Learning for Refugees: Bonding, Bridging and Building Transcultural Capital. *Literacy, 45*(2), 91-97. doi:10.1111/j.1741-4369.2011.00581.x
Hunpage, L., & Marston, G. (2006). Recognition, Respect and Rights: Refugees Living in Temporary Protection Visas (TPVs) in Australia. In N. Yuval- Davies, K. Kannabiran, & U. Vieten (Eds.), *The Situated Politics of Belonging* (pp. 113-126). London: Sage.
Kendi, I. (2017). *Stamped from the Beginning: The Definitive History of Racist Ideas in America*. New York: Nation Books: A Member of the Perseus Books Group.
Massing, C., Kirova, A., & Hennig, K. (2013). The Role of First Language Facilitators in Redefining Parent Involvement: Newcomer Families' Funds of Knowledge in an Intercultural Preschool Program. *Canadian Children, 38*(2), 4-13.
Matthews, J. (2008). Schooling and Settlement: Refugee Education in Australia. *International Studies in Sociology of Education, 18*(1), 31-45. doi:10.1080/09620210802195947
Miller, G., Thomas, C. A. T., & Fruechtenicht, S. (2014). Engaging Refugee Families as Partners in Their Children's Education. *Communique (0164775X), 43*(4), 1-31.
Navarrao, Z. (2006). In Search of a Cultural Interpretation of Power: The Contribution of Pierre Bourdieu. *IDS Bulletin, 37*(6), 11-22.
Noddings, N. (2005). *The Challenge to Care in Schools; An Alternative Approach to Education* (2nd ed.). New York: Teachers College Press.
Noddings, N. (2012). *The Philosophy of Education*. Boulder Colorado: Westview Press.
Nolan, D., Farquharson, K., Politoff, V., & Marjibanks, T. (2011). Mediated Multiculturism: Newspaper Representations of Sudanese Migrants in Australia. *Jouirnal of Intercultural Studies, 32*(6), 655-671.

Nussbaum, M. (2001). *Upheavals of Thought: The Intelligence of Emotions.* . New York: Cambridge University Press.

Pinson, H., & Arnot, M. (2007). Sociology of Education and the Wasteland of Refugee Education Research. *British Journal of Sociology of Education, 28*(3), 399-407. doi:10.1080/01425690701253612

Pinson, H., & Arnot, M. (2010). Local Conceptualisations of the Education of Asylum-seeking and Refugee students: from Hostile to Holistic Models. *International Journal of Inclusive Education, 14*(3), 247-267. doi:10.1080/13603110802504523

Pinson, H., Arnot, M., & Candappa, M. (2010). *Education, Asylum and the Non- Citizen Child: The Politics of Compassion and Belonging.* Basingstoke UK: Palgrave Macmillan.

Reay, D. (2010). From the Theory of Practice to the Practice of Theory. In E. Silva & A. Warde (Eds.), *Cultural Analysis and Bourdieu's Legacy: Settling Accounts and Developing Alternatives.* New York: Routledge.

Saltman, K., & Means, A. Students as Critical Citizens/Educated Subjects but Not as Commodities/Tested Objects. In *The Sage Guide to Curriculum n Education* (pp. 284-301). Retrieved from http://sk.sagepub.com/reference/the-sage-guide-to-curriculum-in-education/i4315.xml. doi:http://dx.doi.org/10.4135/9781483346687.n41

Saltsman, A. (2014). Beyond the Law: Power, Discretion, and Bureaucracy in the Management of Asylum Space in Thailand. *Journal of Refugee Studies, 27*(3), 457-476. doi:10.1093/jrs/feu004

Sayer, A. (2010). *Bourdieu, Ethics and Practice.* New York: Routledge.

Schubert, A., & Wurf, G. (2014). Adolescent Sexting in Schools: Criminalisation, Policy Imperatives, and Duty of Care. *Issues in Educational Research, 24*(2), 190-211.

Stewart, J. (2011). *Supporting Refugee Children: Strategies for Educators.* Toronto, Ontraio: University of Toronto Press.

Tarumoto, H. (2019). Why Restrictive Refugee Ppolicy can be Retained? A Japanese Case. *Migration and Development, 8*(1), 7-24. doi:10.1080/21632324.2018.1482642

Travis, S., Kraehe, M., Hood, E., & Lewis, T. (Eds.). (2018). *Pedagogies of the Flesh.* New York: Palgrave Macmillan.

United Nations High Commission for Refugees. (2019). *Figures at a Glance.* Retrieved from https://www.unhcr.org/en-au/figures-at-a-glance.html

Wadham, B., Pudsey, J., & Boyd, R. (2007). *Culture and Education.* Frenchs Forest, NSW: Pearson Education Australia.

Watt, D. (2012). The Urgency of Visual Media Literacy in our Post-9/11 World: Reading Images of Muslim Women in the Print News Media. *Journal of Media Literacy Education, 4*(1), 32-43.

Watters, C. (2007). *Refugee Children: Towards the Next Horizon* (1 ed.). Florence: Taylor and Francis.

Williams, C. R. (2008). Compassion, Suffering and the Self: A Moral Psychology of Social Justice. *Current Sociology, 56*(1), 5-24. doi:10.1177/0011392107084376

Chapter Six: People: Schools as Safe Spaces

Introduction

This chapter discusses the notion that schools can, and ethically should be, places of safely and support for all students, most especially those with refugee and asylum seeker backgrounds. The climate of the school, the hidden curriculum, the compulsory content knowledge curricula and the ways in which the socio- emotional lives of students are supported are critical to the perceptions that students develop about their schools as welcoming, accepting spaces where they are valued and respected as community members. Maslow (1943), clearly placed the need for safety and security on the second of his five levels of need, second only to the basic physiological needs of food, water, shelter and warmth. This need for security is closely associated with the need for love and belonging. Given that schools are acknowledged as major socializing agents in any society (see, for example, Bourdieu, 1990; Connell, 1977, 1982; Connell et al., 2007; Hamilton & Moore, 2006) and provide multiple opportunities to be involved in social, sporting and other community groups, to develop positive relationship and friendships and to mitigate the impact of negative experiences and emotions, the importance of school context, including the interactions students with refugee and asylum seekers experiences encounters with teachers and peers, is critical to these students' potential to develop socially, emotionally, physically and academically.

School climate

Values and beliefs are also the basis of the discussion around school climate, which has been investigated for over 100 years (Perry 1908 in C. Cohen, McCabe, Michelli, & Pickeral, 2009) as being an important aspect of school life. Although the initial investigations of school climate focus on the organisational and physical aspects of schools, (see, for example, Guion, 1973; Moos, 1973; Tagiuri, 1968), studies gradually began to include the perspectives of other stakeholders and to consider the personal contributions of the school community to the development of school climate, in addition to analysing and categorizing the various contributions into classified groups. Field and Abelson (1982), for example, based their study on the combined findings of the literature. They included the perceptions of all members of the school in their study. From the commonly accepted understanding of a three level model of school climate, they developed a three level model of school climate which focussed on the psychological level of school climate. This revised model was analysed over four common dimensions. The levels identified where that of (i) the organizational climate, ii the group climate and (iii) the psychological climate. The level of psychological climate was found to be the essence of school climate, examining the experiences of individuals in relation to the school climate supporting consideration of their feelings of connectedness and belonging in relation to the school. At the organisational level they considered the degrees of (i) autonomy/control, ii degree of structure, (iii)rewards and (iv) consideration, warmth and support and how this was moderated by the group climate which, in turn modified the personal experiences of school climate at a personal level (Field & Abelson, 1982:186).

This characteristic of school interactions appears to be more inclusive and less dominated by policy than some of the other elusive, aspects of school characteristics. Cohen et al. (2009), described the state that is identified as school climate as;

> the quality and character of school life. School climate is based on patterns of people's experiences of school life and reflects norms, goals, values, interpersonal relationships, teaching and learning practices, and organizational structures. A sustainable, positive school climate fosters youth development and learning necessary for a productive, contributive, and satisfying life in a democratic society. This climate includes norms, values, and expectations that support people feeling socially, emotionally, and physically safe. People are engaged and respected (p. 100).

School climate is perceived as a subtler and more subjective component of school culture which may be considered critical to student success in multiple domains (Kaplan, deBlois, Dominguez, & Walsh, 2016; Loukas & Robinson, 2004; Wang et al., 2014). Walters (2012), summarized the literature that discussed school climate as a matter of priority, indicating that positive school climate is an essential factor in developing young people's capacity to participate fully in democratic societies. In the review, four major dimensions of school life were under consideration. These complemented the comprised,

- Safety (e.g. rules and norms; physical safety; social---emotional safety);
- Relationships (e.g. respect for diversity; school connectedness/engagement; social support; leadership);

- Teaching and Learning (e.g. social, emotional, ethical and civic learning; support for academic learning; support for professional relationships);
- Institutional Environment (e.g. physical surroundings). (p. 4).

These reflected the ways in which school climate had been developed over the decades by number of scholars (see, for example, J. Cohen, 2009; T. Cohen, Guffey, Higgins, & D'Alessandro, 2013; Coladarci, 1992; Cotton, 1996; Tagiuri, Litwin, & Barnes, 1968; Vieno, Perkins, Smith, & Santinello, 2005; Wang et al., 2014), who, at various times in history, had reported on school climate as perceived by educators and by the current perceptions of the role of schools and the roles of teachers and learners. There appears to be a consensus about the importance of school climate for the wellbeing of all students, but particularly those with refugee and asylum seeker experiences (Watters, 2007) and those whose foci are social and emotional wellbeing in schools (see, for example, Watson, Ermery, Bayliss, Boushel, & McInnes, 2012). This is acknowledged in the work of Bradshaw, Waarsdorp, Debnam, and Johnson (2014)., who write,

> There is a growing body of research documenting an association among a positive school climate and prosocial motivation, academic motivation, self-esteem, conflict resolution, and altruistic behaviour. School climate is also a significant predictor of rates of dropout, absenteeism and truancy, suspension, drug use, and violent and aggressive behaviour (Bradshaw et al., 2014 p. 593).

Despite the evolving definitions of this construct (Van Houtte, 2005), it remains a rather elusive aspect of schooling that is examined as a multi- faceted conceptualization . Bradshaw et al. (2014) examined school climate using a model which included twenty- five thousand students' perceptions of school safety, engagement and environment. These major components were further subdivided to include thirteen subsections. These subsections required students to answer specific questions about their perceptions of their school environment in terms of their personal safety, bullying and aggression, drug use, connection to teachers, student connectedness, academic engagement, school connectedness, equity, and parent engagement; rules and consequences, physical comfort, and support, and disorder. The findings of this study revealed that the safety domain was most negatively impacted by bullying, aggression and drug use. In relation to engagement, they found that the relatively unexplored areas of equity and fairness were important to students and that in schools with higher achievement successes, students' perceptions of these dimensions of school life scored highly. Fairness and equity were investigated in the student perceptions of the elements of well- structured school, fair discipline practices and more positive student relationships, which were also elements that scored highly in the schools with least student behaviour problems and where parents were encouraged to build positive relationships with the school. School-wide approaches to violations of the school rules, an orderly, well maintained school site and emotional support from teachers also provided encouragement for students to behave appropriately and succeed academically.

The critical aspect of this research is not that Bradshaw et al. (2014) may have developed a successful framework for examining school climate but that the student participant had opportunities to report their perceptions of the climate in their schools. The dimensions of schooling that were investigated and the means by which this was done elicited responses from the student participants that relied on their affective perceptions of schooling, not directly on the capacity of the school to achieve academic goals, although these were improved considerably by positive and supportive school climate. Students with refugee and asylum seeker experiences not only need to belong to schools with positive school climates, but be aware that they have an important contribution to make to the school climate, irrespective of their experiences of trauma and loss and the subsequent impact of these encounters on their emotional and social wellbeing. In order to achieve this, they need to have school experiences that foster an authentic sense of belonging.

Belonging

The notion of belonging is complex and critical (Angus 2015; Hamilton & Moore, 2006; Stewart, 2011), and some of the literature contributes significantly to ways in which belonging is facilitated or hindered in west centric classrooms. Belonging encompasses feelings of connectedness and positivity (see, for example, Loukas, Suzuki, & Horton, 2006; McMichael, Gifford, & Correa-Velez, 2011; McNeely, Nonnemaker, & Blum, 2002; Shernoff et al., 2016), is differentiated by students into different types of belonging; social and academic (Green, Emery, Sanders, & Anderson, 2016) and is influenced by cultural and socio economic factors in addition to student and staff personalities and character traits (Chiu, Chow, McBride, & Mol, 2016). A simple definition that defies this complexity is provided by Goodenow and Grady (1993 p. 80), who state that belonging is a feeling of being 'accepted, respected, included and supported by others'. There are multiple contexts in which individuals can perceive a sense of belonging. In the context of students with refugee and asylum seeker experiences, many, if not all, these contexts may be lost for them. They may have lost belonging to a family group if they are unaccompanied, lost many of the members of extended family, neighbourhood groups, wider community and identity forming friendships and team memberships and connection to country (Hamilton & Moore, 2006; Pinson & Arnot, 2007; Pinson, Arnot, & Candappa, 2010; Stewart, 2011; Watters, 2007).

As, in many cases, lack of belonging in one context can be compensated by the sense of belonging in other circumstances and environment, the degree to which this can achieved for students with refugee and asylum seeker experiences may be difficult, especially when government policies of detention, dispersal and resettlement do not consider the impact of their decision making on the possibilities of exclusion and belonging. School may be, at least initially, the only place outside the home to which these groups of students have the potential to belong, which presents schools and school communities with considerable responsibility for the emotional welfare and wellbeing of the students in their care (Edgeworth, 2014).

Chiu et al. (2016), in their investigations of school belonging in forty- one countries, identified some of the most pertinent variables that may prevent students with refugee and asylum seeker experiences from initially feeling that they belong in neoliberal classrooms. Amongst these factors where notions of school familiarity and home backgrounds of print materials, students reading competencies, social status such as that identified by refuge and asylum seeker, students and teachers own personalities and economic wealth. These may constitute a significant barrier to students with refugee and asylum seeker experiences who originate from backgrounds of oracy, who had had no previous experiences of schooling, or have interrupted schooling, who have limited experience print materials and who have lost their homes, their parental and extended family livelihoods and economic capital. Interestingly, however, they nominated their most important finding as one that related to cultural norms and practices. In the investigation of whether the sense of belonging was a globally held imperative for wellbeing at school, they found that a sense of belonging at school was contingent on culture. While there existed a number of studies that investigated the sense of belonging at school focussing on the difference in racial groups and various diverse language backgrounds (see, for example, Faircloth & Hamm, 2005; Goodenow & Grady, 1993), the researchers found no investigations that focussed on cultural differences to examine the importance and variations of degrees of belonging at school.

Chiu et al. (2016), investigating from the macro system level of Bronfenbrenner's ecological systems theory (Bronfenbrenner, 1990; Yok-Fong, 2013), found that two aspects of cultural difference were significant in terms of students' sense of belonging at school. These were power distance and the collectivist or individualistic nature of the culture (Hofstede, 1983;1986; 2001). Power distance refers to the degree to which hierarchical structures are incorporated into cultural norms and relationship. A contrasting culture would be an egalitarian culture in which all people, regardless of their wealth, status or education are treated in the same manner in everyday interactions, without undue deference to their position or standing in the society in which they live. In school contexts, students in hierarchical cultures would be expected to obey and respect authority figures because of their positions. They would not expect to develop friendly, everyday conversations with their teachers and other school authority figures as would students in egalitarian societies. Students who view their teachers as superior are unlikely to develop any closeness to them, to expect emotional and social support from them or anticipate that they would cultivate appropriate, personal relationships with them. Individuals who are of dissimilar status and position in hierarchical societies understand each other as different themselves and so making connections with each other is not expected.

Collective cultures provide the opposite effect. There is a strong tendency for students to consider the whole group when making decisions, to work cooperatively and help each other, there exists a great degree of perceived similarity amongst group members and they readily identify with each other. They tend to observe group behaviours such as turn taking and listening carefully to one another. This also leads them greater compliance towards group rules and norms and class standards tend to predict their academic achievement. Unfortunately, Chiu et al. (2016) did not find that collectivist, cohesive cultural inclinations had any impact on the students sense of belonging at school. Unfortunate because many of the students with refugee and asylum seeker experiences originated in communities that had collectivist cultures and this may have provided one avenue; social belonging; by which these students could access a sense of belonging in classrooms that are dominated by students from individualistic cultures, which are characterized by prioritizing personal goals, competition amongst peers and a singular focus on the development and promotion of self above all others. Considering the experiences of refugee and asylum seeker students in relation to provision for their educational needs between the times of dispersal and resettlement, and the individualistic nature of learning success in neoliberal classrooms it may be difficult also for these students to belong in ways described by students as 'academic belonging'(Green et al., 2016).

One other factor was prominent in the study (Chiu et al., 2016), the quality of the supportive, accepting and respectful relationships with peers and, most importantly, with teachers. Once again the question of power distance was considered by students from collective societies and this was observed to be more powerful that the impact of collectivism. This again places teachers in a unique position to support the sense of belonging in school for students of refugee and asylum seeker backgrounds. Not only are they the adults who interact most powerfully and most directly with students, they are also frequently the individuals who determine the attitudes and perspectives of the culture in their classrooms. It is therefore, a significant responsibility for teachers to demonstrate, model and establish the acceptance, respect, inclusive strategies and support (Goodenow & Grady, 1993) that students with refugee and asylum seeker experiences need in order to develop feelings of belonging and connectedness at school. This cannot be achieved without teachers who have genuine feelings of empathy towards the circumstances of their students and their families and communities and are prepared to educate their students for the development of empathy also. In the neoliberal world of efficiencies, economies, competition and accountability, this may appear to be an impossible task. Unless it can be achieved at a whole school level, then students with refugee and asylum seeker experiences will feel excluded from the powerful socializing institution in modern societies.

Empathy

Empathy, like compassion, is a human emotion that is not valued as a priority in current neoliberal classrooms. There is little time or encouragement for teachers to develop relationships with students, given their increased workload as a consequence of unprecedented accountability (see, for example, Ferfolja, 2009; Ferfolja & Vickers, 2010). There exists a wide range of research, studies and theories which include empathy as a desirable, indeed necessary construct for humanity, especially in the realm of teaching and learning (see, for example, Bandura, Caprara, Barbaranelli, Gerbino, & Pastorelli, 2003; Ford, 2014; Gidley, 2016, 2017; Goleman, 1995; Gutstein & Peterson, 2005; Peck, Maude, & Brotherson, 2015; Sarraj, Bene, Li, & Burley, 2015; Savoley & Mayer, 1990). Despite the varying contexts, perspectives and definitions of empathy in these and other academic writing, there is no consideration that empathy itself is both politicised and inequitable. It is taken for granted that empathy is the same for everyone, irrespective of cultural values and person values and beliefs. However, another, more critical understanding of empathy and the ways in which it can be used in public spaces to both create social harmony and divisions is offered by Mirra (2018).

Mirra (2018) differentiates between individual and more public forms of empathy. She discusses individual empathy for other individuals as valuable but asserts that doing this alone can lead to a lack of awareness that the notions of empathy and perspective- taking are in themselves inequitable and politicized. This is because individuals do not grow and develop in a vacuum but are influenced by the many layers of social constructs. These include race, religion, socio-economic status, political views, gender and so forth. Individual empathy seeks to understand or imagine the experiences of others by making meaning within the constructs of their own lives, whether these be lives interpreted through the powerful influence of privilege, or the disempowerment and disenchantment of a marginalized minority. She suggests that a new understanding of empathy is possible, one that is 'explicitly committed to grappling with the inequities in our public life and engagement with democratic power structures (p. 7) and recommends that it replaces the current treatment of civics in school curricula in order to develop more socially aware, active citizenship as critical practice. Using the term *Critical Civic Empathy*, Mirra suggests that this understanding of empathy should be the overarching goal of all educators' work. This model of empathy is characterised by three defining principles. She states

- It begins from an analysis of the social position, power and privilege of all parties involved.
- It focusses on the ways that personal experiences matter in the context of public life.
- It fosters democratic dialogue and civic action committed to equity and justice. (p. 7)

With these in mind, Mirra has developed a four square typography of empathy in which the horizontal axis represents mutual humanization, based on the Freirean (1970) notion that in order to become fully human it is necessary to recognise and respect the humanity of all people, irrespective of differences in social constructs, including race, religion and economic status. The vertical axis indicates a continuum of how predisposed individuals may be taking social or political action as a result of the commitment to humanity. The resultant typology serves the purpose of setting out the various perspectives of empathy in public life. The bottom left hand quadrant shows *imaginative refusal,* which captures the anti- empathic rhetoric often populated by the media in respect to refugees and asylum seekers and may also include the anti- humanitarian policies and statements made by some politicians. Above it is the quadrant labelled *false empathy*, which is frequently used in public arenas by individuals seeking to gain political kudos. These statements often include notions of national values, use the term 'we' to indicate solidarity with similarly minded people, use notions of emphatical language selectively and purport to be declarations of support for social unity but are, when observed critically, divisive and politically manipulative.

The bottom right hand quadrant of the typography shows the relationship of individual empathy to the other constructs. This type of empathy is seen to be fostered by the popularity of social and emotional programs in schools. While it encourages students to be more aware of the plight of those less fortunate than themselves, these programs do nothing to investigate the rules, laws and policies that are so often the cause of inequitable and inhumane treatment of those to be empathized with, in the case of refugee and asylum seeker populations, immigration and border policies. This happens for several reasons. Programs designed to support emotional and social learning are frequently taught as 'soft skills' and have no academic content. These are not used to interrogate the status quo, to unearth the taken-for-grantedness of educational and other practices, or to create more reflective and reflexive students. In reality, the primary purpose of including programs of social and emotional learning in school are to support greater academic performance, which research has indicated can be impacted positively by student wellbeing. There are few, if any, programs that focus exclusively on the development of critical consciousness and action as a result of engaging in the program. Consequently, Mirra argues that individuals are aware that empathy is a desirable and appropriate emotion, irrespective of differences in social stratification, but without any criticality that might lead them to act in any way that is available to them in order to disrupt the policies, laws and social acceptance that serve to perpetuate injustices and inequities.

The top right -hand corner is the space for critical civic empathy. Mirra (2018) advocates classroom practices and activities that investigate beyond the academic. She encourages dialogues that investigate different perspectives and the underlying values and beliefs that influence them. As an English teacher, she proposes that literature is an ideal means by which this can be achieved, but there exist multiple possibilities and opportunities across the curricula to identify spaces in all learning areas where these dialogues may occur. Creating an agenda of critical civic empathy is critical to addressing the ways in empathy can be actioned in schools, the wider public arena and in the decisions that are made by politicians in democratic societies.

What implications are there for students with refugee and asylum seeker backgrounds?

One of the most obvious and self- righteous aspects of school culture is racism (see, for example, Anderson, 2001; Baak, 2019). Related to Foucault's (1991) notion of 'othering', in many cases exclusion from school activities, friendship groups and the sense of belonging is based on the racist beliefs of teachers and peers. Frequently it is based on the colour of students' skins, racial stereotyping or religious discrimination and it adds considerably to the emotional stress that students with refugee and asylum seeker experiences are already undergoing. Appallingly, much of the exclusion perpetuated in schools goes unchecked, whether as the result of an exclusive school climate, an unwelcoming school community or the ambivalence of staff and students (see, for example, Baak, 2019; Bloch & Hirsch, 2017; Carlile, 2012; Edgeworth, 2013; Forrest, Lean, & Dunn, 2016; S. L. Green & Edwards-Underwood, 2015; Gutstein & Peterson, 2005; Levine-Rasky, Beaudoin, & St Clair, 2014; Rasmussen, 2011). Incidences of exclusions that are motivated by personal prejudice are inhumane and lacking in empathy but, irrespective of the extent of distress that they cause, they are without authority and reflect only the limited perceptions of the offenders and the degree to which they lack the capacity to identify with others as members of humanity. Evidence of self- interest and discriminatory practices that impact on students with refugee and asylum seeker experiences are recorded in multiple reports gathered from neoliberal educational contexts (see, for example, Anders, 2012; Buchardt, 2018; Cheah, Karamehic-Muratovic, & Matsuo, 2013; Eastmond, 2011; Fernandes, 2015; Greussing & Boomgaarden, 2017; Iii & Adam, 2017; Madziva & Thondhlana, 2017; Mthethwa-Sommers & Kisiara, 2015).

The more insidious and potentially more critical racism is that with authority; institutional racism. It is objective racism (Zizek, 2008) in that it does not reflect the prejudice of individuals, but is perpetuated through the institutions which are intended to support and assist those with whom they are associated Carlile (2012), discusses this notion using a Foucauldian perspective to interrogate permanent exclusion from school in the United Kingdom. She states,

> institutional prejudice underpins some of the causes of permanent exclusion from school. This prejudice involves the exercising of normative power, because it is expressed through the administrative (mis) representation in paperwork and in professional talk of children and young people at risk of or subject to permanent exclusion. Policy suffuses the activities of

those in the employment of local government with the letter and the spirit of central governmental authority, or as Foucault (1977) puts it, 'the gradual extension of the mechanisms of discipline...their spread throughout the whole social body' (p. 209). (Carlile, 2012).

The evidence indicates that students with refugee and asylum seeker experiences are more likely to be permanently excluded from school. Assessments are made with assumptions of what students need. Age assumptions are most significantly related to immigrant and refugee students, with the result that decisions about student needs 'are found to sometimes be made on the basis of reductive skin-colour labels (Carlile, 2012 p. 175)', and the discussions that are typically engaged with and socially authorized between school and family around these decisions are somewhat arbitrary. Institutional racism appears frequently in government policies which are purported to support refugee and asylum seekers families. These often lead to insensitive and unprofessional decisions being made that impact considerably on the wellbeing of families who have already undergone considerable hardship and distress. In one example, in Australia, the dispersal policy was used by officials to locate a South Sudanese family in rural Tasmania, irrespective of the fact that all Aboriginal Australians were decimated by white people, and the remaining two members of this population died over a century previously, meaning the island had an exclusively white population. The two daughters in the family were effectively isolated at school and excluded from the general community (Edgeworth, 2014).

Students from all walks of life need to feel accepted, feel they belong at either a social or academic level (M. Green et al., 2016). The social aspect of belonging is particularly important for students of otherwise marginalized groups in society (Vasileiadou, 2009) such as students with refugee and asylum seeker experiences. This may easily be because being authentically included produces positive emotions which are critical to health and wellbeing (Seligman, 2011) in addition to facilitating improved potential for learning (Fredrickson, 2000, 2001). Students who are socially accepted and welcomed into school communities with healthy school climates integrate more readily and adapt to their new homelands more easily than those who are not accepted, meet racism and other prejudices and made to feel and remain different from their peers and the school community in general. Anderson (2004) indicates clearly the socializing role of the school. She writes

> Schools are.........points of contact between the refugees and their new country. Schools play a vital part in helping immigrant children understand the new country, find social support, and gain access to trusted people and experience acceptance. This enables them to become a meaningful part of their new home (p. 67).

Becoming a meaningful part of a new society is not just an individual or collective aspiration for specific populations, it is vital for every member of the society that has accepted these newcomers (Sellars, 2017).

The students with refugee and asylum seeker experiences are typically from homelands which have very different cultures to those in which they are settled in developed countries. There are several theories about what happens as the result of these dissimilar ways of doing and being brought together. These are generally focused on either a psychological or an anthropological perspective. A critical feature in both approaches is the degree to which the cultural interaction is voluntary or forced (Berry, 1997; Berry, Phinney, Sam, & Vedder, 2006; Berry, 2009; Berry, Horenczyk, & Kwak, 2006). Forced migration, especially with little or no hope of ever returning to the original homeland, is the most stressful for the immigrants and makes them increasingly vulnerable, through the lack of choice, to developing what Ogbu (1995a); (Ogbu, 1995b)terms 'oppositional cultural frames of reference'. The anthropological model, the original means by which groups of one culture cope with challenges of living in an entirely different culture, has similar considerations to that of the psychological model in the following aspects; the size of the group trying to integrate, the degree of association they have previously experienced with the cultural groups into which they are trying to integrate and the extent of the difference between those who are undergoing change and those belonging to the culture into which these populations are trying to integrate.

These factors can make integration more, or less difficult, for varying groups of students with refugee and asylum seeker experiences. The notion of an 'oppositional frame of reference' can be exhibited by the ways in which they engage in behaviour in their cultural groups which are not acceptable ways of behaving in the majority culture; or of developing negative acculturation attitudes towards intercultural contact as a result of negative interactions such as marginalization (Berry, 1997; Berry et al., 2006). This is a particularly pertinent factor for consideration in schools where students with refugee and asylum seeker experiences are regarded as 'deficit' and are perceived by themselves and others to be at a disadvantage in relation to the other students from the majority culture (Dooley, 2012). Education systems which are developed in the context of the neoliberal economic politics have particular characteristics and processes which serve to privilege specific groups of students and lack the creativity and flexibility to honour diversity and difference (Angus, 2015; Connell, 2013a, 2013b; McGregor, 2009) It is in these educational contexts that many students with refugee students find themselves placed in their newly settled contexts and in which they may, in many instances be at considerable risk of not developing positive acculturation attitudes and processes unless considerable accommodations are made to ensure their acceptance and inclusion (Atasay, 2015; Vickers & McCarthy, 2010).

Experiences with subjective racism and institutional racism in schools may have the impact of encouraging these oppositional behaviours for a considerable time after these students leave schools. Without acceptance, empathy and belonging, students from refugee and asylum seeker experiences will not have opportunities to optimize their integration into cultures significantly different to their own. They will experience continuing stress and trauma, despite their capacities to persevere, to hope (Bešić, Paleczek, & Gasteiger-Klicpera, 2018; Bowden & Doughney, 2010; Correa-Velez, Gifford, & Barnett, 2010; Smith, 2011) and to aspire for better futures (Pinson et al., 2010; Stewart, 2011; Watters, 2007).

Conclusion

This chapter has focussed on the possibility of schools being regarded as 'safe' spaces for students of refugee and asylum seeker experiences. The impact of school climate, which can be defined as the ways in which the school develops culture, implements policies and pedagogies and incorporates all factors that impact on the affective lives of students in schools. The notion of belonging and positivity were also identified as critical to the sense of safety that these students were able to develop in the school context. The idea of critical civic empathy built in the understanding that personal prejudice was not the only negative response made to these students and communities, and examined the reach and significance of institutional prejudice, actioned by those who had the power to do so. 'Othering' and racial discrimination were also discussed as negative and inequitable judgements made by both individuals and institutions which impacted destructively on the wellbeing of these students in their attempts to become integrated in the mainstream culture of schools. The ways in which schools were flexible spaces for learning with staff and student peers who, despite obvious differences, recognised a common characteristic of humanity as pivotal to their school climate were extremely powerful. These spaces of safety are only achieved through whole school actions, supported by the actions and attitudes of the wider school communities and support agencies, together with ethical leadership which holds, as its core values and motivations, care, compassion and empathy. The role of school leadership has never before been so critical to the wellbeing of students with refugee and asylum seeker experiences.

References

Anders, A. (2012). Lessons from a Postcritical Ethnography, Burundian Children with Refugee Status, and their Teachers. *Theory Into Practice, 51*(2), 99-106. doi:http://dx.doi.org/10.1080/00405841.2012.662850

Anderson, A. (2004). Issues of Migration. In R. Hamilton & D. Moore (Eds.), *Educational Interventions for Refugee Children* (pp. 64-82). New York: Routledge.

Anderson, P. (2001). ' You don't belong here in Germany....' On the Social Situation of Refugee Chuildren in Germany. *Journal of Refugee Studies, 14*(2), 187-199.

Angus, L. (2015). School Choice: Neoliberal Education Policy and Imagined Futures. *British Journal of Sociology of Education, 36*(3), 395-413.

Atasay, E. (2015). Neoliberal Multiculturalism Embedded in Social Justice Education: Commodification of Multicultural Education for the 21st Century. *Journal for Critiacl Education, 12*(3), 171- 205.

Baak, M. (2019). Racism and Othering for South Sudanese Heritage Students in Australian Schools: Is Inclusion Possible? *International Journal of Inclusive Education, 23*(2), 125-141. doi:10.1080/13603116.2018.1426052

Bandura, A., Caprara, G. V., Barbaranelli, C., Gerbino, M., & Pastorelli, C. (2003). Role of Affective Self-Regulatory Efficacy in Diverse Spheres of Psychosocial Functioning. *Child Development, 74*(3), 769-782.

Berry, J. (1997). Immigration, Acculturation, and Adaptation. *Applied Psychology: An International Review, 46*(1), 5-68.

Berry, J., Phinney, J., Sam, D., & Vedder, P. (2006). Immigrant Youth: Acculturation, Identity, and Adaptation. *Applied Psychology: An International Review, 55*(3), 303-332.

Berry, J. W. (2009). A Critique of Critical Acculturation. *International Journal of Intercultural Relations, 33*(5), 361-371. doi:10.1016/j.ijintrel.2009.06.003

Berry, J. W., Horenczyk, G., & Kwak, K. (2006). *Immigrant Youth in Cultural Transition: Acculturation, Identity, and Adaptation across National Contexts*. In. Retrieved from http://newcastle.eblib.com/patron/FullRecord.aspx?p=331698

Bešić, E., Paleczek, L., & Gasteiger-Klicpera, B. (2018). Don't Forget about Us: Attitudes towards the Inclusion of Refugee Children With(out) Disabilities. *International Journal of Inclusive Education*, 1-16. doi:10.1080/13603116.2018.1455113

Bloch, A., & Hirsch, S. (2017). The Educational Experiences of the Second Generation from Refugee Backgrounds. *Journal of Ethnic and Migration Studies, 43*(13), 2131-2148. doi:10.1080/1369183X.2017.1286972

Bourdieu, P. (1990). *Reproduction in Education, Society, and Culture*. London: Sage.

Bowden, M., & Doughney, J. (2010). Socio-economic Status, Cultural Diversity and the Aspirations of Secondary Students in the Western Suburbs of Melbourne, Australia. *Higher Education, 59*(1), 115-129. doi:10.1007/s10734-009-9238-5

Bradshaw, C., Waarsdorp, T., Debnam, K., & Johnson, S. (2014). Measuring School Climate in High Schools: A Focus on Safety, Engagement, and the Environment. *Journal of School Health, 84*(9), 593-604.

Bronfenbrenner, U. (1990). Discovering what Families do. *Rebuilding the Nest: A New Commitment to the American Family*. Retrieved from http://www.montana.edu/www4h/process.html

Buchardt, M. (2018). The "Culture" of Migrant Pupils: A Nation- and Welfare-State Historical Perspective on the European Refugee Crisis. *European Education, 50*(1), 58-73. doi:10.1080/10564934.2017.1394162

Carlile, A. (2012). An Ethnography of Permanent Exclusion from School: Revealing and Untangling the Threads of Institutionalised Racism. *Race Ethnicity and Education, 15*(2), 175-194. doi: 10.1080/13613324.2010.548377

Cheah, W. H., Karamehic-Muratovic, A., & Matsuo, H. (2013). Ethnic-group Strength among Bosnian Refugees in St. Louis, Missouri, and Host Receptivity and Conformity Pressure. *Journal of Immigrant & Refugee Studies, 11*(4), 401-415. doi:10.1080/15562948.2013.847684

Chiu, M., Chow, B., McBride, C., & Mol, S. (2016). Students' Sense of Belonging at School in 41 Countries Cross-Cultural Variability. . *Journal of Cross-Cultural Psychology,, 47*(2), 175-196.

Cohen, C., McCabe, E., Michelli, M., & Pickeral, T. (2009). School Climate: Research, Policy, Practice, and Teacher Education. *Teachers College record, 111*(1), 183-213.

Cohen, J. (2009). Transforming School Climate: Educational and Psychoanalytic Perspectives:. *Schools: Studies in Education, 6*(1), 99-103. Retrieved from http://www.jstor.org/stable/10.1086/597659

Cohen, T., Guffey, J., Higgins, S., & D'Alessandro, A. (2013). A Review of School Climate Research. . *Rev Educ Res., 83*(3), 357-385.

Coladarci, T. (1992). Teachers' Sense of Efficacy and Commitment to Teaching. *The Journal of Experimental Education, 60*(4), 323-337.

Connell, R. (1977). *Ruling Class, Ruling Culture: Studies of Conflict, Power and Hegemony in Australian Life*. Cambridge: Cambridge University Press.

Connell, R. (1982). *Making the Difference: Schools, Families and Social Division*. Sydney: Allen & Unwin.

Connell, R. (2013a). The Neoliberal Cascade and Education: An Essay on the Market Agenda and its Consequences. *Critical Studies in Education, 54*(2), 99-112.

Connell, R. (2013b). Why do Market 'Reforms' Persistently Increase Inequality? *Discourse: Studies in the Cultural Politics of Education, 34*(2), 279-285.

Connell, R., Campbell, C., Vickers, M., Welch, A., Foley, D., & Bagnell, N. (2007). *Education, Change and Society*. South Melbourne: Oxford University Press.

Correa-Velez, I., Gifford, S. M., & Barnett, A. G. (2010). Longing to Belong: Social Inclusion and Wellbeing among Youth with Refugee Backgrounds in the First Three Years in Melbourne, Australia. *Soc Sci Med, 71*(8), 1399-1408. doi:10.1016/j.socscimed.2010.07.018

Cotton, K. (1996). School Size, School Climate, and Student Performance. Retrieved 30 November 2012 http://upstate.colgate.edu/pdf/Abt_merger/Cotton_1996_Size_Climate_Performance.pdf

Dooley, K. (2012). Positioning Refugee Students as Intellectual Class Members. In F. McCarthy & M. Vickers (Eds.), *Immigrant Students: Achieving Equity in Education* (pp. 3-20). Charlotte, NC: Information Age Publishing, Inc.

Eastmond, M. (2011). Egalitarian Ambitions, Constructions of Difference: The Paradoxes of Refugee Integration in Sweden. *Journal of Ethnic and Migration Studies, 37*(2), 277-295. doi:10.1080/1369183X.2010.521323

Edgeworth, K. (2013). *Refugees in Rural Schools: Issues of Space, Racism and (Un) belonging.* Paper presented at the Australian Association for Researc in Education Conference, Adelaide, South Australia.

Edgeworth, K. (2014). Black bodies, White Rural Spaces: Disturbing Practices of Unbelonging for 'Refugee' Students. *Critical Studies in Education.* doi:10.1080/17508487.2014.956133

Faircloth, B. S., & Hamm, J. V. (2005). Sense of Belonging Among High School Students Representing 4 Ethnic Groups. *Journal of Youth and Adolescence, 34*(4), 293-309. doi:10.1007/s10964-005-5752-7

Ferfolja, T. (2009). The Refugee Action Support program: Developing an Understanding of Diversity. *Teaching Education, 20*(4), 395-407.

Ferfolja, T., & Vickers, M. (2010). Supporting Refugee Students in School Education in Greater Western Sydney. *Critical Studies in Education, 51*(2), 149-162. doi: 10.1080/17508481003731034

Fernandes, A. G. (2015). (Dis)Empowering New Immigrants and Refugees Through Their Participation in Introduction Programs in Sweden, Denmark, and Norway. *Journal of Immigrant & Refugee Studies, 13*(3), 245-264. doi:10.1080/15562948.2015.1045054

Field, R., & Abelson, M. (1982). Climate: A Reconceptualization and Proposed Model. . *Human Relations, 35*(3), 181-201.

Ford, D. Y. (2014). Why Education must be Multicultural: Addressing a Few Misperceptions with Counterarguments. *Gifted Child Today, 37*(1), 59-62.

Forrest, J., Lean, G., & Dunn, K. (2016). Challenging Racism through Schools: Teacher Attitudes to Cultural Diversity and Multicultural Education in Sydney, Australia. *Race Ethnicity and Education, 19*(3), 618-638. doi: 10.1080/13613324.2015.1095170

Foucault, M. (1991). Governmentality. In B. Burchell, G. Gordon, & B. Miller (Eds.), *The Foucault Effect: Studies in Governmentality.* Chicago: Chicago University Press.

Fredrickson, B. (2000). Cultivating Positive Emotions to Optimize Health and Well being. *Prevention and treatment, 3.*

Fredrickson, B. (2001). The Role of Positive Emotions in Positive Psychology. *American Psychologist March*(56, 3), 218-226.

Freire. (1970). *Pedagogy of the Oppressed.* New York: Continuum

Gidley, J. (2016). *Postformal Education: A Philosophy for Complex Futures.* Switzerland: Springer.

Gidley, J. (2017). Contrasting Futures for Humanity: Technotopian or Human-Centred? *Paradign Explorer: The Journal of the Scientic and Mediacl Network, September*. Retrieved from

Goleman, D. (1995). *Emotional Intelligence*. New York: Bantam Books.

Goodenow, K., & Grady, C. (1993). The Relationship of School Belonging and Friends' Values to Academic Motivation Among Urban Adolescent Students. *The Journal of Experimental Education, 62*(1), 60-71.

Green, M., Emery, A., Sanders, M., & Anderson, L. (2016). Another Path to Belonging: A Case Study of Middle School Students' Perspectives. *The Educational and Developmental Psychologist,, 33*(01), 85-96.

Green, S. L., & Edwards-Underwood, K. (2015). Understanding and Redefining Multicultural Education. *Journal of Education Research, 9*(4), 399-411.

Greussing, E., & Boomgaarden, H. G. (2017). Shifting the Refugee Narrative? An Automated Frame Analysis of Europe's 2015 Refugee Crisis. *Journal of Ethnic and Migration Studies, 43*(11), 1749-1774. doi:10.1080/1369183X.2017.1282813

Guion, R. (1973). A Note on Organisational Climate. *Organisational Behaviou and Human Performance, 9*, 120-125.

Gutstein, E., & Peterson, B. (2005). *Rethinking Schools @ Rethink Schools* Retrieved 25th July 2019 from https://twitter.com/rethinkschools?lang=en

Hamilton, R., & Moore, D. (2006). *Educational Interventions for Refugee Children*. Albington, Oxen: Routledge.

Hofstede, G. (1983). The Cultural Relevativity of Organizational Practices and Theories. *Journal of International Business Studies, 14*(2), 75-89.

Hofstede, G. (1986). Cultural Differences in Teaching and Learning. *International Journal of Intercultural Relations, 10*(3), 301-320.

Hofstede, G. (2001). *Culture's Consequences: Comparing Values, Behaviors, Institutions and Organizations Across Nations* (second ed.). Thousand Oaks: Sage.

Iii, C., & Adam, J. (2017). Attitudes towards Refugee Education and its Link to Xenophobia in the United States. *Intercultural Education, 28*(5), 474-479. doi:10.1080/14675986.2017.1336374

Kaplan, D. M., deBlois, M., Dominguez, V., & Walsh, M. E. (2016). Studying the Teaching of Kindness: A Conceptual Model for Evaluating Kindness Education Programs in Schools. *Evaluation and Program Planning, 58*, 160-170. doi: http://dx.doi.org/10.1016/j.evalprogplan.2016.06.001

Levine-Rasky, C., Beaudoin, J., & St Clair, P. (2014). The Exclusion of Roma Claimants in Canadian Refugee Policy. *Patterns of Prejudice, 48*(1), 67-93. doi:10.1080/0031322X.2013.857477

Loukas, A., & Robinson, S. (2004). Examining the Moderating Role of Perceived school Climate in Early Adolescent Adjustment. *Journal of Research on Adolescence, 14*(2), 209.

Loukas, A., Suzuki, R., & Horton, K. (2006). Examining School Connectedness as a Mediator of School Climate Effects. *Journal of Research on Adolescence, 16*(3), 491-.

Madziva, R., & Thondhlana, J. (2017). Provision of Quality Education in the Context of Syrian Refugee Children in the UK: Opportunities and Challenges. *Compare: A Journal of Comparative and International Education, 47*(6), 942-961. doi:10.1080/03057925.2017.1375848

Maslow, A. (1943). A Theory of Human Motivation. *Psychological Review, 50*(4), 370-396.

McGregor, G. (2009). Educating for *(Whose)* Success? Schooling in an Age of Neo-liberalism. *British Journal of Sociology of Education, 30*(3), 345-358.

McMichael, C., Gifford, S. M., & Correa-Velez, I. (2011). Negotiating Family, Navigating resettlement: Family Connectedness amongst Resettled Youth with Refugee Backgrounds Living in Melbourne, Australia. *Journal of Youth Studies, 14*(2), 179-195. doi: 10.1080/13676261.2010.506529

McNeely, C., Nonnemaker, J., & Blum, R. (2002). Promoting School Connectedness: Evidence from the National Longitudinal Study of Adolescent Health. . *Journal of school health,, 72*(4), 130-146.

Mirra, N. (2018). *Educating for Empathy*. New York: Teachers College Press.

Moos, R. (1973). *Systems for the Assessment and Classification of Human Environments: An Overview.* . Retrieved from Stanford Calif:

Mthethwa-Sommers, S., & Kisiara, O. (2015). Listening to Students from Refugee Backgrounds: Lessons for Education Professionals. *Perspectives on Urban Education, 12*(1).

Ogbu, J. (1995a). Cultural Problems in Minority Education: their Interpretations and Consequences- Part two- The Case Studies. . *The Urbamn Review, 27*, 271-297.

Ogbu, J. (1995b). Cultural Problems in Minority Education: Their Interpretations and Consequences-Part one: Theoretical Background. . *The Urban Review, 27*, 189-205.

Peck, N. F., Maude, S. P., & Brotherson, M. J. (2015). Understanding Preschool Teachers' Perspectives on Empathy: A Qualitative Inquiry. *Early Childhood Education Journal, 43*(3), 169-179.

Pinson, H., & Arnot, M. (2007). Sociology of Education and the Wasteland of Refugee Education Research. *British Journal of Sociology of Education, 28*(3), 399-407. doi:10.1080/01425690701253612

Pinson, H., Arnot, M., & Candappa, M. (2010). *Education, Asylum and the Non- Citizen Child: The Politics of Compassion and Belonging*. Basingstoke UK: Palgrave Macmillan.

Rasmussen, K. (2011). Foucault's Genealogy of Racism. *Theory, Culture & Society,* (5), 34-51. Retrieved from doi:DOI: 10.1177/0263276411410448

Sarraj, H., Bene, K., Li, J., & Burley, H. (2015). Raising Cultural Awareness of Fifth-grade Students Through Multicultural Education: An Action Research Study. *Multicultural Education, 22*(2), 39-45.

Savoley, P., & Mayer, J. (1990). *Emotional Intelligence*: Baywood Publishing Co. Ltd.

Seligman, M. (2011). *Flourish: A Visionary New Understanding of Happiness and Well-being*. New York: Free Press.

Sellars, M. (2017). 'Schools as Institutes of Acculturation: A Question of Belonging', . *Turkish Online Journal of Educational Technology,*, 843-846. Retrieved from

Shernoff, E. S., Frazier, S. L., Maríñez-Lora, A. M., Lakind, D., Atkins, M. S., Jakobsons, L., . . . Patel, D. A. (2016). Expanding the Role of School Psychologists to Support Early Career Teachers: A Mixed-method Study. *School Psychology Review, 45*(2), 226.

Smith, L. (2011). Experiential "Hot" Knowledge and its Influence on Low-SES Students' Capacities to Aspire to Higher Education. *Critical Studies in Education, 52*(2), 165-177.

Stewart, J. (2011). *Supporting Refugee Children: Strategies for Educators.* Toronto, Ontraio: University of Toronto Press.

Tagiuri, R. (1968). *The Concept of Organizational Climate. Organizational Climate: Exploration of a Concept* Boston: Harvard University.

Tagiuri, R., Litwin, G., & Barnes, L. (Eds.). (1968). *Organizational Climate: Explorations of a Concept.* Boston: Division of Research, Graduate School of Business Administration, Harvard University, .

Van Houtte, M. (2005). Climate or Culture? A Plea for Conceptual Clarity in School Effectiveness Research. *School Effectiveness and School Improvement, 16*(1), 71-89.

Vasileiadou, M. (2009). Cooperative Learning and its Effects on Pre-primary, Marginalized Children. *Emotional and Behavioural Difficulties, 14*(4), 337-347. doi:10.1080/13632750903303179

Vickers, M. H., & McCarthy, F. E. (2010). Repositioning Refugee Students from the Margins to the Centre of Teachers' Work. *International Journal of Diversity in Organisations, Communities & Nations, 10*(2), 199-210.

Vieno, A., Perkins, D., Smith, T., & Santinello, M. (2005). Democratic School Climate and Sense of Community in School: A Multilevel Analysis. . *American Journal of Community Psychology,, 36*(3-4), 327-341.

Walters, S. (2012). *School Climate: A Literature Review.* Retrieved from https://docplayer.net/21010292-School-climate-a-literature-review.html

Wang, W., Vaillancourt, T., Brittain, H., McDougall, P., Krygsman, A., Smith, D., . . . Hymel, S. (2014). School Climate, Peer Victimization, and Academic Achievement: Results From a Multi-Informant Study. *School Psychology Quarterly, 29*(3), 360-377. doi:http://dx.doi.org/10.1037/spq0000084

Watson, B., Ermery, C., Bayliss, P., Boushel, M., & McInnes, K. (Eds.). (2012). *Children's Social and Emotional Wellbeing in Schools.* Bristol, UK: The Policy Press.

Watters, C. (2007). *Refugee Children: Towards the Next Horizon* (1 ed.). Florence: Taylor and Francis.

Yok-Fong, P. (2013). Working with Immigrant Children and Their Families: An Application of Bronfenbrenner's Ecological Systems Theory. *Journal of Human Behavior in the Social Environment, 23:954–966, 2013, 23,* 954-966. doi:DOI: 10.1080/10911359.2013.800007

Zizek, s. (2008). *Violence.* London: Profile Books Ltd.

Chapter Seven: People: The School and Leadership

Introduction

The heart of formal education is dictated largely by the school. Schools, their leaders and staff, although components of larger systemic organisations, have considerable differences in their actual interpretation, implementation, and modes of realizing the mandated elements of the systems to which they belong. This chapter seeks to explore how schools may develop as supportive communities for students with refugee experiences whilst remaining within the compulsory, economic ideals of neoliberal educational paradigms. The neoliberal understanding of the purpose of education is productivity, students are predominantly identified as human capital, whose status is reduced in many cases to that of drones, or worker bees, whose entire existence is focussed on working to serve those who are in more privileged roles in the community. As choice is fundamental cornerstone of neoliberalism in the economic sense, it may also provide a focal point around which discussions of productivity, human capital and work can be extrapolated and critiqued in the context of neo liberal educational contexts into which students with refugee experienced are currently placed. All individuals make choices, unless they are in situations where they have no autonomy at all. Unfortunately, many students with refugee experiences and their communities have been found to be in this situation, for several reasons, including dispersal policies which determine where they live and therefore where their children and young people attend school; about which once again, there is no choice. However, in this chapter it is argued that school leaders and their teachers do have choices in the ways in which they interpret, implement, and make meaning from the many conditions, regulations, and compliances that neo liberal educational systems impose.

School Culture

The principal's leadership mode and attitudes towards a number of aspects of professional work can have a significant impact on school culture. Erikson (1987:12) provided a definition of school culture which remains informative. He determined that school culture was;

> ..a system of ordinary, taken-for-granted meanings and symbols with both explicit and implicit content that is, deliberately and non-deliberately, learned and shared among members of naturally bounded social group.

This definition itself illustrates the importance of school culture to students with refugee experiences. It raises questions about how these students may become part of a 'naturally bonded group' in their new educational contexts and how they might gain access to the 'implicit content' which is 'non – deliberately learned'. This may be especially problematic if the situation described by Joyce (1990) and Fullan (1990) remained a concern a quarter of a century later. They recognised, not only the impact that school culture may have but also that very little was known about how school culture developed. To respond to this situation, Leithwood and Jantzi (1990) found, in their Canadian study of collaborative school cultures, that there were six strategies with which the principals engaged systematically to improve and consolidate school culture in addition to the establishment of extensive collaboration in the school. These were identified as (i) strengthening the school culture, (ii) using a variety of bureaucratic mechanisms to stimulate and reinforce cultural change (iii) fostering staff development (iv) engaging in direct and frequent communication about cultural norms, values, and beliefs (v) sharing power and responsibility with others and (vi) using symbols to express cultural beliefs. All of these strategies are amongst those identified and implemented by effective and successful school leaders and are heavily reliant on the personal beliefs and values of individuals as leaders, most particularly in their roles of agents of change.

School culture and school ethos are frequently used interchangeably, but it appears they have different characteristics (Glover & Coleman, 2005; McLaughlin, 2005). McLaughlin (2005) investigated school ethos from a philosophical perspective predicated by its importance to student wellbeing and general education, a growing focus in the current literature of the impact of school ethos in student performance and the need to clarify the nature of school ethos, its assessment criteria, and ways in which it could be improved to have an increasingly positive educative influence on students. Defining ethos was considered problematic. Alder (1993) discussed school ethos, amongst other things, in terms of

> .. human activities and behaviour, to the human environment within which these enterprises take place (especially the social system of an organisation), to behaviour and activity which has already occurred, to a mood or moods which are pervasive within this environment, to social interactions and their consequences, to something which is experienced, to norms rather than to exceptions, and to something that is unique (Alder, 1993:63-69)

Solvason (2005) discussed school ethos as a product of the culture of the school, arguing that culture was more tangible and that ethos was a nebulous term in the context of educational research. This notion was supported by Glover and Coleman (2005:257), who, in their investigation of the interchangeability of the terms school culture, school ethos and school climate, determined that school ethos was a term that was less easily measured, more 'subjective' in nature and was more 'general' than the other terms under discussion. More importantly, however, is the distinction made by Donnelly (2000) between the formal, documented aspects of ethos and the lived reality of this expression in the real contexts of the school classrooms and their relationships. As noted by Eisner (in Mc Laughlin, 2005), there frequently exists an important gap between these two categories of school ethos. These tensions appeared to be inevitable in the complex interactions that constitute formal education processes and environments (Donnelly, 2000; Mc Laughlin, 2005). As both the formal and the experiential notions of ethos are heavily values laden, this lack of congruence between the two can present additional difficulties for students with refugee experiences, accentuating the various interpretations of the core values and foundational rationales under which school operate and obscuring pathways to authentic belonging.

An additional complication is provided by the subcultures that may develop different, conflicting ethos across classroom, departments, or groups of staff or students in schools. Tomlinson, Hogarth, and Thomas (1989) found that students from small minority groups underwent a different experience of school ethos and that it was a variety of classroom and departmental influences or ethos which determined how well their unique learning needs were met, not the overall school ethos. For an commonly agreed whole school ethos, then the leadership model must facilitate a commonly shared school vision and mission, which has been found to be one of the most significant challenges to face school principals (Barber, . Whelan, & Clark, Capturing the Leadership Premium, McKinsey & Company, http://mckinseyonsociety.com/capturing-the-leadership-premium/, 2010). Also central to the discussion is the manner in which school members engage with the articulated ethos of the school. Whilst the lived experience of school ethos may be considered to be a matter for constant negotiation (Donnelly, 2000), the degree to which the school ethos is individually embraced has three dimensions (Donnelly, 2000:151). A superficial, or 'aspirational' attachment is that which is least invested in the aspirations of the ethos. An 'outward' attachment involves a deeper commitment, but it is the 'inward' attachment that is the deepest and most authentic commitment to the values and beliefs expressed as the school ethos. It is this inward attachment to the values of the school ethos which creates both the most significant challenge to school principals and which has the potential to impact most effectively on school communities. A common ethos with deeply engaged communities creates an influential environment for staff and students alike. This common ethos has such impact that it is readily discernible in all aspects of the school environment, acting as a similar influence as that of Bourdieu's notion of habitus, and promoting the values and beliefs espoused as the school ethos (Mc Laughlin, 2005). Fundamental to the development of this ethos is the school leader.

The School Principal

The role of the school principal in contemporary education is multifaceted. To ascertain how this may be analysed and evaluated, two major studies of school leadership are discussed in detail. Each of the studies utilized multiple data sources which included a review of the literature, interview data, and the expertise of those experienced in the area of school leadership. The first study, led by Waters, Marzano, and McNulty (2003), in their analysis and summary of leadership research studies over three decades in the US, succinctly captured the complexity of the role and the importance of the of the personal qualities of the individuals who seek to be school leaders. The question of local leadership and school governance is critical to the discourse around educating students with refugee experiences because of the many ways in which principals dominate, not only highly evident and documented aspects of school life but also those which are implicit. These include school culture, school climate, school ethos, and the hidden curriculum (see, for example,Barber et al., 2010; Cai, 2011; Cotton, 2003; Dimmock & Goh, 2011; Dinham, Anderson, Caldwell, & Weldon, 2011; Giroux & Penna, 1979; Waters et al., 2003). The complex, interpolated nature of all dimensions of schools is reflected in the foundations and predictive attributes of the balanced leadership model (Waters et al., 2003)

> Our leadership framework also is predicated on the notion that effective leadership means more than simply knowing what to do - it's knowing when, how, and why to do it. Effective leaders understand how to balance pushing for change while at the same time, protecting

aspects of culture, values, and norms worth preserving. They know which policies, practices, resources, and incentives to align and how to align them with organizational priorities. They know how to gauge the magnitude of change they are calling for and how to tailor their leadership strategies accordingly. Finally, they understand and value the people in the organization. They know when, how, and why to create learning environments that support people, connect them with one another, and provide the knowledge, skills, and resources they need to succeed. This combination of knowledge and skills is the essence of balanced leadership (Waters et al., 2003:2).

The incredibly complicated balancing act that is described above challenges many of the criteria that are currently in place in educational systems which prioritize compliance, output in terms of student performance in standardized, one size fit all testing regimes, and accountability in terms of maintaining the 'status quo'. The major source of discomfort for school principals attempting to lead in these educational contexts, must be the assumption that effective leaders are agents of change in systems which have revived transmission pedagogies as economical teacher practice and reintroduced curriculum models which prioritize content and do not celebrate student capacities or relative strengths (see, for example,Newmann & associates, 1996; Tyler, 1949; Wiggins & McTighe, 2007; Wiggins & McTighe, 2005). Not only does this resurgence of standardized pedagogy and restrictive curriculum severely impact on the potential for creative and critical individuals to be promoted into leadership positions, it affirms individuals who are strongly invested in 'the pedagogy of poverty' as not only the 'coin of the realm', but as 'the gold standard' (Haberman, 2010:45) and a 'banking model' that serves to disempower many and privilege the few (Freire, 1970). This situation predicates a considerable dichotomy between what is required to achieve a principalship and what is found in the research literature to be the characteristics of effective leaders, not only in the leadership model developed by Waters et al. (2003) but also in the extensive work on school leadership which was conducted internationally by the second study under discussion, that led by Barber et al. (2010). Each study identified key capacities of effective school leaders, many of which are remarkably similar in nature.

Waters et al. (2003) identified defined twenty- one responsibilities of effective school leaders and indicated the impact that improvement in each these responsibilities was found to have on student achievement. Barber et al. (2010) described also found twenty- one characteristics of high performing principals. Waters et al. (2003) discussed two determining variables in the impact of leadership decisions. Ironically, in these contexts, both factors where associated with change. In congruence with the literature that focusses on educational change (see, for example,

Fullan, 2015), Waters et al (2003) discuss the magnitude or the order of the proposed change. If this is misunderstood or miscalculated, then the impact of the change may not be positive in terms of student performance and many even have a negative effect. The primary variable is the focus of the change process itself. In addition to identifying the major areas of school, teacher and student factors which impact on student performance. These writers also determined. from their three knowledge sources; a quantitative analysis of 30 years of research, an exhaustive review of theoretical literature on leadership, and the research team's more than 100 years of combined professional wisdom on school leadership (2003:2); that it was possible to calculate the impact of effective leadership improvement in terms of student academic achievement as calculated on a standard Bell curve (reference). Figure 3.1 illustrates these dimensions of leadership and the degree of impact that one standard deviation of principals' improvement in each of these leadership practices may potentially have on the learning success of the students. The impact is presented as the degree of standard deviation and known as effect size. Additionally, the characteristics that were investigated by Barber et al. (2010) that correlate with these attributes and that were identified as common to high performing principals have been added to the information in Figure 7.1

The seventeen items that Barber et al. (2010) identified from their multiple sources of information, including a survey completed by one thousand, eight hundred and forty school principals in several countries were described as the actions and personal attributes of highly performing school leaders. These items were supplemented by four other characteristics that originated from the survey data. The survey respondents noted that, in their opinions, the major contributors to their success was the capacity to develop and lead a vision for the school, to develop the staff professionally and to effectively manage all the routines, processes and school administration. They also indicated that the most important skill that was needed in the leadership role was the ability to coach and support others. The biggest challenge reported was to improve teaching. While no attempt was made to evaluate or measure the potential impact of these highly performing leaders, it can be seen from the information in Figure 7.1 that some of the responsibilities that Waters et al (2003) found in their research to be powerful in terms of impact on student performance, did not appear to be priorities for the participants of the study conducted by Barber et al. (2010). Whilst responsibilities and actions and attributes are not necessarily synonymous in meaning, the focus of both studies was to develop an understanding of what constituted effective school leadership. With that in mind, detail with which Waters et al (2003) expressly clarify the scope of responsibilities, including what each may entail as first or second order change, provides a window from which to understand more cohesively the impact that school leadership has on the education of students with refugee experiences.

There are several responsibilities shown in Figure 7.1 that were proven to have substantial impact on the students' capacities to learn more effectively. Whilst all the responsibilities need to be undertaken at high levels of proficiency and with an attitude on ongoing professional learning, nine of the responsibilities have an exceptionally high impact of student learning in this model of balanced leadership. These are the responsibilities as;

- Able to accurately complete a situational analysis
- Change agent
- Providing intellectual stimulation
- Input
- *Culture of the school*
- Monitoring and evaluating
- Establishing and maintaining order
- Outreaching to the wider community as an advocate for the school
- Providing resources

Figure 7.1. Responsibilities of principals and effect size (Waters el al. 2003) and characteristics of high performing school leaders

Waters el al 2003		Barber et al 2010
Affirmation (.25)	recognises and celebrates school accomplishments and acknowledges failures	Recognises and rewards achievement
Change agent (.30)	is willing to and actively challenges the status quo	Take risks and challenge accepted beliefs and behaviour
Communication (.23)	establishes strong lines of communication with teachers and among students	
Contingent reward (.15)	recognises and rewards individual accomplishments	
Culture (.29)	fosters shared beliefs and a sense of community and cooperation	Build a shared vision and sense of purpose
Discipline (.24)	protects teachers from issues and influences that would detract from their teaching time and focus	Protect teachers from issues that distract them from their work
Flexibility (.22)	adapts his or her leadership behaviour to the needs of the current situation and is comfortable with dissent	Develop deep understanding of people and context

Focus (.24)	establishes clear goals and keeps those goals in the forefront of the school's attention	
Ideals and beliefs (.25)	communicates and operates from strong ideals and beliefs about schooling	Role-model the behaviour and practices they desire
Input (.30)	involves teachers in the design and implementation of important decisions and policies	Establish effective teams and distribute leadership among school staff
Intellectual stimulation (.32)	ensures that faculty and staff are aware of the most current theories and practices, and makes the discussion of these a regular aspect of the school's culture	
Involvement with Curriculum, Instruction and Assessment (Newmann & associates) (.16)	is directly involved in the design and implementation of curriculum, instruction and assessment processes	Design and manage the teaching and learning program
Knowledge of CIA (.24)	is knowledgeable about current curriculum, instruction and assessment processes	Are self-aware, lifelong learners
Monitor/evaluate (.28)	monitors the effectiveness of school practices and their impact on student learning	Monitor performance
Optimiser (.20)	inspires and leads new and challenging innovations	
Order (.26)	establishes a set of standard operating procedures and routines	Establish school routines and norms of behaviour
Outreach (.28)	is an advocate and spokesperson for the school to all stakeholders	Connect the school to parents and the community
Relationships (.19)	demonstrates an awareness of the personal aspects of teachers and staff	
Resources (.26)	provides teachers with materials and professional development necessary for the successful execution of their jobs	Understand and develop people
Situational awareness (.33)	is aware of the details and undercurrents in the running of the school and uses this information to address current and potential problems	
Visibility (.16)	has quality contact and interaction with teachers and students	

(Barber et al., 2010)

Leithwood, Sun, and Pollock (2017) propose that there are four aspects of leadership that can contribute positively to student success in school. They identify these as the Rational pathway, the Emotional pathway, the Organizational pathway and the Family pathway. In their framework the Family pathway places emphasis on community involvement in a very important and specific manner, unlike the other models of leadership which do acknowledge the wider community but not in a manner that acknowledges this path of leadership has equal impact on students' success as, for example, teacher expertise and attitudes or organizational routines and procedures. In this model, the rational pathway. The pathways are briefly explained as,

> Conditions or variables on the Rational Path are rooted in the knowledge and skills of school staff members about curriculum, teaching, and learning – the technical core of schooling. The Emotional Path includes those feelings, dispositions, or affective states of staff members (both individually and collectively) shaping the nature of their work, for example, teachers' sense of efficacy. Conditions on the Organizational Path include features of schools that structure the relationships and interactions among organizational members including, for example, cultures, policies, and standard operating procedures. On the Family Path are conditions reflecting family expectations for their children, their culture and support to students, and community orientations toward school and general education (p. 3).

These paths are not discrete, but invariably a decision to make improvements that are based on a variable in one path impacts on the other pathways in the framework to a greater or lesser extent. Research findings indicated that variables in three of the pathways were more influential in supporting student success than in the other, the organizational path. Leithwood et al. (2017) propose that authentic school improvement cannot rely exclusively on student results. They argue that, in previous studies, much attention has been paid to the variable that comprise the rational pathway and the organizational pathway, to the neglect of many of the variables that comprise the emotional path and the family path, despite there being significant evidence that these pathways contribute equally to student success. Additionally, they propose that the commonly accepted wisdom regarding the ideal leadership model being dominated by discussion of instruction and strategies is incorrect. They challenge the notion that some components of the rational model can be changed at a school level, as they are dominated by individual classroom practice, indicating that variables such as pedagogical strategies and individual teacher skills with questioning techniques are the current issues that principals are encouraged to improve in their schools but that the principals themselves are frequently less confident about their capacities the do this. Whilst acknowledging that quality instruction will always important in schools, Leithwood et al. propose that addressing one of the variables in family path may have an even greater impact on student success.

The foci on the family path and the emotional path are elements that set this model apart from the other more traditional leadership models described here. These pathways incorporate the components of the affective lives of teachers and student families. The family path was shown to have the greatest impact on student success. In particular, three components were particularly influential. These relate to the educational culture of the home and are specifically described as (i) parental expectations for the children's success at school and after (ii) the quality of communication between the student and the parents and (iii) the parents social and intellectual capital related to school (Bourdieu, 1986), which contributes significantly to the social and intellectual capital that students bring to school, and which is needed by them to succeed (p.306). An important aspect of the communication from the school to the home is that it encourages reasonable disciplinary routines and support and encouragement for the students. The key to developing social capital, according to Leithwood et al, (2017, p. 29) is the ways in which three constructs are developed;

> trust; access to sources of information that promote the common good over individual self-interest; and; norms and sanctions within a community that promote the common good over individual self-interest. Intellectual capital is the knowledge and capabilities of parents with the potential for collaborative action. Many low income parents will differ from middle income parents in two ways that help explain differences in their children's potential for success at school (Bolivar and Chrispeels, 2011). Low income parents often are unable to gain access to and benefit from the resources available in the school; they are less familiar with the "grammar of schooling", for example. In addition, they often do not have opportunities for taking forms of collective action which foster the exchange and development of collective knowledge or intellectual capital; working two or three jobs to "make ends meet" reduces the time available to interact with other parents, for example.

The emotional pathway is also considered as one of the most powerful variants on student success and a critical variable in building better schools (Leithwood & Sun, 2017). The most critical of these were identified as 'teacher trust in others, teacher commitment, teacher collective efficacy and organizational citizenship behaviour '(Leithwood & Sun, 2017 p. 137). The trust that teachers have for the principal, their colleague teachers, the students and their parents was found to be critical in many aspects of effective schools. The principal has a significant part to play in developing these trusting relationships, based on the foundational qualities of openness, reliability, friendliness and capacity to support all others in the relationships. Teacher commitment does not only apply to the individual's capacities for self-efficacy and continuing professional skills, it also includes commitment to student learning, support and wellbeing. Teaching commitment to their workplace and their positive identification with the school, to the students and to teaching are all major contributors to student academic growth and wellbeing. Principals who work to support all aspects of the school community in a holistic manner as opposed to micromanaging staff, students and community by engaging with their values and belief systems are more likely to impact positively on teacher commitment. Organizational citizenship behaviour is characterised by altruism, conscientiousness, sportsmanship, courtesy and civic virtue in the general workplace. These qualities are discussed as one trait in the context of schools (Leithwood & Sun, 2017 p.141). The degree to which teachers develop and maintain these traits depends significantly on the leadership skills of the principal.

Shapiro and Stefkovich (2016) suggest that preparing students to live in the twenty-first century is a complex and demanding role, most especially for educational leaders who may struggle with the inconsistencies and tensions between various codes of ethics and standards that have developed for use by principals, most especially when confronted with dilemmas concerning inequity, injustice and care of young people and children. They advise that educational leaders need opportunities to develop their own codes of ethics, based on their personal experiences and on critical incidents from which they learned more about themselves as individuals and as leaders in schools. In addition to the difficulty of separating personal and professional codes of ethics built on personal values and belief systems, ethical decision making must constantly take into consideration the standards of their professional communities. Ethics leaders should consider all formal frameworks for ethical reasoning and, in the opinion of Shapiro and Stefkovich (2016), optimally build a personally relevant model which includes ethics of justice, care and critique, all of which will have important ramifications for the solving of complex problems and dilemmas.

What implications are there for students with refugee and asylum seeker backgrounds?

Students with refugee and asylum seeker experiences have cultural beliefs, values and practices which may not be congruent with the culture of schools which are operationalized at the expense of other considerations. These students need to be supported with school ethos that has, at its primary focus, their wellbeing, most especially their social and emotional wellbeing. The challenge for many educational leaders is to develop a whole school approach to inclusion and integration of these students as a priority as the contact that students will have initially with the dominant, host country is that of becoming a student in school. Learning to bond with the community of other learners does not imply that the initial culture of students be forgotten or dismissed. Students do need to remain in contact with their heritage language and cultural mores, but they also need to acquire sufficient understanding of the cultural context which is to be their new homeland so they may effectively participate in both the academic and social life of schooling (Hamilton & Moore, 2006).

What are commonly referred to as 'good' schools undoubtedly have strong leaders. The notion of 'good', however, is predicated upon the social and cultural perspectives that are brought to bear on the context. For many non- refugee and asylum seeker students and their parents, 'good' schools are commonly identified using the standards of academic achievement, publicly presented on leadership tables. 'Good' schools in this definition tend to be located in areas of relative wealth and prestige. It is not common that students with refugee and asylum seeker experiences have the economic, social or cultural capital to attend these schools. In fact, a heavy focus on academic achievement may not be the 'best' schools for these students to thrive and have their learning needs appropriately met in tandem with their emotional and social needs. It may be that these students need to be placed with school leaders who understand that to be authentic, schools need to consider the affective components of schooling in order to maximize their work in academic and organisation spheres.

Leaders who acknowledge and effectively design school organisation, implement school wide transactional and transformative pedagogical strategies (Wink, 2011)and promote staff mindsets that appreciated the interconnectedness between emotion and cognition (Sousa, 1995, 2010a, 2010b) are most likely to provide the safe spaces at school that students with refugee and asylum seeker experiences so desperately need and deserve. While this may not be instantly achievable in neo liberal classrooms, and it may be historically a much- neglected aspect of effective leadership. its importance is highlighted in the ways in which effective school leaders achieved school improvement (Leithwood et al., 2017). The affective aspects of school culture are particularly important for students with refugee and asylum seeker experiences.

There are many reasons why the affective components of schooling are important for all students. While the brain is designed to be educated (Blakemore & Frith, 2005), and is literally created by experiences (Suarez-Orozco & Sattin- Bajaj, 2010; Suárez-Orozco & Sattin, 2007). These experiences are all learning experiences, the entire body is involved in the learning, not just the brain (Osgood-Campbell, 2015), and this involves affect. The western notion that the cognition and emotional domains are separate and discrete domains in the brain is highly contested (Briesmaster & Briesmaster-Paredes, 2015; Karagiannidis, Barkoukis, Gourgoulis, Kosta, & Antoniou, 2015; Kristiani, Susilo, & Aloysius, 2015; Maftoon & Sabah, 2012; Parviz & Somayyeh, 2012). One of the most significant features of leadership models which acknowledge the critical aspects of affect and of school leaders who practice these, is that they are cognisant of the reality that the brain cannot function optimally unless it feels 'safe' (Fredrickson, 2000; Medina, 2010; Sousa, 2010b). The critical factor in the work of Leithwood et al. (2017) for many students, but especially for students with refugee and asylum seeker experiences, is the family pathway. The deliberate, persistent efforts to connect the school to the families of these students provide unique opportunities for inclusion and integration, not only for the students themselves but for their parents and caregivers. Principals who design resources, strategies and teacher professional learning with the determined foci of making effective communication, in any appropriate forms, with the students' parents and wider communities have increased potential to include these parents with the mainstream parent community and to include and integrate these students in the school population positively, respectfully and authentically.

Conclusion

The values and beliefs of principals and school leaders, both professionally and personally contribute extensively to developing school culture. Whilst the most difficult task for principals is frequently regarded as the development of a school vision and culture that is shared by everyone in the school, via the staff, it is also the most significant in terms of building school culture. Principals who value critical civic empathy and act accordingly to develop schools which reflect this value throughout in its pedagogical practices, organizational approaches and rational decision- making offer students with refugee and asylum seekers experiences learning contexts in which they can grow holistically. Principals who understand the complexity and contradictions that exist in integrating communities that are significantly different into their current school situations are increasingly likely to persist, to make effective plans for inclusion and to create places where these students and their parents are regarded positively. The considerations given to the families and wider schools communities in leadership models such as those designed by

Leithwood et al. (2017) and Barber, Whelan, and Clark (2010), interpolated with leadership for critical civic empathy provide considerable potential for schools to be developed as safe spaces for all students, most especially those with refugee and asylum seeker experiences.

Schools are not islands of scholarship. They reflect the culture, beliefs and values of individuals who comprise the school community. An accurate assessment of the ways in which teachers, students, parents and the wider community perceive the possibility of receiving students with refugee and asylum seeker experiences into the school community would entail the principal being sensitive to the 'unspoken' in the entire school community. The importance of the ways in change is implemented means there is no standard, set procedures that will be effective in all situations. What is important is that all the stakeholders impacted by the changes that are proposed are invited to have input into the ways that change can be implemented successfully, make decisions with the support of accurate information, intellectual reasoning and, in the case of accepting students with refugee and asylum seeker backgrounds, true empathy and compassion. It is the role of the school principal to ensure that schools and communities are prepared positively to include newcomers who are different from themselves and have diverse ways of knowing and doing.

References

Alder, M. (1993). The Meaning of 'School Ethos'. *Westminister Studies in Education, 16*, 59-61.

Barber, M., Whelan, F., & Clark, M. (2010). Capturing the Leadership Premium, . Retrieved from http://mckinseyonsociety.com/capturing-the-leadership-premium/

Blakemore, S., & Frith, U. (2005). *The Learning Brain: Lessons for Education*. Oxford: Blackwell Publishing Ltd.

Bourdieu, P. (1986). The Forms of Capital. In J. G. Richardson (Ed.), *The Handbook of Theory: Research for the Sociology of Education* (pp. 241-258). New York: Greenwood Press.

Briesmaster, M., & Briesmaster-Paredes, J. (2015). The Relationship between Teaching Styles and NNPSETs' Anxiety Levels. *System, 49*, 145-156. doi: http://dx.doi.org/10.1016/j.system.2015.01.012

Cai, Q. (2011). Can Principals' Emotional Intelligence Matter to School Turnarounds? *International Journal of Leadership in Education, 14*(2), 151-179. doi:10.1080/13603124.2010.512669

Cotton, K. (2003). *Principals and Student Achievement: What the Research Says.* . Alexandria VA: Association for Supervision and Curriculum Development (ASCD).

Dimmock, C., & Goh, J. (2011). Transformative Pedagogy, Leadership and School Organisation for the Twenty-first-century Knowledge-based Economy: The Case of Singapore. *School Leadership & Management, 31*(3), 215-234. doi:10.1080/13632434.2010.546106

Dinham, S., Anderson, M., Caldwell, B., & Weldon, P. (2011). Breakthroughs in School Leadership Development in Australia. *School Leadership & Management, 31*(2), 139-154. doi:10.1080/13632434.2011.560602

Donnelly, C. (2000). In Pursuit of School Ethos. *British Journal of Educational Studies, 48*(2), 134-154. doi:10.1111/1467-8527.t01-1-00138

Erikson, F. (1987). Conceptions of School Culture. *Education Administration Quarterly, 23*(4), 11-24.

Fredrickson, B. (2000). Cultivating Positive Emotions to Optimize Health and Well being. *Prevention and Treatment, 3*.

Freire. (1970). *Pedagogy of theOppressed.* New York: Continuum

Fullan, M. (2015). *The New Meaning of Educational Change* (Fifth ed.). New York: Teachers College Press.

Giroux, H., & Penna, A. (1979). Social Education in the Classroom: The Dynamics of the Hidden Curriculum. *Theory and Research n Social Education, VII*(1), 20-42.

Glover, D., & Coleman, M. (2005). School Culture, Climate and Ethos: Interchangeable or Distinctive Concepts? *Journal of In-Service Education, 31*(2), 251-272. doi:10.1080/13674580500200278

Haberman, M. (2010). 11 Consequences of Failing to Address the 'Pedagogy of Poverty'. *Phi Delta Kappan, 92*(2), 45.

Hamilton, R., & Moore, D. (2006). *Educational Interventions for Refugee Children.* Albington, Oxen: Routledge.

Karagiannidis, Y., Barkoukis, V., Gourgoulis, V., Kosta, G., & Antoniou, P. (2015). The Role of Motivation and Metacognition on the Development of Cognitive and Affective Responses in Physical Education Lessons: A Self-determination Approach. *Motricidade, 11*(1), 135-150.

Kristiani, N., Susilo, H., & Aloysius, D. C. (2015). The Correlation between Attitude toward Science and Cognitive Learning Result of Students in Different Biology Learnings. *Journal of Baltic Science Education, 14*(6), 723-732.

Leithwood, K., & Jantzi, D. (1990). Transformational Leadership: How Principals Can Help Reform School Cultures. *School Effectiveness and School Improvement, 1*(4), 249-280. doi:10.1080/0924345900010402

Leithwood, K., & Sun, J. (2017). Leadership Effects on Students' Learning Mediated by Teacher Emotion. In K. Leithwood, J. Sun, & A. Pollard (Eds.), *How School Leaders Contribute to Student Success The Four Paths Framework* (pp. 137-152). Cham, Switzerland: Springer.

Leithwood, K., Sun, J., & Pollock, K. (Eds.). (2017). *How School Leaders Contribute to Student Success: The Four Path Framework* (Vol. 23). Cham, Switzerland: Springer

Maftoon, P., & Sabah, S. (2012). A Critical Look at the Status of Affect in Second Language Acquisition Research: Lessons from Vygotsky's Legacy. *BRAIN. Broad Research in Artificial Intelligence and Neuroscience, 3*(2), 36-44. Retrieved from

Mc Laughlin, T. (2005). The Educative Importance of Ethos. *The British Journal of educational Studies, 53*(3), 306-325.

Medina, J. (2010). *Brain Rules for Learning*. Seattle: Pear Press.

Newmann, F., & associates. (1996). *Authentic Achievement: Restructuring Schools for Intellectual Quality*. San Francisco: Jossey Bass.

Osgood-Campbell, E. (2015). Investigating the Educational Implications of Embodied Cognition: A Model Interdisciplinary Inquiry in Mind, Brain, and Education Curricula. *Mind, Brain & Education, 9*(1), 3-9. doi: 10.1111/mbe.12063

Parviz, M., & Somayyeh, S. (2012). A Critical Look at the Status of Affect in Second Language Acquisition Research: Lessons from Vygotsky's legacy. *BRAIN: Broad Research in Artificial Intelligence & Neuroscience, 3*(2), 36-42.

Shapiro, J., & Stefkovich, J. (2016). *Ethical Leadership and Decision Making in Education. Applying Theoretical Perspectives to Complex Dilemmas* (4th ed.). New York: Routledge.

Solvason, C. (2005). Investigating Specialist School Ethos … Or do You Mean Culture? *Educational Studies, 31*(1), 85-94. doi:10.1080/0305569042000310985

Sousa, D. (1995). *How the Brain Learns*. Reston VA: National Association of Secondary Principals.

Sousa, D. (2010a). How Science met Pedagogy. In D. Sousa (Ed.), *Mind, Brain and Education: Neuroscience Implications for the Classroom* (pp. 9-26). Bloomington: Solution Tree Press.

Sousa, D. (2010b). *Mind, Brain and Education: Neuroscience Implications for the Classroom*. . Bloomington IN: Solution Tree Press.

Suarez-Orozco, M., & Sattin- Bajaj, C. (2010). *Educating the Whole Child for the Whole World:The Ross School Model and Education for the Global Era*. New York: New York University Press.

Suárez-Orozco, M., & Sattin, C. (2007). Wanted: Global Citizens. *Educational Leadership, 64*(7), 58-62.

Tomlinson, S., Hogarth, T., & Thomas, H. (1989). *The School Effect. A Study of Multi-Racial Comprehensives.* London: Poilicy Studies Institute.

Tyler, R. (1949). *Basic Principles of Curriculum and Instruction*. Chicago: Chcaogo Unversity Ptess.

Waters, J., Marzano, R., & McNulty, B. (2003). *Balanced Leadership: What 30 years of Research Tells Us about the Effect of Leadership on Student Achievement*. New York: ASCD

Wiggins, G., & McTighe, J. (2007). *Schooling by Design: Mission, Action and Achievement*. Alexandria, VA: Association for Supervision and Curriculum Development.

Wiggins, G., & McTighe, m. J. (2005). *Understanding by Design*. Alexandria, VA: Association for Supervision and Curriculum Development.

Wink, J. (2011). *Critical Pedagogy: Notes from the Real World.* Upper Saddlew River, New Jersey: Pearson Education.

Chapter Eight: Pedagogy: Ways of Knowing and Doing

Introduction

Schooling has been part of many ancient cultures in various parts of the world. The nature of the schools may vary considerably from the modern mass schooling that has dominated for over a century. Schools in the past may have provided exclusively for children of the wealthy, most typically for male children only. The knowledge and skills that were taught and learned by pupils in these schools have also changed considerably from the disparate epistemological 'truths' that were foundations of the learning in these different cultural and sociological contexts. People have traditionally sought to make meaning and to interpret their worlds in ways that were culturally and socially unique to their own histories, commonly shared beliefs and ethos. The students with refugee and asylum seeker experiences who enter classrooms in their new neoliberal homelands are no exception. They already have perceptions of the world, ways of making meaning and learning that are congruent with the values and belief systems of their heritage lands and their peoples that are neither arbitrary nor perverse. This chapter explores theories that are related to child development interactions with their environments Bronfenbrenner (1979), understanding cultural difference and its importance in terms of emotional intensity (Hall, 1976), and those which attempt to identify ways of making meaning with geographical influences (Hofstede, 2001; Nisbett, 2005).

Bioecological Theory

Bronfenbrenner (1979) proposed an environmental development theory which has been used extensively as a framework for examining how individuals interact with the wider communities to which they belong. A key aspect of the theory is that the individual at the centre of the system is an active part of all their social experiences. An examination of this model may provide insights in to the ways in students with refugee and asylum seeker students, and their communities, are faced with challenges when attempting to become part of a new society that is substantially different from the one in which they had previously participated. Comprising five systems, the individual remains the centre of the impact of the interactions that each of the systems represent. The microsystem describes the most immediate environmental interactions that children will typically make. These include the family and extended family, perhaps religious institutions, peers, neighbours, early childhood learning contexts and schools. The contact is direct, regular and relatively simple in nature as each of these are considered separate interactions.

The meso-system is a little more complex as it is the interaction of two of the microsystems. The interactions here need to be positive and, for the child, harmonious. For example, the child's interactions at school needs to be supported and congruent with those at home and parents in turn, need to show this by ensuring contact with school leaders and classroom teachers is positive and accommodating so that these two 'worlds' of the child are not in conflict. The exo-system is also about two microsystems interacting, but in this case, only one of the microsystems belongs to the child. The other microsystem belongs to someone close to the child whose microsystems directly or indirectly impact on them. Children with parents who work outside the home, who have carer's responsibilities for extended family members, for example, frequently must make decisions about their microsystems that impact on their children's microsystems. Many of these interactions in the exo-system are the result of the other person's microsystem conflicting with the child's microsystem.

The largest, outside ring of Bronfenbrenner's model is the macro-system. It is the influence of the wider society in which the child interacts. The interactions become less direct but remain an influential aspect of the child's development. The wider societal norms and values of the nation in which the child is active is not as powerful as the macro-system, but it has the potential to influence the ways in which the child understands events, develops attitudes and values, and create their perceptions of their worlds. These attitudes, values and perspectives are not necessarily global. Certainly, in western, developed countries there are standards and principles about specific issues that conflict with those held by people in other parts of the world. The final aspect of the bioecological theory is the chronosystem. This is the influences of significant events that influence the individual over a lifetime. This is not another outer ring but underpins the entire theory as it is applied to each of the systems. This system considers what has happened in each of the individual child's systems that has influenced their attitudes, beliefs and perspectives. These events could have been directly impact as the results of any one or more of the microsystems within which they interacted and are not confined to negative impacts but may include significant changes that are positive. All systems, for example, have been impacted upon by technological advances and the ways they have affected everyday life in a relatively short period of time. In many parts of the world, technology has changed the nature of communications and travel for example, and the entire culture of the people who have extensive contact with it. All of this alters the ways in which children develop from one generation to another. For children in western societies, these may be basically similar types of experiences, depending on the individual's socio- economic status, geographical locations, norms and traditions. For children who have experienced an upheaval in their interactions in the various systems, their development may be very different.

The Cultural Iceberg

The nature of the individual's attitudes, values and perspectives vary in emotional intensity, visibility to others outside of their culture and even in the degree of conscious thought or reflective and reflexive questioning of these personal attributes. The cultural iceberg, attributed to Hall (1976), provides an excellent means by which these personal attributes can be understood by those from different cultural orientations. Like an iceberg, this model indicates that approximately 10% of culture is visible, with 90% remaining as more deeply held beliefs, values and attitudes. The deeper these attributes these are held, the more intensively emotional they are to those who are invested in them. The interesting aspect of this model lies in the ways in which all cultural norms and mores can be examined, including those held by western citizens in developed countries. Items such as national dress, music and dance, food, flags, art and literature, national festivals and other observable characteristics that are easily observed are the surface levels of culture which attract the lowest level of emotional intensity. These aspects of culture are frequently the focus of cultural days in schools and have been heavily criticized as tokenistic where these are the only acknowledgments of diversity in culture that are evidenced in school curriculum, pedagogy and assessment strategies (Cochran-Smith, 1995; Ford, 2014; Hue & Kennedy, 2013; Keddie, 2012; Watters, 2007; Weinstein, Curran, & Tomlinson-Clarke, 2003).

Shallow culture is considered to be unspoken, as are many cultural expectations and norms in western societies and the emotional intensity levels of the aspects of culture at this level are considered to be high, These aspects of culture pertain to conventions of communicating, eye contact, ways in which emotions are managed, notions of personal space and touching, personal contact including body language, facial expression and tone of voice. Also in the level of shallow culture are perceptions of beauty, customs relating to relationships, decision making, leadership and social interaction. These aspects are extrapolated to include practices in childrearing, ideas about adolescence, attitudes towards illness and disease, and concepts of hygiene and cleanliness.

The level of most intense emotional sensitivity is deep culture, which is the level that is so profoundly embedded it is considered that they are unquestionably and unconsciously accepted. These beliefs and values are focussed on notions of obscenity, the roles of caregivers, parents and their dependents, ideas of competition and compliance and concepts of self. Additionally, they include tolerance for pain and hardship, values that are concentrated on the family beliefs, roles and responsibilities and notions of past and future gender, age and social status and occupations. Western beliefs, values and attitudes at the level of deep culture can differ dramatically from those held by individuals in other parts of the world. These include the beliefs, values and attitudes that impact most significantly on educational policies, practices, expectations and measures of success.

Cultural Dimensions Theories

While Hall (1976), presented this early analysis of the ways in which aspects of cultural and social life may more readily be understood, Hofstede (1986; 2001; Hofstede, Hofstede, and Minkov 2010), provides a focus on the major ways in which cultures and societies within these express the characteristics of the beliefs, values and attitudes in what he terms 'cultural dimensions'. Originally four dimensions were identified, but this has gradually expanded to six dimensions with Hofstede (2001), explaining that there may easily be other dimensions that are yet to be identified. The first of his six dimensions is 'individualism versus collectivism'. This dimension is not about egotism but rather about the expectations in some cultures that individuals make their own decisions and choices in life. Conversely, collectivism is about a sensitivity to social order and standing and knowing where any individual is placed in this society; collectivism is about 'knowing your place'. Additionally, students from collectivist societies expect to learn how to do everything in their classes and not to work it out for themselves. They may not speak up individually in class, may not ask questions if they do not understand the lesson, may go to extraordinary lengths to ensure neither they nor their teachers lose face, prefer to work in ethnically homogeneous groups in class and expect that some students may receive deferential treatment from the teacher.

This notion of 'knowing your place' is predicated by what Hofstede identifies as 'power distance'. This second cultural dimension is found to be most widely expressed in societies where it is an expectation that some individuals are more powerful than others and that power itself is distributed unequally. In collectivist societies students are taught to automatically respect their teachers. In a student-teacher disagreement, students may expect their parents to side with the teacher. Students tend to speak only when they are spoken to and rely heavily on the personal 'wisdom' of their teacher, who is also required to provide explicit instruction so the students may learn effectively. Students tend to be passive learners in classrooms.

The third cultural dimension is about societies, not individuals and is termed 'masculine versus feminine'. In masculine societies teachers tend to openly praise 'good' students and use these high achievers as the norm. Failure at school impacts severely on the student's self- image and competition in the classroom is openly encouraged. In masculine societies, both genders are focussed on winning. Size and quantity of goods and achievements important and the society is openly gendered in terms of expectations and emotional role play. Students select academic subjects with a career path in mind. In feminine cultures there is more stress on social adaptation as opposed to open competition at school. The average student is considered the norm, academic subjects are chosen out of intrinsic interest and male students select what others may identify as traditionally feminine subject areas. Students appreciate teacher friendliness and failure at school is not considered as disastrous as in masculine societies. The genders are generally emotionally close than those in masculine societies.

'Uncertainty avoidance' is the fourth cultural dimension in Hofstede's framework. It is not concerned with individual risk taking or compliance to rules. It is a societal attitude towards uncertainty, which can be expressed as comfort and tolerance or anxiety and mistrust. In classrooms, this can be observed in the pedagogical approaches and personal relationships students and teachers share. Weak uncertainty avoidance is found in contexts that have loosely structured learning environments, non- specific learning objectives, broadly defined assignments and flexible timetables. Teachers are allowed to show emotion, as are students, have the option to admit when they don't know something, speak in everyday language when teaching, accept multiple perspectives and award innovative problem solving. High uncertainty avoidance societies have expectations of highly structured learning contexts, strict timetables, precise aims and objectives and highly detailed assignment structures, leaving nothing to chance. Teachers use academic language, are expected to know everything, accuracy is privileged over innovation in problem solving, are expected to engage in their professional work without emotion and consider any intellectual disagreement as disloyalty.

The final two cultural dimensions resulted from a different study than the initial four dimensions. The fifth dimension was added by Hofstede in 1991 but was researched in a relatively small number of countries. By 2010 (Hofstede et al., 2010), sufficient data was available on a large number of countries to include the further two cultural dimensions. They focus on (i) short term orientation (monumentalism) and long- term orientation (flexhumility) which is the fifth dimension and (ii) indulgence, which is the sixth dimension. Long term orientation versus short term orientation focusses on the perspective of the world in relation to change. Societies who believe that the world is constantly changing encourage preparing for the future, emphasising persistence, thrift, saving and having a sense of shame Minkov et al. (2018) discuss this culture as one where individuals have a modest opinion of themselves and where self-reliance and independence are emphasised. Conversely, short term orientation encourages spending to keep up with social pressures, saving face and a preference for quick results. It is heavily focused on the past, valuing tradition and maintaining the social hierarchy more than the future. Minkov et al. (2018) found that these cultures tended to support the notion that individuals are always the same; that they feel good about themselves, and that they make others feel good about them. The most pertinent aspect of the Minkov et al. study is that this cultural dimension appeared as an accurate predictor of academic educational achievement. They hypothesized that this could be for several reasons. Monumentalist cultural traits may not encourage self- improvement as they are basically complacent. It may also be that self -evaluation in complacent cultures does not include accurate assessment of participants' own capabilities. The study indicated that countries that scored highly on international testing were those with high flexibility indexes. While not strongly identified with Monumentalist trends, many of the Westcentric, neoliberal countries associated with refugee resettlement did not score highly in terms of flexibility as a cultural dimension.

The final dimension, Indulgence versus Restraint, appears to be weakly negatively correlated with the previous dimension. The ten characteristics of this cultural dimension include the importance of free speech, leisure, perceptions of personal control over one's life, positive emotions, sport participation and percentage of people who are happy. Additionally consideration was given to maintaining the status quo, birth rates of educated population, availability of food and obesity and, in wealthy countries lenient sexual norms (Hofstede, 2011 p. 16). Cultural contexts that scored highly on the Indulgence scale included the neoliberal contexts into which students with refugee and asylum seeker experiences be resettled. Many of these differences in cultural dimensions may be the foundations upon which notions of geographical differences in ways of making meaning are predicated.

While Hofstede's cultural dimensions indicate that culture is dynamic and ever evolving, it also confirms the importance that cultural and social influences have on individual development, supporting the perspective of Bronfenbrenner's macro system. Hofstede and Bond (1988) and Hofstede et al. (2010) also propose that people living in different cultures do not only have different social and cultural dimensions, but that the think differently. They suggest that western cultures tend to think more analytically, separating the whole to analyse the parts and their relationship to each individually, while eastern Confucian cultures think more synthetically in that they tend to combine ideas and think about a more complete, complex whole. This notion of eastern and western ways of thinking based on Confucius and the ancient Greeks was investigated by Nisbett (2005); Nisbett, Peng, Choi, and Norenzayan (2011). They extrapolate this geographical notion based the historical foundations of ways of thinking and doing in the East and West.

The differences in social structures in the early development of societies is argued to have given rise to differences in cultural traditions of problem solving (Nisbett, 2005; Nisbett et al., 2011). The focus on logic and analytical thinking attributed to the western world is compared with the more consensual, socially harmonious, problem solving strategies employed in Confucian societies. Nisbett and his associates, however, determined that dialectical thinking, the process of debating, identifying positive or strong aspects of the arguments presented and combining these to create a fresh, innovative solution to problem solving, did not reflect the rationality of the western styles of thinking, not only polarizing the understandings of the capacities that individuals and societies possess to solve problems using higher order thinking skills, but nominating the rational, logical more analytical ways of engaging with higher order thinking capacities as more superior. Considering the social context and historical time is an important aspect of understanding different ways of making meaning, as indicated by Bronfenbrenner (1979: 1990) and Hall (1976) and the appropriateness of polarizing eastern and western ways of making meaning has been challenged.

Chan and Yan (2007) for example indicate that they agree with Hofstede (1983; 1986; 2001; 2011; Hofstede & Bond, 1988; Hofstede et al., 2010) that all individuals are rational and use these competencies in response to their particular contexts and that they do this unconsciously in response to their own learning processes. Chan and Yan (2007), in disputing the geographical nature of thought and reasoning whilst respecting the various socio- cultural influences on thinking declare that,

> Logic or reasoning (or critical thinking) is not something homogeneous: there are different ways or forms of reasoning and they are often adaptive strategies in response to particular problems in human life. If students are taught to be more aware of the natural and cultural contexts in which their thinking patterns are embedded, they should become more sensitive to their own ways of thinking and less likely to misapply them or make hasty judgements based on them (p. 400).

In this way they honour the diverse ways in which rational minds can work effectively, without determining that analytical or holistic thinking are hierarchical in the way that's that have been suggested by Nisbett and his associates and by some western scholars (Paul, 2005; Paul & Elder, 2008a, 2008b, 2008c). There may, however, one way of learning that is frequently overlooked in the print laden environments of westernised societies and their schools; that of traditional ways of knowing and making meaning orally. It has been suggested that this has a significant impact on the strategies of learning, knowing and doing utilized by individuals for whom this tradition has been a means by which histories and cultural knowledge's have been learned for generations.

Oracy

The term oracy is used in educational contexts to indicate areas of interest. The first of these is the ways in which students can be interactive in various classroom context by contributing to discussion and engaging in dialogical and dialectic exchanges (Horton & Freire, 1990), an important construct in the movement to give students a 'voice' in an otherwise highly transmissive learning environment (for example, Arnott, 2014; Barry, 2007; Bunyan, Donelan, & Moore, 2003; Coultas, 2015; Gibbons, 2014; Vaish, 2013). In his own context, Freire (1985), acknowledged the use of the students' own native language or heritage language an important tool in emancipation and to any emancipatory education. In societies where oral communication is supplemented by written language, this becomes a basic skill for thinking and expressing ideas critically. Ownership of the students first language is of critical importance as it is considered to be a mastery of language beyond literacy itself and a powerful political tool (Giroux, 1981). Freire was conscious of the complex and formidable nature of he termed 'orality'. He possessed a deep appreciation of the mastery of oracy having the capacities to 'shape and reshape, form, create and recreate, the words and ideas they have inherited and give them new meaning in new performance' (Westerman, 2009 p. 555).

Contrary to popular academic belief, the mastery of oracy as a means by which to communicate effectively was not superseded by the acquisition of literacy skills but, for Freire, remained an important aspect of language along with literacy and was accorded the same status and attention in his language programmes, as where other traditional modes of communicating; dance, music, song and performance. These aspects of cultural life not only highlighted the importance of these traditional ways of presenting these symbolic performances of art and dance, music artefacts, pattern and interpretation, they identified with their critical consciousness in language and cultural artefacts.

What implications are there for students with refugee and asylum seeker backgrounds?

Students with refugee and asylum seeker experiences bring with them all the traditions of their early micro environments. While acknowledging that human development is a process of continuity and change (Bronfenbrenner, 1986a, 1986b), the experiences that individuals undergo in the processes of continuity and change can have a significant impact on their development. Individuals are shaped by their cultural and social contexts in ways that may be transformative or traumatic. Bronfenbrenner's ecological model provides a useful framework for attempting to understand the impact of the personal and environmental factors that impact on students with refugee and asylum seeker experiences. Built on the foundation premise that development is a lifelong process which is undertaken by individuals in the context of continual change and adaptation (Bronfenbrenner, 1988; Bronfenbrenner & Morris, 2006). Generally, for non- refugee and asylum seeker populations, the changes are gradual, and adaptation is a steady process. However, for students with refugee and asylum seeker experiences, the changes are rapid, all embracing and impact on all aspects of their lives. Adaptation then, must be rapid, major and of foremost importance for their future successful development.

From the perspective of the ecological model developed by Bronfenbrenner (1979), the challenges to the individual's micro system have immediate, direct impact on students. In many cases, for students with refugee and asylum seeker experiences, there are appalling, devastating changes to their micro systems. Their worlds are disrupted by loss of homeland at the very least. Common themes in the lives of these students are denial, silence or minimizing the extent and impact of these experiences (Sousa, Kemp, & El-Zuhairi, 2014). This may be because of fear of upsetting their parent or care giver or because it is difficult for them to admit that their remaining source of sanctuary and safety, has been unable to ensure their safety during the ordeal (Hamilton & Moore, 2006). These experiences are also frequently accompanied by loss of family members, loss of neighbourhood relationship, loss of school friends and, sadly, numerous experiences of violence and destruction, which for many of the caregiving adults creates feelings of shame and guilt which contributes significantly to post traumatic stress (The Victorian Foundation for Survivors of Torture, 2005). Additionally, in many cases the child's response to the death of a person to whom they had a close attachment is overlooked or not given suitable recognition, despite research evidence that indicates that a child's identity is more profoundly impacted upon by grief in childhood and grieving may continue for longer periods than adults because the process of development is not yet complete (Hamilton & Moore, 2006). Educationally, these enduring feeling of grief may be manifest in various inappropriate behaviours, withdrawal and excessive fear, including somatic disorders (Davidson, Murray, & Schweitzer, 2010).

Even when resettled, the new, emerging micro systems of these students may remain challenged by communication difficulties, lack of autonomy and the conflict of microsystems at the level of the mesosystems. The wider social contexts of the new society require families to develop new interpersonal relationships, new family roles and new perceptions of what the future may hold for them. The ways in which grief is understood determines a new mindset and a cohesive plan to organise and order family relationships and living successfully in their new context. If the families are able to accept that grieving and flexibility are experienced differently and accept help, then this contributes considerably to the reestablishment of family life (Hamilton & Moore, 2006) and school communities, school leadership and support agencies have major contributions to make to support this process. The acquisition of the host language is imperative for the functioning of families and individuals in their new homelands. There are many variables that can impact on ease and degree of success with second language acquisition for students with refugee and asylum seeker experiences compared to other migrant students (Rutter, 1994a, 1994b; Rutter & Jones, 1998). Students with refugee and asylum seeker experiences arrive in their host countries poorly prepared for learning. They are frequently suffering from trauma, 'and do not arrive in optimal psychological or emotional condition for language learning (Hamilton & Moore, 2006 p. 36)', have various levels of premigration educational experience and many have suffered from disruptions to their schooling and necessitate additional emotional support, specific strategy implementation and empathetic interactions to facilitate language acquisition as newly arrived students and beyond (Brown, Miller, & Mitchell, 2006; Due, Riggs, & Mandara, 2015; Matthews, 2008; Stewart, 2011). Additionally, the general social norms and mores that are characteristic of the culture in which these students and their families have been introduced are typically very different to that which they experienced in their homelands. While these dissimilarities may be evidenced at any level of Hall's (1976) cultural iceberg, even for those with considerable educational experiences pre migration, notions of appropriate schooling may commonly clash as expectations and perceptions of schooling can differ considerably from one cultural context to the next, including views on teacher responsibilities and actions, punishment and discipline, modes of communication and behaviour (Watters, 2007).

The ways in which the unobservable characteristics of the cultural iceberg are expressed are extremely varied and specific to different groups if students with refugee and asylum seeker experiences. They depend on personal preferences, habits and belief systems in addition to the wider cultural and social norms of the social, economic, religious and familial or tribal groups to which they are affiliated. As in all western cultural groups, sensitivities to individual capacities and ways in which students prefer to learn is paramount in supporting these students, using their relative strengths to facilitate learning (Sellars, 2008) and providing appropriate differentiated tasks in order engage successfully and develop their confidence as learners in new educational environments (Sellars, 2017). Understanding that some aspects of the cultural iceberg are highly emotionally charged serves to highlight the importance of some characteristics and attitudes which may not be considered important in Westcentric cultures, but which may be highly sensitive issues in others. A critical aspect of authentically engaging with the aspects of characteristics and customs identified by Hall (1976) is that all people have culture and reflective practices that are the foundation of professional identity for educators, must of necessity, include an interrogation of the cultural practices and norms that are assumed and are subscribed to, both at observable and hidden levels of consciousness (Foucault, 1991; 2003). For educators in neoliberal cultural settings, there may be considerable challenges, not solely in their interpersonal interactions with the expectations of parents and community, but in more individual instances that challenge unconscious ways of doing and believing of a private nature. Mistrust or disapproval, however subtly concealed, of, for example, oil pulling (Sellars, 2018), hair oiling and dressing, and other matters of personal hygiene could undermine the development of sound teacher – student relationships that are so vital to students' feelings of acceptance and belonging (Carlton, 2015; Correa-Velez, Gifford, & Barnett, 2010; Faircloth & Hamm, 2005; Green, Emery, Sanders, & Anderson, 2016; Lam, Chen, Zhang, & Liang, 2015).

Hofstede's cultural dimensions (1983; 1986; 2011; Hofstede et al., 2010) provide educators on neoliberal systems with a comprehensive overview of the six major distinguishing traits that are attached to their own nation. This may facilitate an understanding of how students with refugee and asylum seeker experiences may, with their communities and caregivers, adopt diverse ways of understanding and doing that are counter to the cultural norms of others in the schools. For example, it would be counterproductive to expect that students from societies with large power distance are naturally autonomous learners, that they will ask questions in class, question the perspective of teachers, or that they will not be increasingly respectful of teachers who are older (Chan & Yan, 2007; Hofstede, 1983; 1986; 2001). Similarly, students from collective cultures will avoid 'losing face' and they will ensure that teachers do not 'lose face' either. Groupings need to be harmonious and consensual; awards and merits are to be prized and displayed, more as symbols of status than competence at times and it would be expected that some students would be given preferential treatment depending on teacher preference or parent influence.

Other areas of difference include male students from masculine societies refusing to participate in what they believe to be subject content that is traditionally women's work, that they disrespect all methods of discipline except corporal punishment and that they are typically are very competitive. Students from uncertainty avoidance societies prefer strict, detailed lessons, regimes, timetables and precise learning objectives. They may judge teachers by their capacity to control their emotions, have all the answers and use academic language (Hofstede, 1983;1986; 2001). The additional two cultural dimensions that may impact on the ways in which students with refugee and asylum seeker experiences may be most obvious in the way in which they view themselves and interactions with friends and peers. Students from societies that consider change is constant may be more open to being autonomous learners, modest about their achievements and dedicated to learning more, while those with short term orientations may be complacent about improving their standards of achievement, be confident in the superiority and permanence of their historical cultural foundations and be inclined to be about saving face in their communities and adherence to the social pressures of their communities, preferring quick returns and results for effort. The final dimension of the framework discusses notions of indulgence. Students from societies that restrained may have less choice in life decisions, choose career paths and life outcomes that are dictated by families or communities, spend less time building friendships, engaging in team sports or expecting happiness (Hofstede & Bond, 1988; Hofstede et al., 2010; Minkov et al., 2018).

While the preferred ways of making meaning and finding solutions that are attributed geographically are debated and contentious (Chan & Yan, 2007; Nisbett, 2003; Nisbett et al., 2011), what is apparent is that problems are resolved, cognitive capacities are engaged and that no two brains are identical, irrespective of global location (Coch, Fischer, & Darwin, 2010; Medina, 2010). In its simplest manifestation, individual brains all have millions of nerve cells, known as neurons, that are arranged in 'circuits' in the brain. Circuits are organised in the brain so that, as the result of electrochemical process, neurons contact and create a synapse. There are 'trillions' of synapses which are associate with memory, learning, emotions, reasoning and so forth (Suarez-Orozco & Sattin- Bajaj, 2010 p. 65; Suárez-Orozco & Sattin, 2007). When the synapses occur, the neural pathways along which the neurons have travelled to make contact, and therefore the learning episode, becomes easier to travel and the brain changes to accommodate new learning (White, 2002). This is termed brain plasticity and every new synapse, which occurs in response to an experience, causes the brain to change to accommodate the new learning. Each experience which create new learning changes the functional organization of the brain. To complicate everything further, the individual wiring differences become increasingly complex in formal teaching and learning environments as they are 'also influenced by learning related to personal values, belief systems, social modelling and cultural complexity (Sellars, 2017 p. 74; Wentzel & Romani, 2916). Irrespective of the different wiring circuits, the brain responds to experiences as stimuli in the exactly the same manner.

In the case of students with backgrounds of oracy that is not supported by any written language, all these cultural, personal values and belief systems respond to the social modelling of oral tradition. This is not, as previous determined, an inferior pedagogical strategy based on transmission. It is an interactive performance that engages the learners as active participants of their learning in complex and multifaceted roles. It is rich in demonstration, performance, music and movement, singing and chanting experiences and coordinates part of the brain that are not otherwise connected in less divergent learning and tasks. It is also a very powerful educational tool as its basis is in storytelling and is frequently used to support students with refugee and asylum seeker experiences in both home and school settings (Balfour, Bundy, Burton, Dunn, & Woodrow, 2015; Strekalova-Hughes & Wang, 2019).

Conclusion

The impacts of these vastly diverse cultural perspectives can be totally hidden by the official terms 'refugee and asylum seeker', irrespective of how transient these labels may prove to be. The negotiation of the various worldviews held by students under this banner is not one that may be readily achieved in the learning environments of their new homelands. However, the unsettling, even confusing influences of these dissimilar perceptions and attitudinal values can be mediated by educational systems that acknowledge students with refugee and asylum seeker experiences as holistic learners (Green & Edwards-Underwood, 2015; Miller, 2007; O'Rourke, 2011; Pastoor, 2017; Pinson & Arnot, 2010), have high expectations of school leaders who respect and value all four pathways of their responsibilities (Leithwood, 1992; Leithwood & Janzi, 1990; Leithwood, Sun, & Pollock, 2017), ensure that those employed to teach, mentor and support students with refugee and asylum seeker experiences are empathetic, culturally competent and have the capacities to reflect critically on their own bias and prejudices (Hawkins, 2014; Jones, 2015; Richeson & Shelton, 2003) and have the skills to teach for critical, civic empathy in ways that support all students' healing, sense of belonging and compassion, capacities for tolerance, understanding of global diversity and worldviews and disparate ways of knowing and doing (Hope, 2008; Malm, 2009; Mirra, 2018). Unfortunately, the factory economies of the power, politics, people and pedagogies that dominate neoliberal education systems do not wish and will not afford to do that.

References

Arnott, N. (2014). Substantive Conversations: The Importance of Oracy in the Classroom. *Practically Primary, 19*(1), 13-15.

Balfour, M., Bundy, P., Burton, B., Dunn, J., & Woodrow, N. (2015). *Resettlement: Drama, Refugees and Resilience* London: Bloomsbury.

Barry, B. (2007). How do You say Oracy? *Screen Education, 46*, 66-71.

Bronfenbrenner, U. (1979). *The Ecology of Human Development: Experiments by Nature and Design.* Cambridge, Massachusetts: Harvard University Press.

Bronfenbrenner, U. (1986a). Ecology of the Family as a Context for Human Development: Research Rerspectives. *Developmental Psychology, 22*(6), 723.

Bronfenbrenner, U. (1986b). Recent Advances in Research on the Ecology of Human Development. In R. Silbereisen, K. Eyferth, & G. Rudinger (Eds.), *Development as Action in Context - Problem Behavior and Normal Youth Developmen* (pp. 287-309). Berlin, Germany: Springer Berlin Heidelberg.

Bronfenbrenner, U. (1988). Interacting Systems in Human Development. Research Paradigms: Present and Future. . In N. Bolger, A. Caspi, G. Downey, & M. Moore-House (Eds.), *Person in Context: Developmental Processes* (pp. 25-50). New York: Cambridge University Press.

Bronfenbrenner, U., & Morris, P. (2006). The Bioecological Model of Human Development. . In W. Damon & R. Lerner (Eds.), *Handbook of Child Psychology: Theoretical Models of Human Development* (pp. 793-828). New York: Wiley.

Brown, J., Miller, J., & Mitchell, J. (2006). Interrupted Schooling and the Acquisition of Literacy: Experiences of Sudanese refugees in Victorian SecondarySschools. *Australian Journal of Language and Literacy, 29*(2), 150-162.

Bunyan, P., Donelan, K., & Moore, R. (2003). Writing in the Sand: Drama, Oracy and Writing in the Middle Years. *Literacy Learning: The Middle Years, 11*(2), 61-64.

Carlton, S. (2015). Reprint of: Connecting, Belonging: Volunteering, Wellbeing and Leadership among Refugee Youth. *International Journal of Disaster Risk Reduction, 14, Part 2*, 160-167. doi:http://dx.doi.org/10.1016/j.ijdrr.2015.10.010

Chan, H., & Yan, H. (2007). Is there a Geography of Thought for East-West Differences? Why or Why Not? . *Educational Philosophy and Theory, 39*(4), 383-403.

Coch, D., Fischer, K., & Darwin, G. (Eds.). (2010). *Human Behaviour, Learning and the Developing Brain*. New York: Guildford Press.

Cochran-Smith, M. (1995). Color Blindness and Basket Making Are Not the Answers: Confronting the Dilemmas of Race, Culture, and Language Diversity in Teacher Education. *American Educational Research Journal, 32*(3), 493-522.

Correa-Velez, I., Gifford, S. M., & Barnett, A. G. (2010). Longing to Belong: Social Inclusion and Wellbeing among Youth with Refugee Backgrounds in the First Three Years in Melbourne, Australia. *Soc Sci Med, 71*(8), 1399-1408. doi:10.1016/j.socscimed.2010.07.018

Coultas, V. (2015). Revisiting Debates on Oracy: Classroom Talk – Moving Towards a Democratic Pedagogy? *Changing English, 22*(1), 72-86. doi:10.1080/1358684x.2014.992205

Davidson, G., Murray, K., & Schweitzer, R. (2010). Review of Refugee Mental Health Assessment: Best Practices and Recommendations. *Journal of Pacific Rim Psychology, 4*, 72-85.

Due, C., Riggs, D., & Mandara, M. (2015). Educators' Experiences of working in Intensive English Language Programs: The Strengths and Challenges of Specialised English Language Classrooms for Students with Migrant and Refugee Backgrounds. *Australian Journal Of Education 59*(2), 169-181.

Faircloth, B. S., & Hamm, J. V. (2005). Sense of Belonging Among High School Students Representing 4 Ethnic Groups. *Journal of Youth and Adolescence, 34*(4), 293-309. doi:10.1007/s10964-005-5752-7

Ford, D. Y. (2014). Why Education must be Multicultural: Addressing a few Misperceptions with Counterarguments. *Gifted Child Today, 37*(1), 59-62.

Foucault, M. (1991). *Discipline and Punish: The Birth of a Prison.* . London: Penguin.

Foucault, M. (2003). Society Must Be Defended' (D. Macey, Trans.). In *Lectures at the College de France 1975-1976,* . New York: Picador.

Freire, P. (1985). *The Politics of Education* (D. Macedo, Trans.). South Hadley, Mass.: Bergin and Garvey Publishers Ltd.

Gibbons, S. (2014). The Importance of Oracy. In S. Brindley & B. Marshan (Eds.), *Master-Class in English Education: Transforming Teaching and Learning*. London, GBR: Bloomsbury Publishing.

Giroux, H. (1981). *Ideology, Culture and the Process of Schooling*. Philadelphia: Temple University Press.

Green, M., Emery, A., Sanders, M., & Anderson, L. (2016). Another Path to Belonging: A Case Study of Middle School Students' Perspectives. *The Educational and Developmental Psychologist,, 33*(01), 85-96.

Green, S. L., & Edwards-Underwood, K. (2015). Understanding and Redefining Multicultural Education. *Journal of Education Research, 9*(4), 399-411.

Hall, E. (1976). *Beyond Culture*. New York: Knopf Doubleday Publishing Group.

Hamilton, R., & Moore, D. (2006). *Educational Interventions for Refugee Children*. Albington, Oxen: Routledge.

Hawkins, K. (2014). Teaching for Social Justice, Social Responsibility and Social Inclusion: A Respectful Pedagogy for Twenty-first Century Early Childhood Education. *European Early Childhood Education Research Journal, 22*(5), 723-738.

Hofstede, G. The 6 -D Model of National Culture. Retrieved from https://geerthofstede.com/culture-geert-hofstede-gert-jan-hofstede/6d-model-of-national-culture/

Hofstede, G. (1983). The Cultural Relevativity of Organizational Practices and Theories. *Journal of International Business Studies, 14*(2), 75-89.

Hofstede, G. (1986). Cultural Differences in Teaching and Learning. *International Journal of Intercultural Relations, 10*(3), 301-320.

Hofstede, G. (2001). *Culture's Consequences: Comparing Values, Behaviors, Institutions and Organizations Across Nations* (second ed.). Thousand Oaks: Sage.

Hofstede, G. (2011). Dimensionalizing Cultures: The Hofstede Model in Context. *Online Readings in Psychology and Culture 2*, 1-26. Retrieved from doi:https://doi.org/10.9707/2307-0919.1014

Hofstede, G., & Bond, M. (1988). The Confucius Connection: From Cultural Roots to Economic Growth. . *Organizational Dynamics, 16*(4), 5-21.

Hofstede, G., Hofstede, G. J., & Minkov, M. (2010). *Cultures and Organisations: Software of the Mind*. New York: McGraw- Hill.

Hope, J. (2008). "One Day We Had To Run": The Development of the Refugee Identity in Children's Literature and its Function in Education. *Children's Literature in Education, 39*(4), 295-304. doi:10.1007/s10583-008-9072-x

Horton, M., & Freire, P. (1990). *We Make the Road by Walking: Conversations on Education and Social Change*. Philadelphia: Temple University Press.

Hue, M.-T., & Kennedy, K. J. (2013). Building a Connected Classroom: Teachers' Narratives about Managing the Cultural Diversity of Ethnic Minority Students in Hong Kong Secondary Schools. *Pastoral Care in Education, 31*(4), 292-308. doi: 10.1080/02643944.2013.811697

Jones, J. R. (2015). Infusing Multicultural Education into the Curriculum: Preparing Preservice Teachers to Address Homophobia in K-12 Schools. *International Journal of Multicultural Education, 17*(3), 107-118.

Keddie, A. (2012). Refugee Education and Justice Issues of Representation, Redistribution and Recognition. *Cambridge Journal of Education, 42*(2), 197-212. doi:10.1080/0305764x.2012.676624

Lam, U., Chen, W., Zhang, J., & Liang, T. (2015). It Feels Good to Learn Where I Belong: School Belonging, Academic Emotions, and Academic Achievement in Adolescents. . *School Psychology International, 36*(4), 393-409.

Leithwood, K. (1992). The Move toward Transformational Leadership. *Educational Leadership, 49*(5), 8-14.

Leithwood, K., & Janzi, D. (1990). *Transformational Leadership: How Principals Can Help Reform School Cultures.* Paper presented at the Annual Meeting of the Canadian Association for Curriculum Studies, Victoria, British Columbia, Canada.

Leithwood, K., Sun, J., & Pollock, K. (Eds.). (2017). *How School Leaders Contribute to Student Success: The Four Path Framework* (Vol. 23). Cham, Switzerland: Springer

Malm, B. (2009). Towards a New Professionalism: Enhancing Personal and Professional Development in Teacher Education. *Journal of Education for Teaching, 35*(1), 77-91. doi:10.1080/02607470802587160

Matthews, J. (2008). Schooling and Settlement: Refugee education in Australia. *International Studies in Sociology of Education, 18*(1), 31-45. doi:10.1080/09620210802195947

Medina, J. (2010). *Brain Rules for Learning.* Seattle: Pear Press.

Miller, J. (2007). *The Holistic Curriculum.* Toronto: University of Toronto Press

Minkov, M., Bond, M., Dutt, P., Schachner, M., Morales, O., Sanchez, C., . . . Mudd, B. (2018). A Reconsideration of Hofstede's Fifth Dimension: New Flexibility Versus Monumentalism Data From 54 Countries. *Cross Cultural Research, 53*(3), 309-333.

Mirra, N. (2018). *Educating for Empathy.* New York: Teachers College Press.

Nisbet, R. (2003). *The Geography of Thought: How Asians and Westerners Think Differently ... and Why.* . New York: THe Free Press.

Nisbett, R. (2005). *The Geography of Thought.* London: Nicholas Brearley Publishing.

Nisbett, R., Peng, K., Choi, I., & Norenzayan, A. (2011). Culture and Systems of Thoughts: Holistic Versus Analytic Cognition. . *Psychological Review, 108*(2), 291.

O'Rourke, D. (2011). Closing Pathways: Refugee-background Students and Tertiary Education. *Kōtuitui: New Zealand Journal of Social Sciences Online, 6*(1-2), 26-36. doi:10.1080/1177083X.2011.617759

Pastoor, L. d. W. (2017). Reconceptualising Refugee Education: Exploring the Diverse Learning Contexts of Unaccompanied Young Refugees upon Resettlement. *Intercultural Education, 28*(2), 143-164. doi:10.1080/14675986.2017.1295572

Paul, R. (2005). The State of Critical Thinking Today. *New Directions for Community College, 130*, 27-38.
Paul, R., & Elder, L. (2008a). The Art of Socratic Questioning. *Journal of Developmemtal Education, 31*(3), 34-35.
Paul, R., & Elder, L. (2008b). *The Miniature Guide to Critical Thinking.* Dillon Beach CA: The Foundation for Critical Thinking
Paul, R., & Elder, L. (2008c). Strategies for Improving Student Learning Part 11. *Journal of Developmemtal Education, 32*(2), 34-35.
Pinson, H., & Arnot, M. (2010). Local Conceptualisations of the Education of Asylum-seeking and Refugee Students: From Hostile to Holistic Models. *International Journal of Inclusive Education, 14*(3), 247-267. doi:10.1080/13603110802504523
Richeson, J., & Shelton, J. (2003). When Prejudice Does Not Pay: Effects of Interracial Contact on Executive Function. *Psychological Science, 14*(3), 287-290.
Rutter, J. (1994a). The Emotional Needs of Refugee Children. In *Refugee Children in the Classroom* (pp. 89-98). Staffordshire, England: Trentham Books Limited.
Rutter, J. (1994b). Welcoming Newly Arrived Refugees into Schools. In *Refugee Children in the Classroom* (pp. 59-64). Staffordshire, England: Trentham Books Limited.
Rutter, J., & Jones, C. (Eds.). (1998). *Refugee Education: Mapping the Field.* Sterling VA: Stylus Publishing.
Sellars, M. (2008). *Using Students' Strengths to Support Learning Outcomes: A Study of the Development of Gardner's Intrapersonal Intelligence to Support Increased Academic Achievement for Primary School Students* Saarbrucken, 97: VDM Verlag.
Sellars, M. (2017). *Reflective Practice for Teachers* (2nd ed.). London: Sage.
Sellars, M. (Ed.) (2018). *Authentic Contexts of Numeracy: Making Meaning across the Curriculum.* Singapore: Springer.
Sousa, C., Kemp, S., & El-Zuhairi. (2014). Dwelling Within Political Violence: Palestinian Women's Narratives of Home, Mental Health, and Resilience. . *Health & Place, 30*, 205-214.
Stewart, J. (2011). *Supporting Refugee Children: Strategies for Educators.* Toronto, Ontraio: University of Toronto Press.
Strekalova-Hughes, E., & Wang, X. C. (2019). Perspectives of Children From Refugee Backgrounds on Their Family Storytelling as a Culturally Sustaining Practice. *Journal of Research in Childhood Education, 33*(1), 6-21. doi:10.1080/02568543.2018.1531452
Suarez-Orozco, M., & Sattin- Bajaj, C. (2010). *Educating the Whole Child for the Whole World:The Ross School Model and Education for the Global Era.* New York: New York University Press.
Suárez-Orozco, M., & Sattin, C. (2007). Wanted: Global Citizens. *Educational Leadership, 64*(7), 58-62.
The Victorian Foundation for Survivors of Torture. (2005). Annual Report. Retrieved from http://www.foundationhouse.org.au/rebuilding-shattered-lives-2/
Vaish, V. (2013). Questioning and Oracy in a Reading Program. *Language and Education, 27*(6), 526-541. doi:10.1080/09500782.2012.737334

Watters, C. (2007). *Refugee children: Towards the Next Horizon* (1 ed.). Florence: Taylor and Francis.

Weinstein, C., Curran, M., & Tomlinson-Clarke, S. (2003). Culturally Responsive Classroom Management: Awareness Into Action. *Theory Into Practice, 42*(4), 269-276. doi:10.1207/s15430421tip4204_2

Wentzel, K., & Romani, G. (Eds.). (2916). *Handbook of Social Influences in School Contexts*. New York: Routledge.

Westerman, W. (2009). Folk schools, Popular Education and a Pedagogy of Community Action. In A. Darder, M. Baltodano, & R. Torres (Eds.), *The Critical Pedagogy Reader* (pp. 541-562). Abington, Oxen: Taylor and Francis.

White, J. (2002). *The Child's Mind*. London, New York: RoutledgeFalmer.

Chapter Nine: Pedagogy: Educating for Global Competence

Introduction

The initial discussion of this work articulated the ways in which neoliberal influences had impacted negatively on education (Sardar, 2010; Wilkins, 2017, 2018a, 2018b), creating a mandatory system which privileges specific populations (Connell, 1977, 1982, 2013a, 2013b; Connell et al., 2007) and dehumanizes (Gary, 2017) students and communities who are not included these cohorts (E. W. Ross & Vinson, 2013; W. Ross, 2017). This has resulted in an education system that not only disrespects human capacity, is inadequate preparation for the world in which its students will seek to make meaningful lives and contemptuously classifies what is understood as knowledge and learning to suit an economic agenda, but also serves to significantly handicap the students who are in most need of understanding, empathy and compassion: those with refugee and asylum seeker experiences. Additionally, these education systems do little to address futures; the need for ethical decision making in relation to entire human community, the demand for critical discourse and the consideration of multiple alternatives in individual and community outcomes, irrespective of time and place (Bell, 2002), especially in current context of the global diaspora and its implications for the entire global community. Neo liberal education systems encourage views of the world that are black and white, absolutist and without significant value driven higher purpose. They are inadequate preparation for global engagement, which demands personal and collective qualities which include; global responsibility including ecology, social justice, appreciating and developing multiple perspectives, critical and creative thinking and problem finding.

Education in these contexts has looked backwards, not forwards, and, as such, is totally unprepared for the impact of authentic multiculturalism in which traditional and modern, diverse ways of knowing and doing are honoured and respected as legitimate epistemologies. It steadfastly ignores philosophies and knowledge which bring hope to the urgent task of educating students to cope with inevitable tensions of a 'multi- perspectival world' characterised by change, 'contradiction, chaos and complexity ' (Gidley, 2016 p. 112), which, while important all students, is urgent and critical for students with refugee and asylum seeker experiences whose ontologies already mirror the change 'contradiction, chaos and complexity' of 'the multi -perspectival world' of which Gidley and Kincheloe write and which reflects the 'postnormal world' of Sardar (2010). It is urgent and critical for these students to be integrated into learning contexts that support the development of these Postformal reasoning skills from a young age, as, more than others, they need an education that provides them with opportunities to develop the complexities of thinking and meaning making that will give them the hope to plan productive and constructive futures as wise global citizens. It is argued also that neoliberal societies will need the wisdoms these students bring as part of the heritage and relationship with the natural world. Current education policies and practices in western countries with neoliberal economic agenda does not have the capacities to authentically develop these opportunities for these populations as it disregards the 'global educational priority today' to 'lay foundations in childhood and adolescence' so that people have the 'ability to think more complexly and to hold a paradox in mind' with resorting to abstract rational thinking that splits mind and body and which is the prevalent model of thinking in the western world (Gidley, 2016 p. 113).

Postformal Psychology

Developed from the work of early psychologists, including Jung and Freud, postformal psychology not only focusses on the development of cognitive capabilities that go beyond Piaget's formal thinking, it contributes substantially to critical constructivism in educational contexts. Kincheloe and Steinberg (1993 p. 297-298) write,

> The postformal concern with questions of meaning, emancipation via ideological disembedding, and attention to the process of self-production rises above the formal operational level of thought and its devotion to proper procedure. Post-formalism grapples with purpose, devoting attention to issues of human dignity, freedom, authority, and social responsibility. Many will argue that a post-formal mode of thinking with its emphasis on multiple perspectives will necessitate an ethical relativism that paralyses social action. A more critical Postformality grounded in our emancipatory system of meaning does not cave in to relativistic social paralysis. Instead, it initiates reflective dialogue between critical theory and postmodernism

— a dialogue that is always concerned with the expansion of self-awareness and consciousness, never certain of emancipation's definition, and perpetually reconceptualising the system of meaning.

Working within the context of critical pedagogies, which contest the notion that any education is objective, instead understanding all educational endeavours have a purpose to create particular types of citizens; critical constructivists seek to expose the power dimension of epistemology, its impact on educational practices, theory, curriculum and how this positions those who are not western, white, middle class and male. In current neoliberal educational contexts, students have education 'done to them' as they learn to regurgitate the 'right; answers, follow directions and swallow in its entirety the information that comes from the holders of all knowledge; the teachers; in an effort to be considered successful. The prescriptive content of what is to be considered as 'truth' is sanitized and regulated, tailored specifically to promote and endorse the values, beliefs and ideals of the powerful ruling class. As a seminal theorist in critical constructivism and credited with coining the term postformal, Kincheloe (Kincheloe & Steinberg, 1993) advocates for the importance of contextual awareness in a critical pedagogical model with the capacity to challenge and resist the ways in which capitalist empires use 'knowledge' to exploit and oppress. Malott (2011 p. 53) states,

> Obvious examples of what this looks like in practice at the level of education, of course, are ways schools in the United States teach a social studies of white supremacist manifest destiny that situates Western civilization and industrial capitalism as evidence of progress and Euro-supremacy and, simultaneously, positions Indigenous peoples in America, Africa, and elsewhere, as backwards, primitive, and lucky to be under the protective care of their natural superiors, even if these bosses do have an occasional genocidal mean streak.

Education is underpinned by modern psychologies that perpetuate the notion that intelligence can be measured and therefore controlled, leaving Malott (2011, p. 53) to comment that current educational practices are so antiquated and populated with untruths and fanciful 'realities' that scientific enquiry has long abandoned any attempt to inform or impact upon education as a discipline or a field of study. He states,

> Consequently, the empire must ignore science and work in the less than admirable domain of indoctrination and propaganda and pretend people are robots and the earth is a bottomless shopping mall, and the world will live happily ever after as long as we do not challenge or question the man behind the curtain (2011, p. 54).

However, what Kincheloe (2005) highlights are concept of free will, of personal autonomy and of the consciousness and human agency (also referred to by Foucault, 1977) that is expressed in critical pedagogies and which identifies and condemns what Kincheloe terms the 'machine cosmology' (2005, p. 84) of these modern psychologies under which neoliberal education is predicated. Instead, he promotes instead a dynamic, organic, life-filled ontology. He states,

> With the birth of modernism and the scientific revolution, many pre-modern, indigenous epistemologies, cosmologies and ontologies were lost, ridiculed by European modernists as primitive. While there is great diversity among pre-modern worldviews, there do seem to be some discernible patterns that distinguish them from modernist perspectives. In addition to developing meaningful systems that were connected to cosmological perspectives on the nature of creation, most premodernists saw nature and the world at large as living systems. (Kincheloe, 2005, p. 84).

Much of the wisdom and cosmological perspectives to which Kincheloe is referring is now subjugated knowledge, despite the unique understanding of the interpolated relationships of all living things that is the strength of premodern indigenous epistemologies. However, it is this appreciation of the interconnectedness of the living systems that were understood in their wholeness by premodernist societies that Kincheloe uses to illustrate the extent of the decontextualized school contexts and curricula that pervade current public educational contexts in neoliberal societies. Inherent in these contexts is the perpetuation of so called 'objective truths' determined by those in power. It is challenging this separation of the learning from the learners' identities, from the social, cultural, temporal and political contexts in which learner identity is formed (Kincheloe, Hayes, Rose, & Anderson, 2006), that is the crux of much of Kincheloe's work in critical constructivism; and which lends itself to the importance of the development of postformal thinking as an alternative pedagogy in which multiple epistemologies can be recognised as authentically based in context and act as counter- hegemonic forces in transformative education.

While there are criticisms of critical pedagogy. Darder, Boltodano, and Torres (2009 p. 14-19) have identified six major areas of critique and discussed these in some detail, noting the impact these have had on critical scholars and theorists. However, while some of these concerns may have been mitigated by the new wave of critical theorists, it is in the discussion of 'The Barriers to an Anarchical Postformal Pedagogy' that Malott (2011a p.181) clearly articulates the global dilemma in education when he states,

> It is therefore the challenge of critical postformal educators to demonstrate through our teaching and scholarship the practical reasons why critical theories and practices, such as anarchy, are favourable alternatives to the neoliberal order that currently dominates. People must come to understand that the current neoliberal trajectory is not only unsustainable, but it is dangerously irresponsible. The media has conditioned millions of people to equate democracy and freedom with capitalism rendering the struggle for genuine democracy an incredibly difficult

undertaking. Consequently, many critical pedagogues have given up hope, believing the only way paradigmatic change will come is through the catastrophic physical and economic collapse of the current system.

Presenting this problem as not only the concern of institutions but also of individuals, Malott argues that it is the work of critical theorists to 'demonstrate that the result of a world without oppression and crude exploitation (p.182) is of benefit to all humanity, even those who currently profit from the neoliberally dominated system. One model education that has the potential to prepare answer the critics of critical theory, advocate for the principals of postformal education and prepare students for students to engage in dialogue that reflects the consideration of all peoples and their epistemologies is that developed by Gidley (2008, 2016, 2017). It is a comprehensive framework for transforming educational practice into a process of respect, dialogue and multi-perspectives which facilitates the development of postformal reasoning skills and the honouring of currently subjugated epistemologies.

Gidley's Model of Adult Postformal Reasoning

Influenced by multiple philosophical sources, postformal theorist including Kincheloe and Steinberg, and following the respected tradition of Steiner, Gidley (2016, p.113 – 120) theorizes that postformal reasoning has twelve 'qualities'. These are very briefly summarized as (i) Complexity, which is considered to be a significant aspect of postformal reasoning involves the capacity to consider two seemingly contradictory statements and the possibility that neither or both may reflect the truth. Complexity is important to the development of wisdom. (ii) Creativity, which is the ability to see or to view things in unorthodox ways and incorporates problem finding. This capacity also contributes to the development of wisdom. (iii) Dialogical reasoning, which includes dialectics. Gidley comments on the formal reasoning capacity to present an argument, dialogical reasoning provides solutions that are formulated as the result of considering multiple perspectives and appreciating the thoughts and views of others, as expressed in Kincheloe (2005) notion of bricolage. Kincheloe's work also contributes the understanding of the quality that is (iv) ecological reasoning, which includes the necessary consideration of context, process and organicism. This quality reflects the understanding of the relatedness of the ecological world to other living systems and the need to understand knowledge as organic and dynamic, constantly changing and evolving. (v) Future mindedness (futures reasoning, foresight) is central to the positive psychology movement championed by Csikszentmihalyi (1988; 1991; 2000; Csikszentmihalyi & Lebuda, 2107) and Seligman (2002); (Seligman, 2011; Seligman, Ernst, Gillham, Reivich, & Linkins, 2009) and is critical to emotional wellness. This quality emphasises the multiple opportunities that emerge from considering numerous, varied opportunities for the future and understanding that the future can be created. (vi) Higher Purpose, including values awareness and spirituality is a focus on the role of higher purpose and ego motivation in personal endeavour. It is explicitly linked to notions of fairness and justice in addition to being a manifestation of choice and freedom. Gidley proposes that many corporate endeavours lack higher purpose and that it should be salient feature of educational endeavour. Imagination is a higher order thinking skill that

> 'not only enliven concepts but … bring the significance of life back into centre focus in our lifeworld, enhancing vitality and wellbeing (Gidley, 2006; p.117).

Imagination, especially strong visual imagination, is important to future mindedness as envisioning a future allows for the possible creation of that eventuality. (viii) Integration, incorporating holism and unitary thinking is important to the notion of contradiction and paradox that is found in complexity. The current trends of specialization and siloing of knowledge, context, and aspects of human thought requires students to be able integrate and develop holistic understandings of all the human facilities, cognitive, affective, physical and conative in order to develop wisdom. This is a quality that is written strongly about in Gidley's work. (ix) Intuitive wisdom, a quality that appears to have been lost in the quest for absolute knowledge, is included here as a postformal quality of tacit wisdom, a capacity to synthesize the various forces and influences that are impacting on life swiftly and with unstated wisdom. (x) Language Reflexivity, incorporating construct – awareness, voice and language, described as 'a subtle and advanced postformal quality (p. 119). This quality is aligned with the understanding of the aesthetic, artistic and poetry education that allows multiple meaning and interpretations of language itself and how the world is framed through language. It encourages an awareness of personal language (xi) Pluralism, incorporating non- absolutism and relativism of knowledge and is explicitly linked with quality of complexity, contradiction and paradox. It is a quality that predicates the acceptance of social and cultural pluralism. (xii) Reflexivity, incorporating self- reflection and self- referential thought, is believed to be the most commonly recognised of the twelve qualities of adult postformal thinking and is researched widely. It focusses on the self- reflective, meditative practices of interrogating assumptions about the ways in which, as individuals, meaning has been constructed in personal ways and standing back to view these non- judgementally.

The development of these qualities is proposed through educational practices designed to engage students from a very young age and are founded on four, core pedagogical values. Gidley (2016) states

> ......summarizes the process of my theorizing that led to the distillation of my four core *pedagogical values*: love- an evolutionary force; life – a sustaining force; wisdom- a creative force and voice – an empowering force. By associating the Postformal pedagogies that best align to the evolutionary theme, and partnering them with one of the core values and the keywords that arise in the literature related to these values, I begin to build a picture of evolutionary education (p. 176).

The completed 'picture' of evolutionary education developed by Gidley (2016, p. 177) is developed as a framework. The evolutionary theme of *conscious, compassionate, spiritual development* groups together the postformal reasoning qualities of higher purpose (putting something else before personal self), dialogical reasoning (respecting the views of the 'other') and integration (linking the heart with thinking and action) are grouped together under the core value of love which incorporates service, compassion and heart and the pedagogical core value of Love which is expressed in reverence, care , head and heart. The second theme, *mobile life enhancing thinking* contains the postformal reasoning qualities of imagination (bringing thinking to life), ecological reasoning (respect for the balance of nature) and futures reasoning (responsibility for long term habitability) come together under the core value of life, incorporating vitality, nature and sustainability and the pedagogical core value of Life expressed in imagination, ecology and foresight. *Complexification of thinking and culture* is the third evolutional theme that includes creativity (taking novel and multiple perspectives), complexity (acceptance of contradiction and paradox), and intuitive wisdom (developing one's sense of intuition). These are linked to core value of wisdom which includes novelty, paradox and intuition and the pedagogical core value of Wisdom expressed through creativity, multi-modality and layering. The final evolutionary theme is *linguistic and paradigmatic boundary- crossing* incorporating reflexivity (reflecting on one's own thoughts, feelings and values), language reflexivity (being conscious of our language) and pluralism (recognising power and worth and their many voices). These postformal reasoning skills are brought together under the core value of voice, which combines the capacities for self- knowledge, language and relativism and the core pedagogical value of Voice, expressed as self-reflection, silence and multicultural thinking. It is through the implementation of strategies, tasks, knowledge, discourse and debate in formal and informal (Jackson, 1990) curriculum spaces that Gidley proposes to support the development of these postformal reasoning skills for young learners, students and young people in educational contexts.

Transforming Education

The seminal work in transformative education has been attributed to a small number of eminent scholars, who have influenced a significant number of educational practitioners with their insights in to ways in which education can become an authentic means by which societies, and indeed how the individual, community and global worlds may be better understood to improve the interactions of people, both with each other and with the natural world. Mezirow (1981); Mezirow (1991, 1998); (Mezirow, 2003) offers a ten-step process by which adults may refocus their perspectives with the support of constant, critical reflection and dialogic processes, much of which is based on the distinction made in the theory by Habermas, which distinguishes instructional from communicative modes of learning. The work of Boyd and Myers (1988) focusses on transforming individuals by supporting successful and authentic understandings of self and integrating the self- reflection as a learning tool for the progress of adult learners. However, it is the work of O'Sullivan that allows a more comprehensive view in the possibilities for transforming education at every stage of the formal systems and for introducing the essential foundations of transformative education that directly incorporates the transformation of perspectives in relation to personal, institutional and global agenda as humans living in the natural world. In addressing relationships and interactions between to mankind and the biosphere, O'Sullivan, of necessity, addresses the impact of market driven economies on both mankind and the world on which they are dependent for survival. O'Sullivan (1999 p. ix -xi; 2008); (O'Sullivan, Morrell, & O'Connor, 2002), in his discussion of transformative education begins with a reminder that technology has not, as hoped and planned, stopped wars, alleviated hunger and brought peace and prosperity to all. Instead, in switching biosphere to bytesphere the latter has dominated the former and the traditional balances of populations and the world's resources have been decimated to degree that the market economy and the age of consumerism upon which current western educational practices have been built are not only unsustainable but dangerously unreflective, the result of which may easily prove the reality to Colin Thiele's children's picture book of 1977; *The Sknuks*. O'Sullivan's review of current formal educational practices, identifies the characteristics of this process as the following familiar traits which must be addressed in any plan to transform or change education;

1. A narrowing of what counts as achievement through that which can be measured
2. High stress among teachers and a feeling of being out of control and undervalued
3. The deprofessionalisation of teachers who become technicians instead of reflective practitioners
4. A breakdown or sense of community with a school and of professional collegiality
5. A return to limited learning styles and didactic teaching and the decline of teacher led innovation
6. The marginalization of the arts and humanities subjects
7. The equating of quality and achievement only through measurable results
8. Less sharing of experiences among schools and localities
9. The increasing gulf between the haves and the have nots
10. Less time and ability to respond to differentiated needs among pupils and pupils with social or emotional difficulties
11. A breakdown of community links as children have to travel miles valuing what can be measured instead of measuring what can be valued (2008, p. xiii).

Arguing that what is needed is a 'paradigm shift in sense' (2008, p. xiv) O' Sullivan posits that currently it is time to reinvent what it is to be human and offers insights in what he considers the five central themes in reimagining education for humanity. He values the importance of holistic educational practices in which complexity theory is recognised and demands that students are taught to respond to hitherto unseen contingency and in which creativity is respected as a means by which people become holistically human and develop an awareness of the biosphere and respect for their surroundings. He renews the focus on the notion of the 'web of life', thinking in terms of circles, webs and continuity instead of hierarchies so the people become increasingly connected and can cross boundaries to negotiate and develop solutions that rely on consensus, not only in terms of human matters but in relation to natural world; the biosphere. Challenging the dominance of patriarchal societies, O'Sullivan honours and respects the feminine, even in men, and what women can provide in developing resolutions to break down the destructive forces of war and devastation in the world; the nurture, caring and life-giving forces that are essential for survival.

The wisdoms of indigenous people are an essential theme in the reconception of education, with O'Sullivan stressing that in the 21st century, it is the people whose culture and ancient appreciation of the natural world who will be the educators of those who sought for many centuries to destroy it. This will be essential for people in neoliberal market- driven societies to develop the consciousness that is so difficult to come to terms with (Malott, 2011a, 2011b; Malott, 2011) and so which can only be taught by those who own and honour these ancient wisdoms. The last of the central themes which O'Sullivan discusses is that of spirituality. Not religion, but the mystery of personage. A spirituality that opens individual up to 'what Thomas Berry outlines as differentiation, subjectivity and communion (O" Sullivan, 2008, p. xvi)', and which has diverse articulations, all of which are expressions of the inner spirituality of what it is to be human. In an ever- changing world, however, many educationalists, governments and policy makers appear oblivious to the short sightedness of their decision making and resist notions of change which will improve the capacities of students to live harmoniously and inclusively in a global environment, irrespective of the potential of appropriate theories of educational change that could support the development of postformal and transformative educational outcomes.

One such change theory is posited by Fullan (1993, 2015). This model may be the most appropriate for several reasons. Firstly Fullan, has recognised the need to consistently revise and reformulate his theory in response to the ever-changing societal contexts and environmental conditions under which educational systems operate. From his original themes for change consideration, he has now refined his theory to four, which he terms the 'right drivers' for educational change (Fullan, 2011). Secondly, he has eschewed the hierarchically organised checklists so beloved of factory quality control and failsafe recipes that are intended as a one size fits all panacea for the painful processes of self- evaluation, critical contemplation and flexible, multi- perspectives that are embedded in every change undertaking. Finally, he prioritises the need for a moral purpose in the leadership capacities that may result in effective change. The four drivers are expressed as

> Thus intrinsic motivation, instructional improvement, teamwork, and 'allness' are the crucial elements for whole system reform. Many systems not only fail to feature these components but choose drivers that actually make matters worse (Fullan, 2011 p. 3).

The 'allness' that is referred to here by Fullan is that impact will be positive for all those involved, teachers and students alike. This is reflected in his model for leadership during periods of change, the characteristics of which are framed within the capacities for enthusiasm, energy and hope. Within these attributes, leaders must understand and work with moral purpose, have a sound understanding of the change process, the capacity to build positive relationships and listen and appreciate the wisdom of objections and matters to be considered seriously, the propensity for knowledge creating and sharing and the overall ability to develop and maintain coherence for all those involved, which is the consideration given to the importance of identifying patterns and trends. Indicating that there is direct, reciprocal relationship between the framework of enthusiasm, energy and hopefulness and the five leadership components they frame, Fullan recognises that this process has no linear developmental process, no strategic order and no simplistic implementation (Fullan, 2001). With the exception of the focus on measurable change impacts for students, this may be the first step to authentic and dependable change in the various and diverse contents which are loosely brought together as the education systems that are characterised by the economic efficiencies of factory models common in diverse representations of neoliberal education systems.

It is apparent that school systems in neoliberal contexts need to undergo significant change as the world in all its complexity is increasingly conspicuous in the societies that these systems serve. Students in schools are diverse. They bring with them different cultures, belief systems and values, many of which challenge those of the dominant culture and render the educational process a dismal and unrewarding experience for the children and young people who are mandated to participate. Whilst many may believe that populations with refugee and asylum seeker experiences are fortunate to be resettled in neoliberal countries, for others, the white hegemonic processes of power are seen to further disadvantage individuals who have suffered inconceivably, denying them real opportunities to succeed in school systems that dismiss and disrespect their epistemologies and ontologies. In some pockets of more liberal practice, despite the pressures of constant competition and arduous accountability, students with refugee and asylum seeker experiences are welcomed, their cultures respected, and their communities integrated (Stewart, 2011; Watters, 2007). These schools, however, represent a tiny minority amongst the thousands of schools in wealthy, developed countries in which students with refuge and asylum seeker experiences are enrolled. The inclusion of programmes designed to develop a sensitivity towards other world perspectives and cultures, identified as 'multicultural' programs (see, for example, Convertino, 2016; Danzak, 2015; Ford, 2014; Lopez & Kambutu, 2011; Ramirez, Salinas, & Epstein, 2016; Rizvi, 1986; Ukpokodu, 2009), may have some local impact on students but, delivered as they are in the context of neoliberal education, the limited effect on student awareness is not likely to be sufficiently impressive on a larger scale.

The critical importance of educating students with refugee and asylum seeker experiences is about the 'bigger picture'. It is about behaving humanely towards other members of the human race, despite living in societies that transparently place profit above people. It is about being critical of educational spaces that are blatantly exploiting students without advantage or privilege for the benefit of a few. It is about placing these students, amongst many others in cultural learning environments where there is recognition of sustains life and makes it worth living in the wake of experiences that not only diminish life itself but dull the spirit (Anders, 2012). Engaging with pedagogical love, in a learning context that acknowledges the importance of imagination, creativity and multi modalities and gives voice to those who have been displaced, disempowered and discarded from their homelands is not a small undertaking but it is powerful one that could send a message of a new era, a commitment to humanity in the face of global destruction, ecological disaster and an economy of greed. In the provision of humane educational options for these children and young people, such as that proposed by Kincheloe, Steinberg, Gidley and others, a glimmer of hope is reflected for the future of humanity and the 're-balancing' and restoration of the planet and all living species with which mankind have been entrusted.

Conclusion

The adaptation of school systems to acknowledge the true worth of humanity and of epistemologies and ontologies that are diverse and multi-perspectival is not only an opportunity for students with refugee and asylum seeker experiences to be recognised as a valuable and valued population in schools and societies, it is a reflection of the true meaning and importance of education. Whilst no education can be considered value free, educational contexts that understand the need to model ethical and fair practices, that condemn racism and prejudice in order to authentically care for all students can certainly set a worthwhile precedent in a world that is characterised by conflict, poverty, hunger and destitution for so many of its inhabitants. The prospect of students with refugee and asylum seeker experiences entering schools that are welcoming, that realize the dangers, difficulties and traumas they have faced and that are based in the ethics and philosophies of care and pedagogical love may be a proposition that politicians in neoliberal countries and nation states find too dangerous to contemplate. Nevertheless, it is an opportunity for human progress despite tragedy and a preparation for complex and unpredictable futures.

References

Anders, A. (2012). Lessons from a Postcritical Ethnography, Burundian Children with Refugee Status, and Their Teachers. *Theory Into Practice, 51*(2), 99-106. doi:http://dx.doi.org/10.1080/00405841.2012.662850

Bell, W. (2002). Making People Responsible: The Possible, the Probable, and the Preferable. . In J. Dator (Ed.), *Advancing futures: Futures studies in higher education* (pp. 33-52). Westport, CT: Praeger.

Boyd, R., & Myers, J. (1988). Transformative Education. *Internationsl Journal; of Lifelong Education, 7*(4), 261-284.

Connell, R. (1977). *Ruling Class, Ruling Culture: Studies of Conflict, Power and Hegemony in Australian Life*. Cambridge: Cambridge University Press.

Connell, R. (1982). *Making the Difference: Schools,Families and Social Division*. Sydney: Allen & Unwin.

Connell, R. (2013a). The Neoliberal Cascade and Education: An Essay on the Market Agenda and its Consequences. *Critical Studies in Education,, 54*(99-112). Retrieved from http://dx.doi.org/10.1080/17508487.2013.776990

Connell, R. (2013b). Why do Market 'Reforms' Persistently Increase Inequality? *Discourse: Studies in the Cultural Politics of Education, 34*(2), 279-285.

Connell, R., Campbell, C., Vickers, M., Welch, A., Foley, D., & Bagnell, N. (2007). *Education, Change and Society*. South Melbourne: Oxford University Press.

Convertino, C. (2016). Beyond Ethnic Tidbits: Toward a Critical and Dialogical Model in Multicultural Social Justice Teacher Preparation. *International Journal of Multicultural Education, 18*(2), 125-142.

Csikszentmihalyi, M. (1988). The Flow Experience and its Significance for Human Psychology. In M. Csikszentmihalyi & S. Csikszentmihalyi (Eds.), *Optimal Experience: Psychological Studies of Flow in Consciousness.* (pp. 3-37).

Csikszentmihalyi, M. (1991). Consciousness for the Twenty First Century. *Zygon, 26*(1).

Csikszentmihalyi, M. (2000). Happiness, Flow and Economic Equality. *American Psychological Association, 55*(10), 1163-1164.

Csikszentmihalyia, M., & Lebuda, I. (2107). A Window Into the Bright Side of Psychology: Interview With Mihaly Csikszentmihalyi. *Europe's Journal of Psychology, 13*(4), 810-821. doi:doi:10.5964/ejop.v13i4.1482

Danzak, R. L. (2015). "Sometimes the Perspective Changes": Reflections on a Photography Workshop with Multicultural Students in Italy. *International Journal of Multicultural Education, 17*(3), 56-75.

Darder, A., Boltodano, M., & Torres, R. (2009). Introduction. In A. Darder, M. Boltodano, & R. Torres (Eds.), *The Critical Pedagogy Reader* (2nd ed.). New York: Taylor and Francis.

Ford, D. Y. (2014). Why Education Must be Multicultural: Addressing a Few Misperceptions with Counterarguments. *Gifted Child Today, 37*(1), 59-62.

Fullan, M. (1993). *Change Forces: Probing the Depths of Educational Reform.* . Bristol PA: Falmer Press.
Fullan, M. (2001). *Leading in a Culture of Change.* San Francisco: Jossey Bass.
Fullan, M. (2011). *Choosing the Wrong Drivers for Whole System Reform.* Melbourne, Vic:
Fullan, M. (2015). *The New Meaning of Educational Change* (Fifth ed.). New York: Teachers College Press.
Gary, K. (2017). Neoliberal Education for Work Versus Liberal Education for Leisure. *Stud Philos Educ.* Retrieved from doi:DOI 10.1007/s11217-016-9545-0
Gidley, J. (2008). Beyond Homogenisation of Global Education: Do Alternative Pedagogies such as Steiner Education have Anything to Offer an Emergent Globalising World? In S. Inayatullah, M. Bussey, & I. Milojevic (Eds.), *Alternative Educational Futures: Pedagogies for an Emergent World* (pp. 253-268). Rotterdam, Netherlands: Sense Publications.
Gidley, J. (2016). *Postformal Education: A Philosophy for Complex Futures.* Switzerland: Springer.
Gidley, J. (2017). Contrasting Futures for Humanity: Technotopian or Human-Centred? *Paradigm Explorer: the Journal of the Scientic and Mediacl Network, September.* Retrieved from
Jackson, P. (1990). *Life in Classrooms.* New York: Teachers College Press.
Kincheloe, J. (2005). On to the Next Level: Continuing the Conceptualization of the Bricolage. *Qualitative Inquiry, 11*(3), 323-350.
Kincheloe, J., Hayes, K., Rose, K., & Anderson, P. (2006). Introduction: The Power of Hope in the Trenches. . In J. Kincheloe, K. Hayes, K. Rose, & P. Anderson (Eds.), *The Praeger Handbook of Urban Education:* (Vol. 1). London: Greenwood Press.
Kincheloe, J., & Steinberg, S. (1993). A Tentative Description of Post-Formal Thinking: The Critical Confrontation with Cognitive Theory. *Harvard Educational Review, 63*(3), 296-322.
Lopez, V., & Kambutu, J. (2011). Multicultural Education Within the Era of Internalization and Globalization. *Multicultural Perspectives, 13*(1), 3-4. doi:10.1080/15210960.2011.548173
Malott, C. (2011a). *Critical Pedagogy and Cognition An Introduction to a Postformal Educational Psychology.* London, New York: Springer.
Malott, C. (2011b). The Social Construction of Educational Psychology (Continued): Implications for Teacher Education Critical Pedagogy and Cognition. In (Vol. 15, pp. 79-94): Springer Netherlands.
Mezirow, J. (1981). A Critical Theory of Adult Learning and Education. *Adult Education Quarterly, 32*(1), 3-24. doi: 10.1177/074171368103200101
Mezirow, J. (1991). *Transformative Dimensions of Adult Learning.* San Francisco: Jossey - Bass.
Mezirow, J. (1998). On Critical Reflection. *Adult Education Quarterly, 48,* 185-198.
Mezirow, J. (2003). Transformative Learning as Discourse. *Journal of Transformative Education, 1*(1), 58-63. doi:10.1177/1541344603252172

O'Sullivan, E. (1999). *Transformative Learning: Educational Vision for the 21st Century.* London: Zed.

O'Sullivan, E. (2008). Preface. In M. Gardner & U. Kelly (Eds.), *Narrating Transformative Learning in Education* (pp. ix-xvii). New York: Plagrave Macmillan.

O'Sullivan, E., Morrell, A., & O'Connor, M. (2002). *Expanding the Boundaries of Transformative Learning.* . NY: Palgrave.

Ramirez, P. C., Salinas, C., & Epstein, T. (2016). Critical Multicultural Citizenship Education: Student Engagement toward Building an Equitable Society. *International Journal of Multicultural Education, 18*(1), 1-6.

Rizvi, F. (1986). *Ethnicity, Class and Multicultural Education.* Melbourne: Deakin University Press.

Ross, E. W., & Vinson, K. (2013). Resisting Neoliberal Education Reform: Insurrectionist Pedagogies and the Pursuit of Dangerous Citizenship. *WORKS AND DAYS, 31*(1 & 2), 1-32.

Ross, W. (2017) *The Fear Created by Precarious Existence in The Neoliberal World Discourages Critical Thinking/Interviewer: M. Abdelmoumen.* American Herald Tribune.

Sardar, Z. (2010). Welcome to Postnormal Times. *Futures: The Journal of Policy Planning and Future Studies, 42*(5), 435-444.

Seligman, M. (2002). *Authentic Happiness: Using the New Positive Psychology to Realize Your Potential for Lasting Fulfillment.* New York: Free Press.

Seligman, M. (2011). *Flourish: A Visionary New Understanding of Happiness and Wellbeing.* New York: Free Press.

Seligman, M., Ernst, R., Gillham, J., Reivich, K., & Linkins, M. (2009). Positive Education: Positive Psychology and Classroom Interventions. *Oxford Review of Education, 35*(3), 293-311.

Stewart, J. (2011). *Supporting Refugee Children: Strategies for EDucators.* Toronto, Ontraio: University of Toronto Press.

Ukpokodu, O. (2009). Pedagogies that Foster Transformative Learning in a Multicultural Education Course: A Reflection. *Journal of Praxis in Multicultural Education, 4*(1), 1-8.

Watters, C. (2007). *Refugee Children: Towards the Next Horizon* (1 ed.). Florence: Taylor and Francis.

Wilkins, A. (2017). *The New Political Economy of Neoliberal Education: "Private Monopoly' Chain Effects and Multi Academy Trusts.* Paper presented at the BERA, Bristol.

Wilkins, A. (2018a). Assembling Schools as Organisations: On the Limits and Contradictions of Neoliberalism. In M. Connelly, C. James, S. Kruse, & D. Spicer (Eds.), *SAGE International Handbook on School Organization.* London: Sage.

Wilkins, A. (2018b). Neoliberalism, Citizenship and Education: A Policy Discourse Analysis. In A. Peterson, G. Stahl, & H. Soong (Eds.), *The Palgrave Handbook of Citizenship and Education.* Basingstoke: Palgrave.

Index

A
ageism 26–27
agency 55
asylum seekers
    defined 53
    demonized in Western society 73–75
    global numbers 70
    health 1
    see also students with refugee and asylum seeker backgrounds

B
belonging, politics of 72–73, 80–81
belonging, sense of 88–91, 95
bioecological theory 121–23, 129
biopower 22–23
Bourdieu, Pierre, theory of social capital 4, 5, 76–80
brain plasticity 133
Burundian family 28–29

C
capital 4, 5, 76–80
care, ethic of 8–12, 63
change
    preparing for 126
    school principals as change agents 108, 117
change theory 149–50
child development
    bioecological theory 121–23, 129
    developmental trauma 57–58
    western perspectives 28
childhood, Western perspectives 26–27
choice of school 3–4, 39
classical liberalism 3, 35–36
classification of students 26–27
Cold War 69
collectivism 90, 124–25, 132
communication and ethic of care 10–11, 12
compassion 54–56, 71–72, 80–81
complexity 144, 146
confirmation principle 12
creativity 144, 146
critical constructivism 141–44
critical thinking 127–28
cultural capital 76–77
cultural dimensions theories 124–28, 132–33
cultural iceberg 123–24, 131
cultural integration 95–96

D
deep culture 124
deregulation 3
detention centres 2, 73–74
developmental trauma 57–58
dialogical reasoning 13, 144, 146
dialogue and ethic of care 10–11, 12
difference 72
differentiation of students 26–27
disability 25
disciplinary power 22, 24
discourse (definition) 20
dispersal policies 73
displaced peoples
    countries hosting 2
    demonized in Western society 73–75
    global numbers 1, 69–70

displacement 56
documentation in schools, mandatory 24

E

ecological reasoning 144, 146
economic rationalism 3, 38
education
   alternative models 6, 7–8
   postformal psychology 141–44
   power relationships 19–20, 23–24
   purpose of 4–9
   quality of 6
   reforms 8–9, 43
   in refugee camps 1–2
   transformative education 147–51
education policies 2–4, 6, 13, 36, 37–43, 75–76, 140–41
emotional and social learning 92–93
emotional health of refugees 1
emotional intensity and culture 123–24
emotional learning 115–16
emotional pathway in teaching 112, 113–14
emotions 78–80
empathy 91–93, 116–17
English Language Learners (ELLS) 43–44
environmental development theory 121–23, 129
equity 87, *see also* inequity
ethical conduct 79, 80
ethics in leadership 114
evolutionary education 146

F

fair trade 37
fairness 87
family involvement in schools 112–13, 116
feminine cultures 125, 148

forced labour 37
Foucault, Michel
   biopower 22–23
   disciplinary power 22, 24
   discourse (definition) 20
   governmentality 24–25, 27
   institutional power 19–24, 29–30, 63
   juridical power 21
   knowledge/power relationships 23–24
   normative power 21–22
   panopticon theory 3, 4, 5, 22
   racism 24–25
   summary of power analysis 31–32
free trade 3, 35, 37
future-mindedness 144, 146

G

global engagement, educating for 140–41
globalization 70
governmentality 24–25, 27
governments, neoliberal *see* neoliberalism
grief 56–61, 130

H

habitus 77, 78–80
Haiti, slavery in 37
haute cuisine model of education 38–39, 42
health of refugees 1
hierarchical structures in schools 89–91
higher purpose 13, 145, 146
holistic education 148
human capital 4, 76

I

imagination 145, 146

immigration policies 37, 55–56, 70–71, 73
independent schools 3
indigenous peoples, wisdom of 148–49
indigenous world views 143
individualism 75–76, 124
indulgence versus restraint 126–27, 132–33
industrial cuisine model of education 38–39, 42
inequity 9, 76, *see also* equity
institutional power 19–24, 29–30, 39, 63
institutional racism 94–95, 96

integration
   cultural integration 95–96
   postformal reasoning 13–14, 145, 146
intergenerational transmission of trauma 59–60
interpersonal trauma 59
intuitive wisdom 145, 146

J
juridical power 21

K
Keynesian policies 2
knowledge economy 76
knowledge/power relationships 23–24

L
language acquisition 130–31
language intervention programs 43–44
language reflexivity 145, 146
leadership by school principals 105, 107–17
learning experience 6

liberalism 3, 35–36, *see also* neoliberalism
life as pedagogical value 7, 146
life skills 6–7
long term and short term orientation 126, 132
loss 56–61, 130
love as pedagogical value 7, 12–14, 146
love, ethic of 9–12, 54

M
mandatory documentation in schools 24
masculine cultures 125, 132
mass education 2–4, 7–8
media, influence of 73, 74–75
mental health of refugees 1
migration, forced 70
moral conduct 79, 80
moral education: ethic of care 8–12
mutuality and ethic of care 11

N
natural environment connectedness 147–48
neoliberalism
   21st century practice 36–37
   dispersal policies 73
   economic policies 2–3
   education policies 2–4, 6, 13, 36, 37–43, 75–76, 140–41
   education practice 142, 143
   and food production 38–39
   foundational theory 35–36
   immigration policies 37, 55–56, 70–71, 73
   purpose of education 4–6
normative power 21–22

157

O

oracy 128–29, 133
'othering' (perceived difference) 27–28

P

panopticon theory (Foucault) 3, 4, 5, 22
pedagogical love 7, 12–14, 146
performativity 40
physical health of refugees 1
pluralism 145, 146
politics of belonging 72–73, 80–81
postformal psychology 141–44
postformal reasoning 7, 12–14, 144–47
power
    biopower 22–23
    Bourdieu's theory of social capital 76, 78
    disciplinary power 22, 24
    Foucauldian analysis 31–32
    institutional power 19–24, 29–30, 39, 63
    juridical power 21
    knowledge/power relationships 23–24
    normative power 21–22
    power distance 89–91, 125
private schools 3
privatization 3, 39
problem solving 127–28, 133
productivity 5
public opinion re displaced peoples 73, 74–75
purpose of education 4–9

R

racism 24–25, 63, 93–95, 96
reflexivity 145, 146
refugee and asylum seeker status 52–53
refugee camps, education in 1–2
refugees
    defined 52–53
    demonized in Western society 73–75
    global numbers 70
    health 1
    see also students with refugee and asylum seeker backgrounds
religious schools 3
resettlement 70
resilience 62–65
restraint versus indulgence 126–27, 132–33

S

school climate 85–88, 95
school culture 104–7, 116
school ethos 105–7, 114–15
school principals 105, 107–17
schools
    alternative models 6, 7–8
    choice of 3–4, 39
    as commodity 39
    function of 37–38
    instilling sense of belonging 89–91, 95
    leadership *see* school principals
    management of 39–40
    mandatory attendance 2
    mandatory documentation 24
    role in positive environment 65
    as safe spaces 85, 97
    see also education; education policies
self-identity 59, 64
self-interest 54–55, 79
shallow culture 123–24
short term and long term orientation 126, 132
slavery 37
social and emotional learning 92–93
social capital 4, 5, 76, 77, 113
social development 121–23, 129–33

social fields 77–78
social justice 9, 71
social norms 22, 24, 36
spirituality 149
stateless people 70
stressors, responses to 57–58
structural violence 30
students
    empowering 7, 11
    performance measures 4
    reciprocity of care 11
students with refugee and asylum seeker backgrounds
    access to schools 38
    adaptation 129
    ageism 26–27
    appropriate schooling 115, 131
    belonging, sense of 88–91, 95
    benefitting from effective leadership 114–16
    bioecological theory 121–23, 129
    Burundian family 28–29
    change 129
    classification and differentiation 26–27
    collective cultures 132
    cultural difference 132–33
    cultural iceberg effects 131
    emotional learning 115–16
    family involvement in schools 116
    grief 130
    humane education of 150–51
    indulgence versus restraint 132–33
    institutional power impacts 26–30
    integration 114–15
    language acquisition of host country 130–31
    language intervention programs 43–44
    learning challenges 44–45
    loss 130
    masculine cultures 132
    oracy 133
    problem solving 133
    racism 93–95
    resilience 62–65
    school ethos 114–15
    short term and long term orientation 132
    social and cultural development 129–33
    teacher relationships 131–32
    trauma 56–61
    uncertainty avoidance 132
success, measuring 76
symbolic capital 76, 77
symbolic violence 78

T

teachers
    desensitization 30, 54
    identity and professionalism 40–41
    inculcating sense of belonging 90–91
    leadership 10, 11
    neoliberal policy impacts 40–43
    student relationships 131–32
    see also school principals
teaching standards 41–42
thinking, ways of 127–28
transformative education 147–51
trauma 56–61

U

uncertainty avoidance 125–26, 132

V

virtue ethic 11
voice as pedagogical value 7, 146

W
wisdom as pedagogical value 7, 146
wisdom, intuitive 145, 146
wisdom of indigenous peoples 148–49
workers, humans reduced to 5–6, 7

Marta Kowalczuk-Walędziak
Alicja Korzeniecka-Bondar
Wioleta Danilewicz
Gracienne Lauwers (eds.)

**Rethinking
Teacher Education for
the 21st Century**

*2019 • 402 pp. • Pb. • 76,00 € (D) • US$105.00 • GBP 67.00
ISBN 978-3-8474-2241-9 • eISBN 978-3-8474-1257-1*

This book focuses on current trends, potential challenges and further developments of teacher education and professional development from a theoretical, empirical and practical point of view. It intends to provide valuable and fresh insights from research studies and examples of best practices from Europe and all over the world. The authors deal with the strengths and limitations of different models, strategies, approaches and policies related to teacher education and professional development in and for changing times(digitization, multiculturalism, pressure to perform).

The book is an **Open Access** title (DOI: 10.3224/84742241) , which is free to download or can be bought as paperback.

www.barbara-budrich.net

Petra Strehmel | Johanna Heikka
Eeva Hujala | Jillian Rodd
Manjula Waniganayake (eds.)

Leadership in Early Education in Times of Change

Research from five Continents

2019 · 308 pp. · Pb. · 36,00 € (D) · US$50.00 · GBP 32.00
ISBN 978-3-8474-2199-3 · eISBN 978-3-8474-1224-3

The collection brings together the latest work of researchers from Australia, Africa, Asia, and Europe focusing on early childhood leadership matters. It covers different aspects of leadership in early education: professional education and development, identity and leadership strategies as well as governance and leadership under different frame conditions.

The book is an **Open Access** title, which is free to download or can be bought as paperback.

www.barbara-budrich.net